THE
Approachable
ARGUMENT

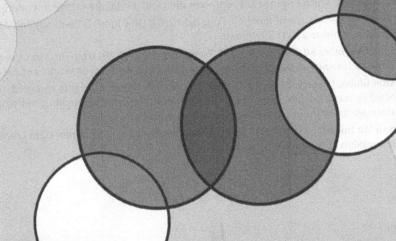

MICHAEL G. LEIGH
Third Edition

Kendall Hunt
publishing company

Kendall Hunt
publishing company

www.kendallhunt.com

Send all inquiries to:

4050 Westmark Drive

Dubuque, IA 52004-1840

Copyright © 2005, 2007, 2011 by Michael G. Leigh

ISBN 978-0-7575-9136-5

Printed in the United States of America

10 9 8 7 6 5 4 3

CONTENTS

Introduction .... *v*

CHAPTER 1: A FIRST LOOK AT ARGUMENT 1

CHAPTER 2: CRITICAL THINKING PITFALLS 33

CHAPTER 3: FINDING AND USING EVIDENCE 67

CHAPTER 4: "SPIN" 101

CHAPTER 5: WAYS THAT WE REASON AND WAYS THAT WE FAIL 153

CHAPTER 6: BUILDING SPEECHES: FACT, VALUE, & POLICY 191

CHAPTER 7: A BRIEF WORD ABOUT ORAL ADDRESS 231

CHAPTER 8: REFUTATION AND DEBATE 251

Appendix: Sample Speeches *295*

Glossary *319*

INTRODUCTION

I recall being told by a favorite professor that they didn't give diplomas at Oxford University. He was asked, "then how do you know if someone went there?" He replied, "You talk to them." His point was simply that diplomas are less important than education itself. The search for knowledge for its own sake seems to be an increasingly archaic value, though.

I worry about my students today. They are so concerned about a grade or a test score, but they haven't really learned how to learn. They've learned how to be obedient and ask questions like, "What do you want me to do for an A?" They memorize, regurgitate, and expect that entrance to a good college or a certificate of some kind will guarantee them a good life. They move dutifully, obediently through rote learning processes yet never really learn why they have the opinions they do or how to defend those opinions in anything but the most cliché manner.

Grades guarantee very little. There are many well-degreed yet unemployed people among us today. Practicing disciplined argument and developing critical thinking, however, can give us something. People who learn to think critically tend to be more assertive and independent. They have higher credibility among work associates and greater likelihood of job success, including promotions. Even arguments in the more mundane sense of personal quarrels become more manageable when we learn how to think rationally (1). In sum, learning to be argumentative without being aggressive is a predictor of personal and professional success.

This text focuses on *simple approaches to argument* rather than on a lot of theories. The primary goal is to help students find arguments less threatening, more approachable. The writing here is as conversational as possible without being academically irresponsible. That's not to say that there is no new vocabulary. There is a *language of argument* that students need to learn. This specialized vocabulary will aid in building arguments and in better appreciating the arguments of others.

We'll examine this new language by paying close attention to the concepts shown in *bold italics throughout this text*, as well as in the glossary. These bold italics are equivalent to the underlining or highlighting of a book that some students may practice on their own but that many do not. A good basic study method would be to review all the highlighted items and then study the vocabulary list at the end of each chapter.

We'll learn a simplified version of argument form as designed by logician **Stephen Toulmin**, focusing mainly on his primary triad of "claim, warrant, and grounds." We'll also use "qualifiers" from his secondary triad, which are necessary because they help us limit the extent to which a claim is true.

We'll learn how to structure three different kinds of speeches, defending **propositions of fact, value, and policy**. There are at least two sensible approaches to understanding these kinds of propositions. There's a certain natural progression from determining facts, to assessing our values in relation to facts, then creating a policy, a social action to take. However, since there are close structural similarities to arguing fact and policy, it's also reasonable to learn the more difficult and less formulaic ways of arguing values last. Your teacher will determine which is best.

Many practical examples of real world argument are provided here to ground new vocabulary in common student experience. There will be references to web, magazine, and newspaper articles about current events. Such articles model how arguments should and should not be made in public, provide frameworks for class discussion, and suggest current topics for written and spoken research assignments.

Another goal is to **involve students in current events** and to invite them to enhance their knowledge through the research process. Honestly, students simply don't read as much as they used to, and that decline is linked to poorer test scores and lesser income (**2**). Accurate awareness of civics and of public events is declining. Fewer than 27% of those born after 1977 read the news, either in print or online. That's less than half the participation of those born after 1946. Only 43% of all Americans say that the loss of a local paper would hurt civic life, and only 33% said they'd miss reading the local paper if it folded (**3**).

A Michigan college professor surveyed his classes on basic civics over three years and discovered that less than a third could name their state senators; one sixth could name one. Only half could name the three branches of the federal government (the executive, the legislative, and the judicial). Only about a sixth could name either the Secretary of Defense or of State, and **less than half knew that there were 50 states.** Guesses ran from 51 to 54.

A sixth could not name our first president. "Lincoln" was a common guess. Over a third could not answer the old trick question, "Who is buried in Grant's tomb?" Yet these are questions that an immigrant seeking citizenship would typically have to answer (**4**). I just read in this morning's local paper that nearly a quarter of high school graduates couldn't pass military entrance exams (**5**). The military used to be where kids who didn't graduate were encouraged to go to find a career.

When I was young, wild, and hitching around Europe, I had a memorable encounter with some German children. I was sleeping away my deck passage on a night crossing from Brindisi, Italy, into Dubrovnik of what was then Yugoslavia. I and my bag of sad sandwiches were stepped on by three kids who didn't notice me curled up in a sleeping bag. I roared like a bear about my squashed food, and the kids ran off. Later they came back with some sandwiches, apologized, and asked if they could ask questions about American politics. They were very afraid that President Reagan really was a kind of nuclear cowboy and would start a war. They could name members of his cabinet and a couple of bills before our congress, too. They were ages eleven, nine, and seven.

Students may say, "I'm not really 'into' the news," but ***the news is into you.*** Our daily lives are shaped by advocates who speak in the news media. As speakers, we also have a responsibility to research what we say in public, not just repeat what we've heard from "a guy I know," or what is popular in the moment to say. Repeated rumor and innuendo can't replace research.

Politicians have a distinct advantage over us if we don't understand the rules by which they play. They may prey on our unreasoned fears to take us in directions that we wouldn't support if we truly understood their methods. Frankly, I felt a civic responsibility to write this third edition after the terrible argument practices we witnessed in the 2010 midterm elections.

Many of our views have been unconsciously reinforced by media and social conditioning. We hear unexamined slogans so often that we utter them automatically, yet we are often unable to defend them with verifiable facts. These are uncertain and challenging times, yet the tendency to oversimplify our condition seems more common. "It's those darn Democrats." "It's those crazy Republicans." The truth is so much more complex, and it is our civic responsibility to understand that.

Lack of critical thinking can hurt us economically. Advertisers grapple for our dollars with *"persuasion,"* the use of imagery and subjective appeals to motivate audiences. Persuasion is a practical tool. Yet it can be used to motivate us to purchase substandard goods and services. Much of our current economic struggle is due to the unscrupulous persuasion of banks that led us into unsound mortgages and other shaky investments. Our savings have been decimated by credit card companies that entice us with cheesy commercials into incredible interest costs.

How can we defend ourselves? We can learn about **critical thinking**, a more self-aware and self-reliant approach to the appreciation of argument and persuasion. Critical thinking is learning to think for oneself. It is also a framework for developing good attitude and sound ethics in argument, each of which should be practiced more often by public figures today.

Critical thinking is *an open-minded and searching process.* It has to be because we seldom discover absolute truth about difficult social issues. We deal more often in relative truths heavily influenced by varying social conditions. For those of us who are strongly attached to unfounded beliefs about public issues and consider them absolute truths, a little effort, patience, and courageous self-examination can help us see anew.

One measure of human intelligence is certainly that we can change our minds in the face of new or superior evidence that challenges our opinions. *Critical thinkers may have ideas, but we don't allow our ideas to have us.* We can change and adjust ideas in the face of superior arguments or new research and be O.K. with that. We don't lack integrity, yet we are flexible.

Ultimately, there is *something transformational* about the study of critical thinking. Disagreement may even be mutually illuminating to those who disagree. The flint and steel of opposing arguments may strike the spark by which we better see our own positions. We may improve their defense. We may modify our views in the face of superior arguments from another.

Personal growth is a wonderful by-product, if not a goal, of this study. We may discover for the first time ideas worthy of our eager support. We may very well change our opinion of ourselves. As our argumentative abilities increase, we may find that our confidence, integrity, and self-respect grow, too. We may not feel compelled to leap to the lectern and proclaim our world vision, but we'll become better consumers of public speech. One natural result may be ***more responsible social action.*** We may feel better qualified to participate in elections and other community responsibilities.

May such transformations visit you as you work with this text. At least, I hope, you'll find argument slightly less intimidating, more approachable.

Now get started on building some arguments of your own.

REFERENCES

1) Colbert, K.E. "The Effects of Debate Participation on Argumentativeness and Verbal Aggression." Communication Education 42 (1993): 206–214.
    Infante, D.A. "Trait Argumentativeness as a Predictor of Communicative Behavior in Situations Requiring Argument." Central States Speech Journal 32 (1981): 265–272.
    Infante, D.A. "Aggressiveness." In J.C. McCroskey and J.A. Daly (Eds.), Personality and Interpersonal Communication, (pp. 157–192). Newbury Park, CA: Sage Publications, Inc., 1987.
    Shutz, B. "Argumentativeness: It's Effect In Group Decision-Making and Its Role in Leadership Perception." Communication Quarterly 30 (1982): 368–375.

2) "Study Links Drop in Test Scores to Decline in Time Spent Reading," New York Times, November 19, 2007.

3) "Many Americans Wouldn't Care a Lot if Local Papers Folded," Pew Research Center Publications, March 12, 2009.

4) "Schooled but not Educated," The Detroit News, November 18, 2010. http://www.detnews.com/article/20101118/OPINION01/11180354/1008/Schooled-but-uneducated

5) "23% of high school grads fail Army entrance exam," Arizona Daily Star, December 22, 2010.

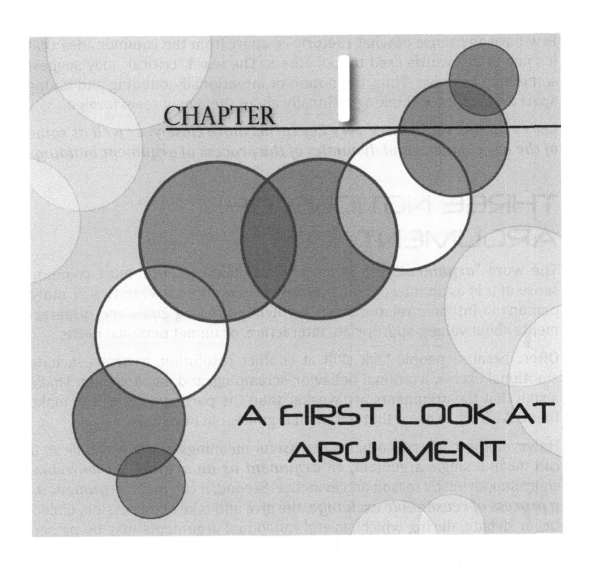

CHAPTER I

A FIRST LOOK AT ARGUMENT

"YOU HAVE TO STAND FOR SOMETHING, OR YOU'LL FALL FOR ANYTHING."

THE CHARACTER OF "WISEMAN"

IN THE 2011 FILM "SUCKER PUNCH"

When we hear the terms *"argument," "rhetoric," and "critical thinking,"* we may get intimidated. To the average Jack and Jill, arguments are unpleasant personal conflicts involving emotional pain. Yet argument can be a reliable and approachable skill used to create intelligent opinion.

Few have any sense of what rhetoric is, apart from the common idea that it's just pretty words used to fool others. The word "critical" may suggest something negative. Thus, the notion of intentionally building and taking apart arguments or thinking rationally about them may seem foreign.

Let's examine these three very key terms more closely, as well as some of the key elements and dynamics of the process of argument building.

THREE NOTIONS OF ARGUMENT

The word *"argument"* has at least three meanings. Our most common sense of it is as an interpersonal *quarrel,* a conflict between two or more persons in intimate relationships, involving differing goals and disagreements about values, appropriate interaction, or unmet personal needs.

Often, because people lack skill at conflict resolution, quarrels include emotional excess, irrational behavior, screaming, and name-calling. That's a sign that the arguments are weaker than the participant's will to make them. We'll try to avoid that notion of argument in our study.

However, there are two other more useful meanings of the word. First, it can mean a single argument, an *argument as an artifact*, an individual claim supported by reason and evidence. Second, it can mean *argument as a process of reasonable exchange*, the give and take of discussion, dialectic, or debate, during which several individual arguments may be passed back and forth, pro and con. Managing the first is a matter of learning a basic format. Managing the second has format, too, but it requires that we learn new communication skills and develop a self-aware use of them.

The difference between a quarrel and an argument, in each of the two senses, is that quarrels often consist of dirty fighting, fallacies, and attacks addressed to people rather than to their ideas: "You're dumb," rather than "I think differently." Here we will learn to *attack ideas, not people.* That is not always well modeled for us in public speaking today. In fact, our most recent elections, the very place where we should expect the best of argument, have included fairly shameful exhibitions of this skill.

Yet if we *learn how to fight fairly*—one of our goals—our interpersonal relations may improve along with our ability to discuss public issues. Learning about formal argumentation can help to improve, even elevate, interpersonal quarrels, as well as build our confidence while discussing issues facing the human community. There is also good evidence that using this particular format of argument has a direct link to improved critical thinking, which has not been proven to be true of syllogisms and more traditional forms of logic instruction (**1**).

TOULMIN'S FORMAT

Let's begin with individual arguments, *the basic building block for speeches.* We'll consider argument as a process of discussion, dialectic, and debate in the debate chapter. The individual argument form we will use is a simplified version of that designed by logician Stephen Toulmin (**2**). Using Toulmin effectively will take a bit of time. So, let's begin now.

The most basic format parts are:

CLAIM: THE IDEA TO BE PROVEN

WARRANT: ANALYSIS OR REASONING THAT LINKS THE CLAIM TO ...

GROUNDS: EVIDENCE OR PROOF OF THE CLAIM

We state in a single sentence that something is true. We explain reasons for believing the claim in warrants by analyzing how the sum of the evidence supports the claim, and we use evidence from research to prove the claim in grounds. **A claim is one sentence** and one sentence only, preferably a simple declarative sentence, not a compound one. Compound sentence claims tend make arguments confusing, especially for beginners. Here's a simple example of a Toulmin argument:

Claim: I want to see movie A, instead of movie B.

Why?

Warrant: The actors are better in movie A.

Who says?

Grounds: Well, two have been nominated for both Golden Globes and Academy Awards, and the National Critics Association picked the cast for best ensemble acting. Look, here's a review in last week's *Time* saying ...

That's how we might use an argument in everyday situations. You may already do something like this instinctively. In formal arguments, though, grounds consist of quoted material from reliable research sources, and those *sources are carefully cited in an oral manner*, not just in the bibliography. Your audience can't hear a bibliography. The minimum citation requirement would be the *publication and the date. Expert qualifications also matter.*

Claim: Offshore drilling is hazardous to the environment.

Warrant: The drilling process uses fluids that are toxic. These fluids may spread due to oceanic currents and have long-term effects on biodiversity.

Grounds 1: According to an August 19, 2010, *Houston Chronicle* report on the BP oil spill in the Gulf of Mexico, toxic fluid is used to "lubricate the drill bit as it drills through the layer of hard rock of the outer continental shelf. A toxic soup is formed when the fluid blends with rock, mud, and naturally occurring radioactive materials, which can spread at the minimum of a thousand meters from the rigs. Such threats are affecting the quality of the marine water, harming the organisms that stay on the bottom of the ocean, and ultimately, having negative impacts throughout the region, which includes changes in the abundance richness and diversity of the marine life from both the physical and toxic effects."

While a claim may only be one sentence, the warrant may be more. It can be a several sentence long analysis or preview of what the quoted material will say in grounds. It must remain relevant to that specific argument, not just the overall speech topic.

Quoted material only appears in grounds. Use quotation marks. Claims and warrants are written in your own words. For the time being, just think of the claim as the general statement of what you intend to prove and the warrant to be a more specific explanation of your thinking.

Multiple warrants and multiple grounds are typical in longer speeches about serious social issues. For instance, consider this more elaborate version of the previous oil spill argument:

Claim A: Offshore drilling is hazardous to the environment.

Warrant A-1: The drilling process uses fluids that are toxic and have long-term effects on biodiversity. The effects may be widespread because these fluids may spread due to oceanic currents. Some fluids stay hidden.

Grounds A-1-a: According to an August 19, 2010, *Houston Chronicle* report on the BP oil spill, toxic fluid is used to "lubricate the drill bit as it drills through the layer of hard rock of the outer continental shelf. A toxic soup is formed when the fluid blends with rock, mud, and naturally occurring radioactive materials, which can spread at the minimum of a thousand meters from the rigs. Such threats are affecting the quality of the marine water, harming the organisms that stay on the bottom of the ocean, and ultimately, having negative impacts throughout the region, which includes changes in the abundance richness and diversity of the marine life from both the physical and toxic effects."

Grounds A-1-b: According to the *New York Times* of June 1, 2010, indicated that there were vast plumes of oil permeating the Gulf, even reaching to the bottom and coral reefs, "The reef lies just 20 miles northeast of BP's blown-out well, making it one of at least three extensive deepwater reefs lying directly beneath the oil slick in the gulf. Yet it is not the slick that troubles scientists. They fear a more insidious threat: vast plumes of partly dissolved oil apparently spreading in the deep ocean. The latest research team in the gulf to detect these plumes observed one extending roughly 22 miles northeast of the well site."

Warrant A-2: Oil spills leave chemicals and carcinogens that remain in the water and even after the oil is visibly removed. As people later eat seafood from the apparently "clean" area, their health could be compromised.

Grounds A-2-a: According to *Scientific American of* May 14, 2010, "The toxic compounds in oil vary, but largely fall in the group known to chemists as polycyclic aromatic hydrocarbons.... All are known human carcinogens with other health effects for humans, animals, and plants. 'These hydrocarbons are particularly relevant if inhaled or ingested,' says environmental toxicologist Ronald Kendall of Texas Tech University. 'In the bodies of organisms such as mammals or birds, these aromatic hydrocarbons can be transformed into even more toxic products, which can affect DNA.'"

Grounds A-2-b: According to an EPA report on their website, May, 2010, report from the Environmental Protection Agency "The increased level of toxins in the animals can cause poisoning further up the food chain."

The part labels may seem a little daunting, but it's *the same numbering and lettering you use when you outline.* Since we will not be writing speeches of less than two arguments, we need to identify the claims as 1 or 2, A or B, etc. When we actually read the speech, we can simply say, "My first claim is...my first warrant is...etc." *Please, don't use the words "claims" and "arguments" as synonyms.*

While you're learning Toulmin, though, it's important to clearly identify the parts to show your understanding. It's not the kind of writing you've done in your English classes. It's more like an outline with evidence. Your instructor may later choose to move to a more conventional prose form, perhaps with parts identified in a parenthesis at the end of each sentence or paragraph— (C) (W) (G) - as you would with internal citation on a term paper.

I actually require my students to *speak the parts out loud* as they deliver the content. "This is my first claim," etc. Eventually, students develop not only a tongue for argument, but an ear as well. Listening to and understanding argument structure is at least as important as writing and speaking it.

Don't worry. Seeing more examples will make this easier. There will seldom be a need to make an argument that's any more complex than the one you've just seen.

To start with, embrace this key principle: No claims without some grounds. That is your minimum argument format: a claim supported by some grounds. We have a research obligation to prove what we argue.

A claim unsupported by warrants or grounds is called an *assertion.* Merely exchanging assertions can be frustrating and unproductive. People who operate with assertions have the idea that "my opinion is just as good as yours," but how do we know? We know by examining arguments and discovering which have *the preponderance of evidence* behind them, not just the most evidence, but also the most reliable.

Warrants are a bit more difficult to grasp and will take some time to understand. Be patient with yourself. It will probably be after you study the basic patterns of reasoning in a later chapter before you really start to grasp warrants. Even theorists describe warrants differently, as we'll see when we discuss reason more specifically.

The taproot to understanding warrants is the concept of **an inference,** an analytical conclusion drawn from a combination of data or grounds. For instance, the second warrant in the argument above says that humans may be harmed by oil spills. None of the grounds say specifically "oil spills kill humans." However, when you put together that spills dump "known human carcinogens" into the water affecting our future seafood and the idea that the carcinogens can get absorbed "further up the food chain," it's not unreasonable to presume that humans could be affected.

Another example of inference can be observed *in science.* Has anyone ever actually seen a living dinosaur? No. Yet they've been depicted in film and documentaries with increasing detail. As paleontology advances, inferences made about dinosaurs have changed dramatically. We may now see some dinosaurs depicted with feathers, and we think of them as similar to birds rather than reptiles. We may hear them described as warm-blooded and smarter as we collect more samples of dinosaur remains. DNA sampling allows scientists to determine some relationships between more recent or still living animals and these ancient creatures of the past (3). Yet these depictions are all **inferences—not facts—inferences.** The difference between facts and inferences is very important. Facts can be confirmed, but inferences have an element of subjectivity and can be mistaken. We sometimes take great logical leaps from data into what we'll come to understand as *fallacies*, errors in reason and persuasion.

The order of Toulmin argument parts may change according to medium. Toulmin himself placed grounds after claims and placed warrants last. This is partially because some grounds so directly supports the claim that no further reasoning is required. For instance, what if the U.S. Department of Health said, "X numbers of humans were killed by eating seafood after the Valdez Oil Spill. We expect similar results with the BP spill?" We might not need a warrant beyond presuming that the U.S. Department of Health is a sound authority and has made a sound analogy. Then, to the degree that we assume sources to be reliable, we may say that the *warrant is implied.*

Making speeches is different than writing an argument in a paper, though. *We're writing for the ear, not the eye.* The eye can reread material. The ear cannot review rapidly passing speech. It's possible to have so many grounds that listeners may forget the claim before you get to the warrant. Thus, it's useful to go from claim to warrant to grounds for the sake of preview; it's easier to see the relationship of multiple grounds to a claim.

There are other elements of Toulmin's complete argument form. We're going to **concentrate on the "primary triad"** in this beginner's class. We will be using one concept from his "secondary triad," that of **"the qualifier,"** which simply limits the extent to which the claim is true: it's true most of the time, some of the time, exactly 20% of the time, etc.

The format may be a little confusing at first. That's O.K. It's worth the trouble, as Toulmin's approach to argument has been directly linked to improvement in critical thinking as well as basic skills such as reading and writing **(4).** Why? Because we'll come to understand the structure of rational thought itself and improve our listening skills.

RHETORIC

Formal argument is part of a broader field of study called *rhetoric.* The name comes from "The Rhetoric," the first comprehensive study of speech by the Greek philosopher Aristotle. He called rhetoric, "the faculty of observing in any given case the best available means of persuasion **(5).**" Great. But what do we mean by persuasion? *Persuasion* is the motivational aspect of argument, trying to get others to agree with our position and to act upon it. Persuasion includes use of imagery and colorful language to make our arguments more lively and engaging. Formal argument coupled with persuasion impacts social events in a direct and powerful way by creating public opinion.

Rhetoric is *instrumental speech*—speech with a practical purpose—or speech as a tool for uniting and motivating audiences. Donald C. Bryant, one of my professors, often said that rhetoric is the process of adjusting messages to particular people at particular times and particular places. Different audiences and occasions demand different persuasive tools. We don't use the same language, for instance, trying to persuade our parents to do something as we would a close friend of our same age. Effective persuasion involves *adaptation to the audience and the moment.*

On the anniversary of the peace with Japan, September 8, 2006, the *Los Angeles Times* said that President George Bush took note of time and place in an address about the Iraq War. Standing in the shadow of the "Ronald Reagan," a naval vessel named after one of our most popular presidents, he took the occasion to compare our efforts in the Iraq War with the rebuilding of Japan after WWII. While the analogy was strained, due to the more international nature of WWII, his message was clear. "Look. I'm like President Reagan," a president talented at unifying people behind him.

In January 2011, just after the attempted assassination of Representative Gabrielle Giffords, Arizona Governor Jan Brewer set aside her State of the State address to memorialize those killed, acknowledge the heroism of those involved, and to call for more peaceful political interactions.

Aristotle emphasized the importance of referring to communal connections between the speaker and the audience, or what we call **common ground,** as an important aspect of persuasion. He saw persuasion as imbedded in **appeals**: the ethical character of the speaker (**ethos**), appeals to emotion (**pathos**), and appeals to logic (**logos**). So, we're not just practicing dry logic. Our sense of ethics and our feelings are involved, too.

While reporting about Hurricane Katrina, CNN filmed itself interviewing Kathy Everhard and her young daughter in Waveland, Mississippi, on September 1, 2005. Beyond showing the misery of the two people sorting through a flattened home, the field reporter sorted through the wreckage with the twelve year old girl looking for her dolls. They then carried the dolls to the mother and hugged her while she cried. There is an emotional depiction of the hurricane's effects, pathos, the individual face impacted by disaster, but one can't mistake a second rhetorical message layered under the report. "We're the news station that cares."

Many things are rhetorical. Political speeches or a newspaper editorial page are obvious examples, but songs, films, even clothing can have a persuasive purpose. Toby Keith's country song "Courtesy of the Red, White, and Blue" salutes soldiers who give their lives to support our freedoms. It also entertains and makes a lot of money for the artist. The documentary films of Michael Moore certainly intend to entertain with irreverent humor, but they also make political points. "Capitalism: A Love Story" comments on our current financial crisis at the same time that it pokes fun.

Even a film made apparently for entertainment often has a rhetorical message. It was no coincidence that the film "Good Night and Good Luck," about how famous reporter Edward R. Murrow stood up to the House Un-American Activities Committee's violation of human rights, was made soon after the passage of the Patriot Act, which many thought violated our search and seizure protections. This year's "Fair Game" depicts the story of Valerie Plame, a CIA agent whose identity was revealed by the Bush administration when she questioned intelligence asserting that Iraq had weapons of mass destruction. On one level, the film is about the pressure this event placed on Valerie Plame's marriage, but the film also examines a discounted propaganda effort to justify war with Iraq with WMDs. Two years ago, "Nothing But the Truth" told the story of the reporter who wrote the story outing Plame. The film had a similar message about the lengths government may go through to get what they want, but it also functions as the story of a woman willing to go to jail to protect freedom of the press and the right to keep her sources secret.

Even wearing a T-shirt proclaiming concert attendance has rhetorical purpose, perhaps to announce that our favorite band is the best, or to show others that we're simpatico with them because you share a common interest.

Rhetoric is a kind of social glue that can bring us together and create community. It is a way of sharing ideas and lifestyles. It creates a basis for conversation with like-minded people. However, once we've arrived at the most reliable approximate truth about an issue, it's our usual impulse to confirm our conclusions with others and to persuade those who don't agree to cooperate. It also helps to resolve social conflict, since we don't always agree. In fact, **we are often forced to consensus** whether or not we share common ground. Then we require debate to sort things out and help our society to function in as unified a manner as possible.

Thus, except on mainly ceremonial occasions, it matters less that we form arguments persuasive to those who already agree with us. It's easy to pick a few slogans for one side and repeat them like a cheerleader. Yet the result will be little opinion change. The real challenge is to encourage people to consider positions with which they disagree. To manage that, we each have to accept that our own **opinions may be challenged and changed in a free exchange of ideas.**

Rhetoric can encourage personal growth and communal learning. Yet we may become **defensive** when someone challenges our deeply held beliefs and values, which makes arguments both less pleasant and less productive

(6). We may also use **poor ethics** in argument or unconsciously commit **fallacies** consisting of unfair persuasive appeals or bad logic. There is clearly such a thing as unethical persuasion or misused rhetorical skill. This is where critical thinking comes in.

CRITICAL THINKING

You may be used to classes in which someone lectures then students memorize material and regurgitate it on tests. The purpose of critical thinking is to get beyond mere rote learning.

Critical thinking study urges you to think for yourselves, to search out information, and to analyze it sensibly. Learning to think for oneself is not always comfortable. It's not uncommon for students to look worried when I tell them to find their own topics for speeches. "But what do YOU want me to do?" they ask urgently, the subtext being, "what do I have to do to please you to get a good grade." What really matters is that we discover our own integrity and find something worth arguing about and defending.

The critical thinking movement gained widespread interest among educators during the 1980s. International conferences, such as those held at the Center for Critical Thinking and Moral Critique at Sonoma State University, explored the subject and set some standards listed below.

R.H. Ennis focuses on instrumental functions of critical thinking, defining it as, "reasonable reflection that is focused on what to believe or do." He suggests the following actions (7):

1. Judge the credibility of sources.
2. Identify conclusions, reasons, and assumptions.
3. Judge the quality of an argument.
4. Develop and defend a position on an issue.
5. Ask appropriate and clarifying questions.
6. Plan experiments and judge experimental designs.
7. Define terms in a way appropriate for the context.
8. Be open-minded.

9. Try to be well informed.

10. Draw conclusions when warranted, but with caution.

According to California Educational Code, ***critical thinking goals include:***

A) To identify hidden presumptions, ideas that we assume to be true without knowing how we came to believe them or why we believe them. These are what we try to identify in Toulmin warrants.

B) To apply sound logic to problem solving in daily situations.

C) To learn to structure arguments.

D) To understand the language of argument in everyday text and speech.

E) To build issue-oriented texts dealing with modern social problems.

F) To develop and practice appropriate attitude for applying these skills.

That's quite a list, and there's much more to be said about it in Chapter 2. We'll discuss both positive and negative examples of rhetoric, some blocks to critical thinking, common fallacies, and the dangers of propaganda there.

A PROPOSITION: THE SEED OF ARGUMENT

As soon as you've chosen an issue to discuss, ***matters of format*** will become important. Think of format as the menu for speech development, a kind of cookie-cutter you use to shape the raw dough of your research. Format creates guidelines for writing. You don't know where to start? Then follow the format. Once you understand even a handful of standard forms, they will become models for the future generation and understanding of arguments.

The basic "seed" of argument is the proposition (8). A proposition is simply a complete sentence that announces the point to be proved. A proposition ***answers an issue, a key question*** about that topic.

A proposition cannot be a question, nor can a proposition be a phrase. If we use a phrase it will usually be to announce a topic, as in, "The way we think about space exploration, but that's not focused enough for a proposition."

Both the thesis and the claims are propositions. The main proposition will become the thesis of the speech, while the subsidiary propositions needed to prove the thesis will be the claims for your arguments. ***However, we'll use the term "proposition" to refer to the thesis.*** We will use the word "claim" when referring to particular Toulmin arguments.

Put your thesis proposition at the beginning of the speech after a brief introduction. I've observed something about student writing style lately. There's a tendency to discover the thesis in the process of research and writing then pull the real thesis out in the conclusion. We don't have any room for suspense in argumentation. Few audiences will have the patience for long Socratic musings gradually leading to a point. We establish our point early so that we know what we're debating about, or, as I sometimes say, ***"Hang a sign on your shop."*** Let folks know what you're selling.

A good proposition should be ***a simple declarative sentence.*** That sentence will not be, "I'm going to talk about space exploration," or "I'm going to talk about" anything. It will be something like:

> The space program has made inventions for civilian use.

> Space exploration is a waste of taxpayer money.

> We should spend more funds on a manned trip to Mars.

Keep it simple. Use the fewest words possible "per square inch of idea." You're writing for the ear, remember, not the eye. Also, what you write you also have to say out loud in a conversational and comprehensible way. You may trip yourself up with big words or elaborate sentences used to impress (or used to cover up that you're not clear about your message).

Make a positive statement. Prove what's so, not what's not. Say what you do want us to do or to believe, not what you don't want us to do or believe. Don't say we shouldn't do something; say instead that we should limit it somehow or prohibit it, an affirmative action rather than a denial.

Use neutral phrasing. Propositions should be stated in sufficiently moderate language that each side can hold reasonably equal ground. For example, if you argue that "Child molesters should be kept away from children," that wouldn't leave the opponent much ground. What would the other side argue? "They should be encouraged to baby sit?" What is debatable is a more specific topic about ways to treat and/or punish such people, as well as how best to protect children. We should avoid the now common use of language that taints the issue in our favor. **Avoid colorful adjectives** like, "We must avoid the hideous, immoral, and unjust practice of X."

Specify the direction of change from a current belief, attitude, or social action. It's not sufficient to say, "We should change Y." Be clear about the manner of change, as in we need "more security," "less restriction," or "greater funding for." We want to "establish," "abolish," or "curtail" X. For reasons explained in a legal analogy below, the direction of change should be *away from the present way of looking at the issue.*

Perhaps the most important quality of a well-written proposition is that *it defines the argumentative ground,* establishing not only the point you intend to defend, but what you do not mean to bring up. That also limits the scope of debate and *helps to determine sides.*

ARGUMENTATIVE GROUND

How do propositions limit the scope of debate? Let's use an obvious yet difficult topic, that of abortion. We'll use a *military analogy* to explain. Consider this illustration of *a fort to designate the argumentative ground*, the particular position that you choose to defend (Figure 1).

Let's say *proposition A* is the most inclusive approach, occupying the largest ground to defend. The proposition representing that territory is:

> **All abortion should be illegal.**

Operate in the spirit of a *thesis-antithesis-synthesis format*; identify with the position and its opposite. Yes, identify with your opposite, because one of the best ways of focusing and adjusting your proposition is to imagine what both an advocate and *an imaginary opponent* would argue.

You might call this kind of thinking *an interior dialectic.*

It could also be thought of as *empathy, perspective taking, and compromise.*

So, we would think, what are some questions about or arguments against your proposition A that an opponent might make?

"What about cases of rape or incest? It isn't right to make someone bear the child of one who attacked them, especially knowing that there are some genetic factors to human aggression. How would you feel if your child was a daily reminder of so traumatic an event? Incest is a terrible sin and risks serious genetic problems for a child. Why punish the child for the crime of the father? What if the victim is seriously underage? Would she be able to cope with the pressures of motherhood?"

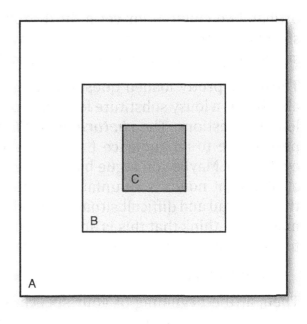

FIGURE 1-1.

The person in favor of proposition A might say that none of this matters; abortion is always wrong. "To use your own argument against you, if the sins of the father shouldn't be visited on the child, why is it right for the sins of the father to be transferred to an innocent baby? Are you saying that we should abort someone with a genetic defect? The brilliant scientist Stephen Hawking has Lou Gehrig's disease, which is inherited. Where would we be without contributions to our knowledge of the universe?" On the other hand, an advocate might think that these were reasonable challenges and modify the position to **proposition B** in Figure 1:

Abortion, except in cases of rape or incest, should be illegal.

You would have tightened the argumentative ground and **preempted an argument** that his opponent might have raised. Or, to further our military metaphor, you would have built **a slightly smaller but more defensible fort.** Let's take that a step further from the imaginary opponent's side.

"Yes, but what about cases of endangering a mother's life? Say you have a single mom with two other kids, and a doctor says she risks her life by having a baby. Would you force her to possibly, even probably, give up her life and orphan two children for yet a third orphan? Even if the mother survives, she may be struggling financially with two and is economically incapable of supporting a third without becoming a welfare burden to the state."

Those are pretty loaded questions, and I suspect most would agree that abortion is a lousy substitute for birth control anyway, but opponents raise loaded questions. The **rhetorical challenge** becomes how to bring your perspective to an audience that may perceive you to be unsympathetic, even cruel. Maybe you argue back that everybody is owed an equal chance at life. Right now, it's an unfair advantage for the mother. You may agree that it's a sad and difficult situation but that adoption remains an option. Or maybe you think that this is another fair set of challenges, and you submit to one more reduction of argumentative ground, **proposition C:**

> **Abortion, except for very specific exceptions, should be illegal.**

Then, at the beginning of your speech, you could define "exceptions" as cases of incest, abortion, or medically documented risk to the mother's life.

It may be we have to "downsize" our territory because of research limits. We don't always find the evidence to prove our original desired position. Whether by virtue of empathy, rhetorical strategy, or limits to research, our **argumentative ground is refined by two factors: definitions and qualifiers.**

DEFINITIONS

The degree to which you propose change can be imbedded in the way you define your terms (9). There are several ways to define your terms in a succinct manner, but we must **first decide which terms require definition.** Reconsider our abortion proposition C:

> **Abortion, except in very specific circumstances, should be illegal.**

Three terms would be important, as they are either vague or controversial enough to require clarification. They are "abortion," "specific exceptions," and "illegal."

The simplest approach would be to use **definitions from dictionaries.** For instance, *Webster's New World Dictionary* defines abortion as, "Premature expulsion of a fetus so that it does not live, especially if induced on purpose." This would probably exclude miscarriages, which may also be included in some definitions of the word "abort."

Often definitions from general dictionaries are too broad to be useful, but a *field-specific dictionary*, like *Dorland's Illustrated Medical Dictionary*, can also be used. *Black's Law Dictionary* may be even more useful here, since abortion is a legal issue. Black's definition includes the key elements of Roe v. Wade, the Supreme Court decision that forms a legal barrier to banning abortion:

> Prior to approximately the end of the first trimester of pregnancy the attending physician in consultation with his patient is free to determine, without regulation by state, that in his medical judgment the patient's pregnancy should be terminated, and if this decision is reached such judgment may be effectuated by an abortion without interference by the state (**10**).

So, making abortion illegal would necessarily include the reversal of Roe v. Wade. By understanding **the present threshold of the law**, we've found a more useful definition. This will become especially important when we build policy positions.

You may also define terms with **quotations from experts in the field** that may turn up in your research.

You may give **inclusive/exclusive definitions**. In other words, you may define by listing what your issue focus does and does not include. In proposition C about abortion, our definition of "specific exceptions" could be stated this way:

> Exceptions" include abortions involving rape, incest, or a severe risk to the health of the mother. That definition excludes financial or emotional reasons for exemption. Under no conditions does it include third trimester abortions.

This brings up one more approach, **operational definitions,** which are descriptions of the actual operations or actions your proposition intends. Just specify what you intend to do. For instance, you could specify how you intend to determine health risk to mothers:

> If there is a chance of risk to the health of the mother, such risk shall be determined by two state licensed doctors.

Or consider an operational definition for "illegal":

> "Make illegal" means that we should reverse Roe v. Wade at the federal level, pass a national law banning abortion on demand, and support states in authorizing selected clinics to determine exceptions.

These are operations or actions you would perform to enact the word "illegal." Simply listing the elements of your solution to a problem as the definition of your policy proposition would be another example of using operational definitions, but that is relevant to one type of speech, policy.

The clearer and more concise your definitions are, the less confusing discussion and debate will be. You want to spend your speaking time defending the proposition, not explaining it. "NOW I understand you. Oops. Time's up!"

QUALIFIERS

There is *a secondary triad* in Toulmin's argument form besides the primary one of claim, warrant, and grounds, but we'll only use one additional element as it helps focus proposition and claim word choice, the qualifier.

Qualifiers describe the degree to which something is true and help us adapt our opinions to audiences.

When dealing with social problems, qualifiers matter because we are not speaking absolute truth so much as opinion. *Speakers usually estimate probability, rather than certainty.* So, we have to use qualifiers to relate our propositions to the degree of probability with which we speak. In a sense, we can say that qualifiers are the primary means by which we determine the size of our " fort."

For instance, there's this *simple declension of descriptive terms* down from "in all cases," to "the vast majority of cases," to "most," to "many," to "some." There is also the phrase "in a few specific cases," to account for exceptions, or even "under certain exact conditions."

Toulmin himself mentions *modal qualifiers,* which are words or phrases that show what kind and degree of reliance is to be placed on propositions (**11**).

He refers to them as adverbs, adverbial phrases, or prepositional phrases that modify the action of the verb:

Sometimes

Perhaps

Maybe

Presumably

Necessarily

Certainly

In certain cases

In all probability

With the exception of

We should also mention the word *"possibly,"* which would certainly limit the degree of probability with which we hold the proposition to be true, and it may be important in discussions of new discovery or scientific matters at the frontiers of knowledge.

Of course, it would be better to use more ***specific statistical thresholds:*** "We should spend another million on this project," or "Increase funds by 10%," rather than "We should spend significantly more money."

For instance, the lame-duck congress of 2010 has been caught in a debate over whether to extend the Bush tax cuts. Republicans want to extend them to everyone. Obama originally supported the cuts for everyone with incomes below $250,000, but he adjusted the threshold to those making less than a million. Finally, all the cuts were extended, but only for two years.

Another modal qualifier is ***"at this point in time."*** We sometimes need to qualify propositions in time, place, and circumstances. If a social problem is imminent, we may need to offer a deadline to achieve something by a given date or year, like our government's deadline to return Iraq to sovereignty. The Bush tax cuts were set for a specific period of time and were meant to expire on January 1, 2011.

We may also ***limit a proposition geographically*** to a specific city, county, state, region, or the nation. We may propose international...or, theoretically, interplanetary change, depending on the planet from which you've come.

We can focus the topic to **include or exclude specific classes of people**:

> Citizens living in flood planes are at significant risk.
>
> Taxation is wrong for those who are unemployed.
>
> All persons over 70 should take semi-annual driving tests.

The limits of **specific circumstances or criteria** under which a proposition may apply can be exemplified by legal criteria. For example, murder in the first degree happens when there is forethought about the act and the slayer lays in wait for the victim. Murder in the second degree includes acts of aggression in the moment, what are often called "crimes of passion." Third degree murder, or manslaughter, occurs when someone causes death by negligent or irresponsible acts without any particular intent to kill.

Qualifiers are simply practical, as they **limit the ground you have to defend** in order to win your position and clarify the point of debate. The broader the position, the more ground you have to defend and the broader the avenues of counter-attack. So, sharpening your proposition not only focuses discussion, it helps one anticipate defenses by considering what attacks may be made against a broader proposition.

RULES & ROLES: A LEGAL ANALOGY

We can use a legal analogy to explain some the **rules and roles** of the debate process better than the military one. It's appropriate because we really are learning **a legalistic form of reason.**

There are three relevant comparisons with **legal terms: presumption, burden of proof, and prima facie case (12)**.

The first key concept is **presumption.** We're commonly aware of the idea that "the accused is innocent until proven guilty." The status quo, the present way of perceiving and doing things, is innocent until proven guilty. **Presumption is the single most distinct advantage in a debate.**

To the degree that our propositions challenge the status quo, the person who defends the proposition in question is **the advocate**, and his role is like that of a **prosecuting attorney.** His position in debate is called **the affirmative** because he affirms the proposition in question. Most importantly, he also **challenges presumption.** The advocate gets a balancing advantage to presumption. He speaks first and *lays out the argumentative territory* upon which the debate proceeds.

The adversary to the proposition is *the opponent,* and he functions very much like the *defense attorney* defending presumption. So, the idea of presumption also explains who goes first in a debate. The *advocate goes first*, because he is advocating against a presumption of innocence. There is no reason to speak unless there is "a charge." The *opponent speaks second*, like a defense attorney, but only once we've heard the prosecutor's case.

However, speaking first also involves an obligation, *the burden of proof.* Advocates, like prosecuting attorneys, must support their position with proof sufficient to give a reasonable audience, the jury, or us in this case, cause to doubt the innocence of the status quo. That is, there should be sufficient evidence to temporarily suspend presumption during a debate.

This is not to say that the opponent doesn't have to have any evidence. It just means that the affirmative must support his case decisively, or the negative wins by virtue of presumption. *A tie, or "reasonable doubt,"* means the advocate loses and the opponent wins.

How do we measure whether someone has met the burden of proof? That involves another legal term, *prima facie case*. In Latin the term literally means "on first face." As Professor Jack Perella of Santa Rosa Community College noted, there is more than one way to define this concept (**13**).

A traditional definition would go something like this: A prima facie case is *a set of arguments that, without refutation, would convince a reasonable person to adopt the proposition*. This definition relies on the notion of "a reasonable person," such as a jury member who might be selected by lawyers trying a case.

Another definition goes like this: *A primary facie case is one that is convincing enough that it temporarily suspends presumption.* In other words, it leaves us suspicious enough to hear a case against the accused. Presumption, as the first definition also acknowledges, can be regained with refutation, or arguments against the affirmative case.

We can even define it as *a case sufficient to meet the burden of proof.*

Yet none of that is very helpful in telling you what to do, is it? However, we have a more specific guideline in the concept of **stock issues.** In the types of propositions section of this chapter, you'll learn that each type of proposition has its own set of questions that need to be answered. Those can be regarded as **check lists** for what must be argued to achieve a prima facie case. If you have well-evidenced arguments that answer each of those questions, that's a reasonable standard for an adequate case.

It's not just about being convincing; you also have to be complete to achieve a prima facie case.

TYPES OF PROPOSITIONS

There are **three types** of propositions. Each type will be the "seed" of one of the kinds of speeches you'll do this semester. Each type is associated with a particular set of *"stock issues,"* questions that have to be answered in every speech of that type.

Propositions of fact argue what does or does not exist, what has or has not happened, and what may occur in the future. For instance, let's say we raise an issue of fact:

Has the Iraq war hurt the U.S. economy?

If you answer the question, "Yes, the Iraq war hurt the U.S. economy," then you'd have a proposition of fact. There are **two stock issues** in discussions of fact:

1. What **significant event** has happened, is happening, or will happen?
   A) Something is happening.
   B) It is a significant phenomenon in terms of its effects.
2. What is **the cause** of this significant event?

Basically, it's a speech that **reasons from cause to effect.** Sometimes we discuss both the short and the long-range effects. That can simply be seen as a division of the second stock issue into two parts. We could argue that something is significant both for immediate and for long-range impact. It may also be that something is not damaging in the present but will have serious long-range effects.

Propositions of value deal with what's **right and wrong**, ethical or unethical, moral or immoral, and good or evil. Concerns over **human rights,** for instance, typically may be expressed as propositions of value.

> **Denying equal employment opportunities to the aged is wrong.**

Value propositions also suggest **a sense of priority** among our values. For instance:

> **We emphasize foreign military action too much over domestic needs.**

For another example, we have a Bill of Rights, which is available on the web and should be read by every student, but those rights often come into conflict. That's one reason we need the Supreme Court to determine if one right is more important than another. So, we might argue that:

> **Fair trial rights are more important than the right to free press.**

We might also argue that fair trial rights are equal to free press rights and that we should balance the two equally. The key point is that value debates are often easier to see in concrete terms if we **place two values in conflict.**

There are **three stock issues** in a value speech:

1. **How do we define the values in conflict?** This is difficult, since values are often abstractions like justice, love, honesty, etc., and we may have very different ideas about what they mean.

2. **By what standard shall we compare values in conflict?** Like the Supreme Court, which uses a body of legal precedent and the constitution itself, we must reason from a clear, objective standard to arrange our priorities. The standard itself may be a point of argument in the debate, in which case we have to determine which side in the debate offers the more reasonable and appropriate standard.

3. **When comparison is made, which value is superior?** As for standards, which we'll discuss in detail later, we're looking for a basis for decision in the debate, some specific socially principle, preferably acceptable to both sides, by which we can declare a winner. We might take, for instance, **"the survival of the Republic"** as the standard for decision for the debate about priorities on foreign military spending

versus domestic spending. The ***criterion for decision*** could then become that the value which better serves the survival of the country and its democratic systems is the superior value.

Let's say that the priorities in conflict are domestic spending vs. military spending. If I defend the proposition that domestic spending on social programs is the higher priority, I might argue that poverty and discontent at home threatens the survival of the Republic. We could be able to defend ourselves from enemies abroad but lose to revolutionary impulses from within. There was 9/11, but there was also Oklahoma City. If I defend the proposition that military defense is the higher priority, I might argue that having richer entitlement programs at home would matter little if we were taken over by foreign powers. Terrorism is a genuine threat.

When we try to compare competing values as "better," we have to consider how to ***make the benefits concrete to an audience.*** Examples of how a value can make our lives better in practical terms is useful. Values aren't just about ideals. They're about ways of life. ***The proof of the value is in the living.***

Finally, there are ***propositions of policy***, which deal with what we should or should not do as a matter of practical social action. We discuss a social ***problem*** and come up with a practical ***solution***. That solution would be summarized as your policy proposition. Propositions of policy could include:

> ***We should reduce required medical care coverage for Americans.***
>
> ***We should increase foreign aid to Africa.***
>
> ***We should commit more funds to alternative fuel development.***

The ***four stock issues for policy*** overlap those for a proposition of fact, though with a slightly different emphasis.

1. Is there a significant ***harm***, a social damage that requires solution?

2. What are the ***causes*** of the harm?

3. What ***workable solution*** would eliminate or diminish the harm?

4. Are there any ***side effects*** of the solution, for good or ill, for which we should claim or for which we should account?

The order of the proposition types is somewhat progressive. We discover what the facts are. Then we look at the facts in terms of our values. Finally, we look at policy, what we should do, given the facts and values we've examined. Policy analysis includes issues of fact and value and is the most complex and complete discussion.

The issues themselves are not just systems of organization; they're means of what we call ***invention,*** the act of creating arguments. Invention is one of five terms used by Aristotle to characterize the parts of the rhetorical process. Even in your off-the-cuff discussions, form can help you to "invent" arguments (**14**). You ask the stock questions and brainstorm your way to appropriate arguments as answers.

The other terms in Aristotle's rhetorical process are ***arrangement***, or organization; ***style***, or the personality in writing; ***memory***, such as during rehearsal; and ***delivery***, the act of saying the material out loud to an audience. We'll discuss each concept over the next few chapters, though in less formal ways than Aristotle had in mind.

For the time being, realize that these stock issues are not just to help you organize what you already have. You can generate arguments by asking the questions and researching about them. That's why stock issues can also be called ***inventional systems.***

I am the great swami and will predict the future! That is not an example of a serious proposition, by the way. It's a prediction that you are going to be confused by these types of propositions for awhile. Thus, we'll spend some time looking at grammatical clues for each type.

THE GRAMMAR OF PROPOSITIONS

Initially, you may have ***trouble distinguishing the three proposition types***. You'll propose something is fact, because you feel deeply about it, but it's really a value. You'll propose what you think is a moral position, a strongly held value, but you can't help arguing what we ought to do, which leads you into policy.

Here are a few somewhat reliable *"key word clues."* We'll use these grammar clues for difficult concepts throughout the text.

Propositions of Fact: These involve forms of the verb *"is," "does," "has," or "will."* That's natural as you argue the nature of what is occurring, what does exist, and what has happened or will happen.

You are also trying to quantify phenomena, so adjectives like *"more," "fewer," "increasing," or "decreasing"* may be used.

> *Global warming is increasing.*
>
> *More people are enlisting in the armed forces.*
>
> *Voter interest has decreased significantly in recent years.*

Adjectives like "growing," "consequential," or "significant" may be used to emphasize topic importance.

> *Poor tests scores in schools are a growing problem.*

By the way, it's a perfectly reasonable proposition of fact to say, "This is a problem" You just have to stop there. You can't go on to propose solutions, which is the province of policy discussions.

Propositions of Value: Since these are essentially comparisons of ideas on a scale, we often find phrases like *"more important than," "more valuable than," or "is the highest priority."* Value also involves *abstract nouns* like "loyalty," "freedom," "democracy," and the like. If you hear language that sounds like the Boy Scout Oath - thrifty, clean, brave, reverent, etc. — you're dealing with values. There will also be "virtue words": *"right," "wrong," "immoral,"* etc.

> *Honesty is more important than courtesy.*
>
> *Medicare is the most important of all social programs.*
>
> *The poor deserve priority for tax breaks more than the rich.*

Value propositions are challenging to defend since we come to them in such subjective ways. Defending values sometimes requires a fair amount of contemplation about why you hold them to start with, or even what your most important values are.

Propositions of Policy: These are perhaps the easiest to recognize, as they almost always use the verbs like *"should," "must," or "ought to"* to motivate social action. Since we're talking about instituting solutions, nouns like *"plan," "program," or "system"* may also come into play.

These are just rough hints for beginners. ***Many exceptions to these word clues occur***, as lines between these proposition types are not rigidly drawn.

Loyalty is the most important human virtue.

Though this proposition employs the word "is," it isn't a proposition of fact. It suggests a sense of priority regarding abstract terms. Thus, it is a value.

We should pay more respect to education.

Just because the word "should" appears doesn't necessarily make this a policy. "Respect" is not a social action, let alone a practical program of policy to solve a problem. It's more an issue of value.

WHAT SHALL WE ARGUE ABOUT?

What issues of the day are worth the attention that this process requires? In the context of a critical thinking class, the subject should be a social, scientific, economic, or political issue. I don't mind hearing a fact speech about sports for a warm up, but part of the purpose of this study is to put you in touch with currents events.

Choosing and researching topics early is key to your success.

Why do we bother to talk about particular public issues? We do so because there is ***rhetorical demand,*** an impending necessity in the community that calls for us to speak and for audiences to listen with interest. Elections are coming up. There's been a catastrophic event. New social conditions demand that we adjust to survive. There's some pervasive injustice that we can't ignore.

General subject matter for the twenty-first century might include:

> *Bioethics*
> *Crime and punishment*
> *Economics*
> *Education*

Election to public office
Environmental problems
Foreign and domestic policies
Human rights
Immigration
Scientific discoveries and medical cure
The war on terror

Consider this list now. You may already have ideas. Ask specific questions about any of these, and you'll probably find an issue to discuss.

The first speech should be about an issue of fact. It's the simplest kind to build, and we can use it to learn more about Toulmin arguments. So some issues of fact might be:

Bioethics: Is rationing health care necessary to bring health costs down?

Crime: Are our drug enforcement policies working?

Immigration: Can we sustain the growing illegal immigrant population?

Material for our subjects are mostly found in non-fiction essays, journalism, editorials, and speeches. We can certainly make arguments about literature, sports, house or dress design, or any area of study, though the nature of the argument may vary from field to field.

Check out the **websites and library references that provide pro and con positions** on various topics at this footnote in the back of the chapter (**15**). Begin a broad subject search to consider topics you wish to use for this class.

It's fine to brainstorm about three or four subjects worthy of discussion and suggest issues to be answered. *However, don't just sit in your room daydreaming.* Go to a newsstand or a bookstore, browse through the magazines dealing with current events, find out what's going on right now. Read some current events sources. DO NOT start thinking about recycling your old legalize marijuana, reduce the drinking age, abortion, and obesity speeches that you did as papers in high school or in another class. Unless there's been some serious change in those old topics requiring us to adjust our presumption, let's **discover something that's happening right now**. It will be much more interesting if we inform each other with new information rather than the tired old clichés we've been throwing around for years.

There are some practical considerations. Choose a topic that is appropriate to the type of speech. If you have a topic you are so passionate about you cannot help but discuss solutions, don't use it for fact. Save it for policy. The fact speech will simply say that there's something happening and explain why in the most objective of terms. Saying that something is morally wrong is not appropriate to a fact speech. Values are opinions, not facts. Your teacher can help you choose what works best.

Also, realize that your speeches will probably range in length from 4 to 10 minutes, so choose something that you can handle in that amount of time.

Of course, since this is a rhetorical activity, think about your audience. We've learned that rhetoric is an adaptive process of shaping messages to particular audiences at particular times and places. Consider certain factors in choosing your topic, as well as your evidence and appeals:

Consider the age of your audience. This will be easy if you're in a class of contemporaries who are likely to be involved in similar events and invested in like concerns. For instance, I can count on my younger students to discuss the challenged future of Social Security and to propose private investment alternatives. Older students in my night classes are more likely to defend the Social Security system, since they've already paid into it.

Consider the education and interest level of your audience. Being in the same class setting already gives you some common interests of time and place. However, some topics are more difficult or require more expertise than your audience may possess. You may be accomplished at something that involves a lot of technical jargon. It's second nature to you or your profession, but will it be right for an audience that lacks your knowledge? It's good to start from your own interests. You may be more likely to speak with enthusiasm. Yet you have to find a way to **make your interest both valuable and accessible to other listeners.**

Consider the prevailing values of your audience. That is not to say that you shouldn't choose controversial issues. Controversy is the best reason to speak. Yet you have to be aware of ideas to which your audience may be sensitive. For instance, teaching in Orange County, California, a Republican stronghold, I have to be thoughtful about my criticisms of conservative policy. I can speak in a free exchange of idea, but I have to be more respectful than I would in a room of flaming liberals. Simply listening to the ideas of classmates can give you hints about how to adapt.

Consider the prominent circumstances of the moment. Sometimes we speak on special occasions, and it's customary to observe the occasion appropriately. If I'm speaking on the fourth of July, I don't show up in a Santa suit and talk about the productivity of my elves. If I'm giving a speech close to the anniversary of Pearl Harbor, I might choose to encourage greater respect for our veterans as a topic, or at least acknowledge their presence in the audience. At minimum, be aware that you may offend if you don't acknowledge events that impact your audience in the moment.

Though your first speech will be one of fact, your best first assignment is to find one proposition on different subjects for each type of speech. You can change later, but having something early will help you gather information as the semester goes and help you avoid last minute work.

Do that right away, please.

VOCABULARY

Advocate/Affirmative/Prosecuting Attorney

Burden of Proof

Claim/Warrant/Grounds

Confusion, Controversy & Conflict

Definitions

Direction of Change

Imaginary Opponent

Inclusive/Exclusive Definition

Invention

Issue

Kinds of Propositions: Fact, Value, Policy

Operational Definition

Opponent/Negative/Defense Attorney

Presumption

Prima Facie Case

Proposition

Qualifiers

Rhetorical Demand

Standards

Stock Issues

Thesis/Antithesis/Synthesis

REFERENCES

1) Gottman, J.M. Marital Interaction: Experimental Investigations. New York: Academic Press, Inc.,1979. http://www.wku.edu/Dept/Support/AcadAffairs/CTL/booklets/critthnk.htm

2) Toulmin, S. The Uses of Argument. London: Cambridge Press, 1958.
Toulmin, S., Rieke, R., Janik, A. An Introduction to Reasoning. New York: Macmillan, 1984.

3) Ellis-Christensen, Tricia. "In Science, What is an Inference?" November 10, 2010. http://www.wisegeek.com/in-science-what-is-an-inference.htm

4) Write Away! (February 1996) Volume 1, No. 2. The Problem of Writing Knowledge. http://wac.colostate.edu/books/
Teaching Blog. "Reading and Toulmin." http://www.ndsu.nodak.edu/ndsu/kbrooks/blog/.
"Creativity & Critical Thinking Skills." http://www.au.af.mil/au/awc/awcgate/awc-thkg.htm
"Critical Thinking Across the Curriculum." http://www.nwrel.org/scpd/sirs/3/snapll.html
"Critical Thinking: The Scientific Method." http://sdb.bio.purdue.edu/SDBEduca/dany_adams/'
"Critical Thinking in Social Studies." http://www.ericfacility.net/databases/
ERIC Digests. "Overcoming Obstacles to Critical Thinking in Your Organization." http://www.phptr.com/articles/
"Teaching CT: Some Lessons from Cognitive Science." http://www.philosoph.unimelb.edu.au/reason/papers

5) Solmsen, F. The Rhetoric and Poetics of Aristotle. New York: Random House, 1954.

6) Festinger, L. A Theory of Cognitive Dissonance. Stanford, California: Stanford University Press, 1957.

7) Ennis, R.H. "A Taxonomy of Critical Thinking Dispositions and Abilities. In J.Baron & R. Steinberg (Eds.) Teaching Thinking Skills: Theory and Practice, pp.9-26. New York: W.H. Freeman, 1987.

8) Ehninger, D., and W. Brockriede. Decision by Debate. New York: Dodd Mead, 1967.

9) Freeley, A. J. Argumentation and Debate: Critical Thinking For Reasoned Decision Making. Belmont, CA: Wadsworth, 1990.

10) Black, H.C. Black's Law Dictionary. St. Paul, MN: West Publishing Co, 1979.

11) Toulmin, et al., p. 85

12) Church, R. T., and C. Wilbanks. Values and Policies in Controversies: An Introduction to Argumentation & Debate. Scottsdale, AZ: Gorusich-Scarisbrick, 1986.

13) Pirella, J. The Debate Method of Critical Thinking: An Introduction. Dubuque, IA: Kendall-Hunt, 1987.

14) Lauer, J. Invention in Rhetoric and Composition. UC Santa Barbara, CA: Parlor Press and the WAC Clearinghouse, 2004.

15) ***Websites with pro and con issue discussion***:
   http://www.twinlakes.k12.in.us./info/library/connection/
   http://www.issuesprocon.org/
   http://www.schoolwork.org/issues.html
   http://wally.rit.edu/pubs/guides/contro.html
   http://www.multicolib.org/homework/sochc.html#gen
   http://lii.org/search/file/socialissues
   http://library.sau.edu/bestinfo/Hot/hotindex.htm
   See also these library reference works:
   CQ Researcher (print version). H35 .E35 (1991-)
   Congressional Digest. H35.E36
   Encyclopedia of Applied Ethics. BJ 63 E 44 1998 (Ref)
   Encyclopedia of Bioethics. QH332 .E52 2004 (Ref)
   Encyclopedia of Ethics. BJ63 .E45 2001 (Ref)
   Greenwood Encyclopedia of Women's Issues Worldwide.
   HQ1115 .G74 2003 (Ref)
   Check library for these pamphlet and book series:
   Contemporary World Issues
   Current Controversies
   Opposing Viewpoints
   Taking Sides

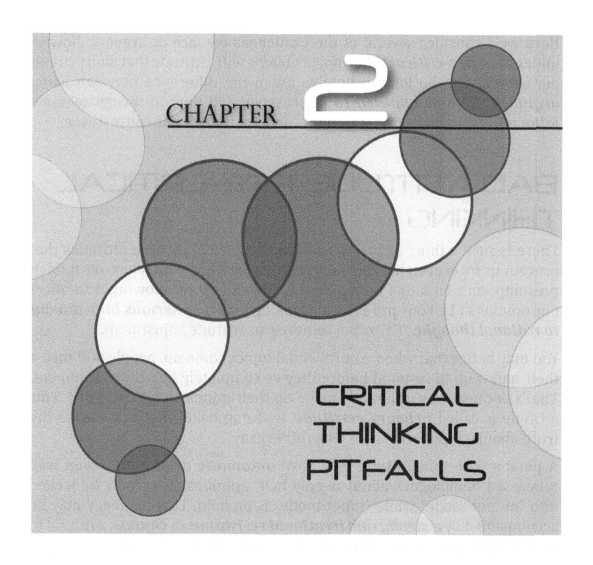

CHAPTER 2

CRITICAL
THINKING
PITFALLS

"DEMOCRACY REQUIRES A CERTAIN AMOUNT OF COMMON
GROUND. I DON'T BELIEVE YOU CAN SOLVE COMPLEX
QUESTIONS IF YOU HAVE TOO MUCH EXTREMISM OF RHETORIC
AND EXCESSIVE PARTISANSHIP. TIMES ARE CHANGING TOO FAST.
WE NEED TO KEEP OUR EYES OPEN. WE NEED TO BE FLEXIBLE."

– PRESIDENT BILL CLINTON –

These are such highly partisan and emotionally charged times that it's
difficult to be a good critical thinker. We're bombarded with bad examples
all the time.

Here we'll consider several of the challenges we face as arguers: how to understand *pre-critical thinking*, problems with attitude that short circuit our attempts to be logical; how to grasp the difference between being *argumentative as opposed to aggressive*; and how to recognize some *fallacies* that damage our arguments and the tone of our conversation.

BAD ATTITUDE: PRE-CRITICAL THINKING

There is such a thing as pre-critical thinking. We may have attitudes that prevent us from even hearing new information that challenges our hidden presumptions, let alone taking data in objectively or allowing it to affect our opinions (1). Poor pre-critical thinking may be *a serious impediment to rational thought.* "CT" often requires an attitude adjustment.

You may notice that when controversial topics come up, people will thrust their hands up to respond before they've completely heard the argument. That's because they've already made up their minds about that topic. This attitude is called *primary certitude*, a strong belief that one knows the truth about a topic, no matter what others say.

A person with this attitude may have *automatic arguments*, even well rehearsed monologues about deeply held opinions. They may be locked into "output mode" while "input mode" is on hold. This tendency may be accompanied by *a strong and irrational resistance to change*, a refusal to alter deeply held notions, even when they're proven to be incorrect.

Sometimes primary certitude may lead to a kind of *mind reading*. You may have had interpersonal altercations with someone who "knows what you really think." They may assume your position and respond to it defensively without getting what you really mean. The same can happen in debate, a forced misinterpretation of an argument, followed by a fallacious response. Rush Limbaugh often makes statements on his radio show like, "Liberals always argue X," though his description of the position he opposes is a misrepresentation of what most folks to Limbaugh's left may really feel.

On the other hand, *open-mindedness* is the appropriate attitude for critical thinking. You have to hear the other person out before you disagree, even be able to offer *a fair paraphrase* of their position before you offer your own. That's how educated people act. ***If you already "know," you can't hear.***

Primary certitude may also accompany oversimplifications, like "you're for me or against me." We call this **either or thinking**. We may long for simple answers, but they're not often there. Social issues are usually complex, not black or white. I recently heard an Arizona man on talk radio say of illegal immigrants, "We need to send them all back or accept them into our homes."

A book by commentator Sean Hannity is called *Let Freedom Ring: Winning the War of Liberty over Liberalism.* Since when are liberty and liberalism really mutually exclusive? Bill O'Reilly's book *Pinheads and Patriots: Where You Stand in the Era of Obama* makes a similar error. If you agree with me, you're a patriot; if you don't, you're a pinhead.

The **pro-life vs. pro-choice** debate, for instance, is one of our most polarized national discussions. Each side tends to stereotype the other, as religious bigots in one case, as murderers in the other. Yet it is unlikely that a person believing in the right to abortion would say, "Yes, I'm anti-life. I just wish everyone who disagrees with me would die." It is equally unlikely that an anti-abortionist would say, "Oh, yes. I hate human choice. I want us all to be mindless robots." These labels are oversimplifications that allow each side a sense of righteous superiority. Thus, it's an ongoing conversation that creates more heat than light. Indeed, it is a defining value conflict of our age.

What we should appreciate is that **there are various possible opinions along a range of belief between "for" and "against."** For instance, it's possible to be pro-choice, allowing others the freedom of their view yet not choose abortion and believe other choices, like adoption, are better. It's also reasonable that we wouldn't want our tax dollars spent on a practice we find morally reprehensible yet defend the freedom of others to behave with the same liberty we grant ourselves, as long as they pay for it.

In contrast to either or thinking, **tolerance of ambiguity** is characteristic for good critical thinkers. That is, in the face of doubt, conflicting data, or lack of information, we suspend premature judgment and search further for the truth. Since there are few clearly right or wrong opinions when dealing with practical public affairs, it's useful to **sit in the presence of uncertainty**, until we're satisfied that we know. Be patient like a good fisherman. Don't jump to conclusions. Let the conclusions come to you through careful listening and the research process (**2**).

Scientists working toward an understanding of neutrino particles speak openly about the need for this trait in pushing at the frontiers of knowledge. Consider the patience of an astronomer waiting for the secrets of the universe to unfold, or the quantum physicist who actually observes that more than one truth is possible at a time. For them, the quality of the journey is more important than jumping to conclusions along the way (**3**).

The ideal critical thinker might have similar patience, within the limits of making assignment deadlines, of course. One benefit of the effort is that tolerance of ambiguity is positively associated with enhanced management ability and employee satisfaction (**4**).

We may feel threatened about our public image in the face of counter-argument, or think that it's somehow a personal assault. "You tore me apart," a student may say when his arguments are taken to task. This kind of feeling is most common when we actually feel like our opponent has made a strong point or even realize that they're right and we're wrong. Yet we don't tend to say, "Hey, you know what? That's a great point."

Unfortunately, that's less likely than having a **reaction formation.** Instead of acknowledging the validity of our opponent's idea, we go overboard on insisting the correctness of a position that we now doubt (**5**). You may have had an argument with a friend who says something that hurts us. We want their friendship and fear its loss, but we say something like, "Oh, get lost. Who needs a friend like you anyway?" A gay person in denial, for another example, may act extra hard to look hetero, even macho. A guy who is really fearful, maybe even a coward, may try to be bully.

In a real life case, California State Senator Roy Ashburn voted vigorously for anti-gay legislation for 14 years. Only recently after a DUI arrest was it discovered that Ashburn is gay (**6**). After Katie Couric took Sarah Palin apart in their famous television interview before the last presidential election, Palin began to use the term "lamestream media," though she was the one unable to answer fairly simple questions about public policy on television, such as being unable to name a single magazine or newspaper that she read to prep herself for debates (**7**). Since then, she has become increasingly aggressive with news media at a distance, while refusing interviews from any but the friendliest sources. Whether Couric was being aggressive by trying to set Palin up is another question.

ARGUMENTATIVE VS. AGGRESSIVE

Being argumentative is not the same as being aggressive (8). People who are argumentative are ***assertive*** and capable of expressing ideas and feelings, but they do so in reasonably ***inoffensive language***. They listen carefully. They believe that appreciation should precede criticism. They try to paraphrase what people say before they argue back. The point for them is not just winning but understanding the relative strengths and weaknesses among the pro and con arguments, so that they can arrive at the best approximate truth about difficult social controversies.

Aggressive people argue against people rather than to the point. They use personal attacks, are prone to ***belligerence***, lack objectivity, and tend to be emotionally reactive. Name calling and yelling are common. They tend to ***interrupt***, an all too common tendency among news interviewers today. This loss of self-control mars intelligent debate.

These opposing sets of behavior have ***nonverbal dimensions*** as well. While an argumentative person maintains a relaxed and positive manner while discussing ideas, aggressive people may roll their eyes, look away, and shake their heads. They may ball up their fists in anger. Their tone may become sarcastic. They may move into the physical territory of those they oppose. They may tap someone with a pointed finger. There's a push, then someone edges their way closer to becoming an assault statistic.

In fact, most murders occur following some degree of aggressive social interaction between victim and murderer. Murders generally happen within the context of interpersonal relations, and most victims know their murderer. It's a sad fact that most American murders occur within the family (9). Apart from pathology as a cause, many of these physical encounters begin with poor communication. Unable to express themselves in more rational and constructive ways, people degenerate into violent behavior.

Yet disagreeing with someone doesn't have to create enemies. Critical thinking discourages aggression at the same time that it encourages argument. An argumentative person practices a ***basic pattern of critical thinking: thesis, antithesis, synthesis.*** Offer your thesis, consider the antithesis, the other person's viewpoint, then generate a synthesis that accounts for the best of both sides. Throughout this text, this process will be referred to as ***using your imaginary opponent.*** Even when you're forming your own arguments, take some time to look at them from the opposite point of view. This is also called ***dialectical thinking.***

If we have trouble controlling our impulse to be aggressive, try to remember that we may be most aggressive when we're fearful, when we're worried about "losing face" because we feel attacked. However, ***we are not our arguments.*** We mold arguments, hold arguments, improve them, or abandon them. Ideas are something we can have, or not, but it sometimes seems as if our ideas have taken possession of us, we're so attached.

Critical thinkers come to look at arguments as tools, perhaps even toys to play with. That's right. ***Argument can be fun if we approach it like a game.*** You are not the ball when you play baseball. You don't grab your head screaming when someone hits the ball. Neither are you your argument.

FALLACIES OF APPEAL

At extreme levels of aggression, our impulse may even be to dislike the messenger as much as the contradictory message. The next natural reaction might be to offer ***ad hominem attacks***, or "arguments to the person." That is, we attack the speaker rather than respond to the speech. This is one of the most prominent of a group of fallacies called "fallacies of appeal." These fallacies employ emotional gimmicks that ***short-circuit logic*** before it gets a chance to gain traction and provoke irrational response.

Our recent mid-term election was a carnival of ad hominem attacks. It was a season of horrible ads that are the antithesis of everything this book intends to teach about fairness, honesty, and balanced thinking. Here are but a few:

Running against Dr. Minyard for coroner in New Orleans, Dr. Dwight McKenna used a scandal regarding the sale of body parts out of the morgue by depicting the incumbent as Dr. Frankenstein, complete with Igor toting body parts (**10**). Dr. Minyard was not directly involved in the scandal.

Representative Barney Frank was portrayed as a man "dancing around the issues" in suggestive moves spoofing his openly gay status (**11**).

California Governor Jerry Brown's campaign group was overhead on a recorded conversation calling his opponent Meg Whitman "a whore." The comment was made in the context that Whitman had been making deals with unions to get votes. It was unclear whether Brown himself or an aide had made the comment, but the comment was made in his presence (**12**).

Outside of the campaign, syndicated commentator Don Imus took ad hominem a step further, calling the Rutgers women's basketball team, "some nappy headed hoes." He was fired from CBS for the comment but remains widely broadcast (**13**).

The **bandwagon argument,** also called "argumentum ad populum" in Latin, or "appeal to the people," exploits the popularity of an idea or action. If the crowd believes it, it must be true. Variations of this fallacy include **tu quoque**, or "you did it, so I get to, too." Yet two wrongs do not make a right. The common language of this fallacy includes **"everybody's doing it," or "everybody knows."** Peer pressure to use drugs often includes "everybody's doing it" as an appeal.

Bandwagon is a familiar staple of TV commercials. They show a lonely guy with Brand X beer looking across at a Budweiser party. The guys drink "Bud" surrounded by gorgeous girls in bikinis in the snow. It's the amazing Swedish Bikini Team cavorting around in sub-freezing temperatures. (Yea. That always happens.) The appeal is to our need to belong, our desire not to be different. It doesn't necessarily make Brand X any worse than Bud.

Billy O'Reilly made a rather bold "everybody knows" argument in an interview with Christine O'Donnell (**14**):

REILLY: "Everybody knows that scientists have enough knowledge to clone a human being if they wanted to..."

O'DONNELL: "They are—they are doing that here in the United States."

Really? Scientists will surely be excited about their previously unknown progress. Science fiction writers may have gotten ideas after O'Donnell proceeded to say that scientists are cross breeding men and animals and have produced a fully functioning human brain in a mouse. Amazing. That would be a snug fit. Yet throwing around the "everybody knows" language is a common way of not having to prove your positions.

As far as the scientific community knows only a few doctors, widely considered to be crackpots, argue that they can clone babies in the near future. A Dr. Zavos claims to have transferred cloned embryos into human wombs, which is considered a serious ethical breach, and even he says that it will be a few years down the line before cloning is possible, "if we can intensify our efforts… but I don't know if we can intensify our efforts to that extent **(15)**."

Another variation of appeal to the people is the **"just plain folks"** approach. George Bush, Sr., and his wife Barbara gave a very classy interview to Don King, one of his last. Barbara, when asked about Sarah Palin, said that she thought Palin was happy in Alaska doing what she's doing and should probably stay there, a subtle way of saying that Palin wasn't ready for the presidency. They then endorsed Mitt Romney for the next presidential election. Palin called them, "the blue bloods who want to pick and choose" who should be on the Republican ticket. In other word, we common folks who aren't blue bloods know much better than the former first lady, not to mention a former president, ambassador to China, and director of the CIA **(16)**. Sarah Palin herself, you may recall, has completed one term as the mayor of a small Alaskan town and resigned her first term as governor.

The complementary fallacy would be *appeal to snobbery*, which occurs when one tries to show that only a few exclusive people would understand. We're so smart or special that we'll rise above the norm when we are privy to this knowledge, have access to a special place, or own a "premium" product **(17)**. Country clubs with limited membership get people to pay outrageous golfing fees with this appeal. The classic contrast to Bud would be Michelob beer, an "upgraded" product from Budweiser. Instead of the Swedish bikini team, you get an actor in a tuxedo talking about the refined taste of this beer. Expensive jeans are a bit ironic. You pay for the pricey label and act as moving advertising for the brand. They're all just denim, which runs about five bucks a yard.

Another common fallacy of appeal is the *appeal to pity and fear.* This is an exploitation of pathos, one of Aristotle's three appeals. There's a point at which pathos goes beyond passion to *"**bathos**,"* which is insincere and excessively sentimental pathos. One of my favorite examples comes from judicial history. A teenage male brutally murdered his own parents. His attorney, showing equal parts of originality and gall, actually argued for mercy on the grounds that his client was an orphan. The jury didn't bite.

I learned this fallacy the hard way. In high school, I agreed to chair a youth drive for *a certain famous charity*. I spent many hours getting other young people to join and spoke for the drive, equipped with the usual, touching poster of a child on crutches in leg braces. Only after the campaign did I discover that 96% of the money raised actually went back into the charitable organization, while only 4% wound up with the children pictured in the posters. Basically, it was an employment program and an excuse for travel junkets. The name has been left out to protect the guilty, since they've cleaned up their act. More modern charities, like the United Way, have a better balance in expenditure, but there are still many charity scams and manipulations that rely on our pity.

There was an incident at my college during *a demonstration against the Vietnam War.* A group of radical protesters distributed a handbill that said they would napalm a dog in the college square to show what we were doing to people over there. A large crowd gathered, shaking their fists in total ire over the threat to a dumb animal. Of course, there was no dog. There was only a guy at the mike, telling us, "Look at how angry you got over one dog. Why aren't you angry about the thousands of human lives lost in Vietnam?" A few people thought it was creative persuasion. Others stayed around, somewhat skeptically, to listen. Most of us were repulsed because we felt manipulated by an unfair appeal to pity based on a lie.

There have been continual assertions that the Obama White House has a communist agenda and wants to redistribute the wealth in a Marxist manner. Newsman Glen Beck has compared Obama to both Karl Marx and Hitler, a communist and a Facist, which is self-contradictory as well as an appeal to fear. Beck has interspersed pictures of Obama and Karl Marx on his program, suggesting an analogy that the two are the same. Fear of communism is deeply rooted in the American psyche, but the notion that the President is a closet communist is absurd. Speaking of President Obama, Beck has said that he has "a deep-seated hatred for white people or white culture (**18**)." Playing the race card is another common appeal to fear.

The mental action of **appeal to tradition** is simple: "We must continue to do something merely because we've always done it this way." You may have suggested a different way of doing something to a boss and had him say, "Well, we've done pretty darn well doing things the old way." By that reasoning, we should stay away from all new schools of art, new scientific discovery, virtually any new manufacturing process, even if it creates jobs and cheaper products, simply because it's new.

A story about cooking shows the folly of appeal to tradition. There was a woman who, when preparing ham, always began by cutting off one end of the ham and throwing it away. When this strange behavior was questioned by a friend, she admitted that she did it only because her mother did it that way. Becoming curious herself, she asked her mother why she cut the end off the ham. The mother, in turn, said that it was how her mother did it. When the grandmother was questioned, she revealed that she only cut the end off the ham because it wouldn't fit in her pan.

Here's some of the language you'll hear that announces this fallacy: "our forefathers," "from the dawn of time," "we have always." On the other hand, "it's new," "it's the latest fashion," "it's cutting or bleeding edge," etc., may be an **appeal to novelty**. To argue, "let's do it because it's new," is equally fallacious. The fact that it's the latest thing, the latest fashion, the latest technology, doesn't necessarily make it better. Chrysler once had a very effective low tire pressure indicator. A picture would appear on the dash and the pressure in each tire was numbered. You knew which specific tire required air and how low it was, a remarkably accurate feature. A newer version just said, "tire pressure low," but it didn't indicate which tire or give a number for how low it was. Chrysler owners then had to get out of their newer model and try each tire to find out which was low. Thanks, Chrysler. I especially enjoyed that improvement in the rain.

Walk down the detergent aisle in your market and count how many boxes say "new and improved." We don't know what's actually been improved, but the appeal itself is popular. "New and improved" seems never to come off some brands. Old ideas aren't necessarily better. Yet new ideas aren't necessarily better. Better ideas are better, as measured by their effects.

The fallacy of appeal to ignorance is often confused by students. They hear an argument that they think is dumb and label it as this fallacy. The mental action is simpler; it's *a reversal of the burden of proof* discussed in the first chapter. The language typically works like this: You make a claim and then, in lieu of providing grounds, you ask your adversary to prove the claim wrong. Often it is seen in discussions of the supernatural and speculations about the unknown. You can almost hear Leonard Nimoy intoning on one of those unsolved mystery shows: "But as for the yeti, to this day, nobody has proved that it doesn't exist." It's not our burden to prove that the yeti does not exist. If you say that something exists, the burden of proof is yours.

The appeal to humor walks a fine line between being good style and a fallacy. If we simply try to make fun of the opponent's position without offering a sound argument of our own, it's a fallacy. An audience may consider it enjoyable, but it's a fallacy. If we're funny and we have an argument, it may be considered good style.

Historically, appeal to humor might sometimes be classified as *wit*. During a duel in British Parliament, Disraeli faced off with an adversary who said:

> "Sir, you will either die of syphilis, or on the gallows!"

> Disraeli coolly replied, "That depends, sir, on whether I embrace your mistress, or your principles."

Game. Set. Match. Disraeli returned a vicious ad hominem with a clever retort. Apart from his strong credibility and the fact that he had other arguments, Disraeli also didn't strike first. A spontaneous rejoinder in self-defense is often considered witty and the sting deserved by the attacker.

It's actually in the mind of the audience, the ultimate arbiter of effective speaking, whether it's a fallacy or style. *Fallacies are perceived in a subjective manner*, and there is often disagreement about them. If you're a conservative and listen to Rush Limbaugh, you may think he's hilarious, even as he says something like, "The difference between Los Angeles and yogurt is that yogurt comes with less fruit," or "Feminism was established so as to allow unattractive women easier access to the mainstream of society (**19**)." If you're more liberal, you may think that Bill Maher is both funny and politically correct commenting on why the Republican party doesn't support a too liberal Arnold Schwartzenegger: "Karl Rove said if his father wasn't a Nazi, he wouldn't have any credibility with conservatives at all (**20**)."

Maher even skewered friend Jon Stewart and Steven Colbert's "Rally for Sanity," dedicated to "toning it down a notch," a satiric response to the fervent rallies of Glenn Beck and the Tea Party. After Stewart's funny encouragements that we should be more moderate and non-partisan in our political debate, Maher took him to task for what he regarded as a hidden presumption in their "can't we all just get along" message: that the left and the right are equidistant from a search for a centrist common ground.

Stewart's response was to suggest another rally: "Rally To Determine Precisely The Percentage Of Blame To Be Doled Out To The Left And The Right For Our Problems Because We All Know That The Only Thing That Matters Is That The Other Guys Are Worse Than We Are...." (21).

But these guys are professional entertainers. What happens when politicians try to use humor against opponents? You be the judge as to whether it's wit or an unfair use of humor to avoid supporting your point:

George W. Bush on his last election against John Kerry: "It's been a little tough to prepare for the debates, because he keeps changing his positions, especially on the war. I think he could spend 90 minutes debating himself."

Senator Kerry on Bush after being told he took a spill on his mountain bike: "Did the training wheels fall off (22)?"

Kerry also said, "I want to start by saying something nice about President Bush. Of all the presidents we've had with the last name of Bush, his economic plan ranks in the top two (23)."

President Obama responded to attacks about him at the Republican convention with, "I've been called worse things on a basketball court."

Concerning references to his relative newness to politics and doubts about whether he was a U.S. citizen: "Who is Barack Obama? Contrary to the rumors you have heard, I was not born in a manger. I was actually born on Krypton and sent here by my father Jor-El to save the Planet Earth."

He also poked fun at Sarah Palin's mention that she can see Russia from Alaska as a foreign policy qualification. He was at the Al Smith dinner at the famous Waldorf-Astoria Hotel. "I do love the Waldorf-Astoria, though. You know, I hear that from the doorstep you can see all the way to the Russian tea room (24)."

FALLACIES OF LANGUAGE

The words we choose to express our arguments are important. *Eloquence*, the ability to say just the right words at the right occasion, contributes to both clear argument and good persuasion.

Fallacies of language are words that intentionally distort meaning, exploit vagueness, or incite emotion in an unreasonable way.

We sometimes use *equivocations* in our word choice, making phrases that can be interpreted in at least two ways. That can be a source of interpersonal and argumentative misunderstanding.

"I really love you." Play with that one for a while. Is that, I love you like my good bud? I love you like, get in the back seat right now? I love you in the sense of agape, brotherly love? I want to marry you? Love ya, mean it, let's do lunch? What?

There are always the usual, innocent human misunderstandings. For instance, people aren't always careful with their *pronouns.* Talking about two female friends, we might tell a story that goes something like, "Well, she did this, but then she did that, so she got really upset." You would have to ask, "Which she is she?" The speaker would then adjust to proper nouns, Sally and May, and we could sort the story out. The fallacy occurs when we intentionally equivocate to avoid close scrutiny of our arguments or actions.

Bill Clinton's response to his Monica Lewinsky affair, "I did not have sexual relations with that woman" attempted to parse definitions of "sexual relations." In his equivocation, oral sex doesn't qualify as sexual relations; only intercourse does.

"Outside of the killings, Washington has one of the lowest crime rates in the country," said Mayor Marion Barry of Washington, DC. Of course, since he's been videotaped smoking crack, he may have been having an off day.

"I haven't committed a crime. What I did was fail to comply with the law," offered David Dinkins, New York City Mayor, answering accusations that he failed to pay his taxes (**25**).

Obama was also called equivocal when he reversed an administration promise to release photos of detainee abuse at Guantanamo Bay (**26**).

Abstract and value-laden words often have equivocal effects, since our understanding of these terms is subjective. These include what may be called *glittering generalities*, values so vague but good sounding that you can't quite argue against them even though you're not sure what the arguer really means. How can you be against "God and Country," unless you're agnostic or atheist? How can you be against "liberty," a word commonly thrown around today? But what do they really mean by liberty? In some cases it seems like liberty from taxation; in others it seems like liberty from regulation of unethical business practices used to take advantage of consumers, liberty to export jobs to other countries for the profit of a few, even liberty from bipartisan cooperation.

It's hard to argue against a word like "patriotism," but what do we mean by that? My country, right or wrong, or the courage to stand up, use your freedom of speech, and disagree with the crowd? Acts of heroism like Medal of Honor Winner Jason Dunham who threw his body on a grenade in Iraq to save his friends? These can all be good words when meaningfully defined. The problem is that unscrupulous people throw them around to conceal more insidious intent, and we go along with them because we appreciate our own sense of the word. As the great Samuel Johnson said, "Patriotism is the last refuge of scoundrels."

Congress was so intimidated by the very name of "*The Patriot Act*," that they passed it without reading it after the very emotional events of 9/11. Three hundred and fifty seven House members said aye to only sixty six nays, including Representative Ron Paul, a Republican candidate for president in 2008 who called it "The Un-Patriot Act." Only one senator, Russ Feingold of Wisconsin, said nay. "While it contained many provisions that I supported," Feingold said, "I voted against the bill because I was concerned that several provisions failed to adequately respect constitutional rights and protections (**27**)." In 2006, a majority of congressmen came to agree with him, and the act was modified with many more nays. After three terms, Senator Feingold lost in 2010 to a wealthy plastics manufacturer with no political experience who spent over $40 million on his campaign.

Here is a list of "generalities" that candidates were told to use when speaking about themselves or their policies in recent presidential elections (**28**):

Change	Commitment	Common Sense
Courage	Crusade	Dream
Duty	Fair	Family
Freedom	Hard Work	Help
Initiative	Lead	Liberty
Light	Mobilize	Moral
Passionate	Peace	Pioneer
Precious	Preserve	Prosperity
Protect	Strength	Success
Truth	Unity	Vision

These are really nice words, but we interpret them so subjectively that we seldom know what candidates really mean by them.

I'll leave glittering generalities with one more example. Note that the key words are capitalized for emphasis:

> This is an institution of Chivalry, Humanity, Mercy, and Patriotism; embodying in its genius and its principles all that is chivalric in conduct, noble in sentiment, generous in manhood, and patriotic in purpose.

Sound appealing? It's from the "Principles of the Klu Klux Klan (29)."

Closely associated to glittering generalities is **jingoism**, the use of overly simple but highly charged phrases. It's a kind of political chauvinism, blind patriotism or nationalism, which I like to call "***bumper sticker logic.***" One of my old favorites that I haven't seen in awhile is "Guns don't kill people; people kill people." Well, sure, a gun doesn't jump out of a drawer and stalk you with murderous intent, but it can be dropped, go off, and kill you by accident. A more accurate bumper sticker would be "People with guns kill people, especially when they misuse them." Guns do make it a lot easier to kill somebody, something I have to remember as a gun owner myself.

At a Tea Party Rally featured in *Time* magazine, you can see a variety of signs in the crowd that say things like, "Guns = security, freedom, equality, democracy," "Stop Socializing America" with a hammer and sickle on it, "We need a truth czar – fire the others," and the common "Take America back." I'm still trying to figure out where America went that it had to be taken back. Where and when did we lose it? Glenn Beck says Woodrow Willson's presidency, though we started to stray with Andrew Jackson **(30)**. Boy, we've been lost a long time. It's a wonder we're still here. Maybe we should don coonskin caps, get in a time machine, and go straighten "Ol Hickory" out. (And, yes, that is an appeal to humor).

The other day I saw a bumper sticker referring to President Obama, who campaigned on a need for change: "You keep the change. I'll keep my money." This is a response to continual references to the president as a communist or a socialist and belief that he somehow, in two years, single-handedly created the debt that he inherited.

These phrases get repeated over and over again, and people come to believe them by sheer force of saturation. Yes, I know, I'm picking on Sarah Palin, but her continual repetition of "Barack HUSSEIN Obama" in her speeches has serious effect **(31)**. This jingo was stopped by Senator John McCain during their 2008 presidential campaign together, but she's resumed it with force. People actually believe the implication that the president is a Muslim, perhaps even a relative of Saddam Hussein, the deposed dictator of Iraq, and, hence, sympathetic to terrorists. A Pew Research Center poll showed that 18% of Americans believe that he is, in fact, a Muslim. Only 34% said that he was a Christian, down from 48% last year **(32)**. After this was published and Obama was seen attending a Protestant church with his wife and children, it was called a "cynical ploy" by FOX news reporters.

Glittering generalities and jingoism are close relatives to the more general fallacy of **emotive language,** using "hot words" that provoke or incite negative emotion and irrational response. They may be intentionally chosen to excite people beyond reason, but we have to acknowledge that we use passionate words legitimately in the pursuit of pathos, and some theorists don't even count emotive language as a fallacy, since it isn't an argument. Technically, the same could be said of ad hominem, even though Aristotle called it "argument to the man," because simple name-calling or insults aren't arguments either.

What's emotive for an audience is, of course, ***subjective***. It may be something as simple as being called "a girl" when you want to be acknowledged as a woman of equal status. Dropping the word "fat" around someone who struggles with their weight may have an entirely different meaning for them than your intent.

However, **the intentional use of "hot words" to exploit irrational audience response** is at least irresponsible. Jerry Falwell called Mohammed a terrorist on the CBS news show 60 Minutes and implied that he was a pederast because he had many young wives. He later apologized for it, but the effect of associating, not just specific groups, but an entire religion with terrorists was incendiary. Perhaps somebody pointed out to Falwell that the Biblical hero David had a number of young wives. Anyway, nobody can say the word "terrorist" today without evoking some kind of negative emotion. Can we have any rational thoughts about a term like "child molester"?

The 2010 election introduced a new wrinkle in emotive language, use of the term **"man up."** On October 14, 2010, the term "man up" began to steamroll its way into becoming a campaign tool. It was used by female candidates to challenge the masculinity of opponents and suggest that they were less than men (**33**).

Sharron Angle said of her opponent in Nevada, "Man up, Harry Reid. You need to understand we have a problem with Social Security."

In Missouri on the same day, Democrat Robin Carnahan spoke of Roy Blunt's desire to repeal health care reform and renew insurance company protections. She told him, "Man up. Repeal your own bad health care legislation, and do what you're asking other people to do."

Sarah Palin directed the term on an October 18 rally against mainstream Republicans who weren't throwing their weight behind the Tea Party, "Hey, politicians who are in office today you... need to man up and spend some political capital to support the Tea Party candidates."

Many a foolish young man has been goaded into a fight because someone called him, well, "a female part."

The other side of the coin is that female candidates are even more likely to receive degrading sexist comments. Men have been making emotive references to female candidates somehow going crazy during their periods for a long time (**34**).

Gordon Liddy said of Supreme Court Justice Sonia Sotomayor, "Let's hope that the key conferences aren't when she's menstruating or something, or just before she's going to menstruate."

Secretary of State Hillary Clinton got this shout from an anonymous audience member during her bid for the presidency: "Iron my shirts."

Candidate Joe Miller made this thinly veiled suggestion to opponent Lisa Murkowski: "What's the difference between selling out your party's values and the world's oldest profession?"

Recently, there has been continual use of **"anchor babies"** and "the anchor baby racket," references to children of illegal immigrants who are granted citizenship upon birth in the United States. The suggestion is that the babies "anchor" an illegal family to use benefits afforded citizens **(35)**.

Glittering generalities, jingoism, and emotive language appeal to our base, unconscious instincts. **Jargonese**, the abuse of technical language to make arguments obscure, attempts to exploit the superior education of the user. This may happen when a specialist in a field describes something in such complex terms that you can only take his word for it. Some doctors may be more interested in your compliance than your understanding of medical treatments. It's a time issue for them to explain, so they may overwhelm you with new terms then ask you to trust them that certain treatments are necessary. Garage mechanics may also dazzle you with technical terms about why you need a lot of engine repairs, or new suspension, or whatever. The chances are good that you have paid for at least some unnecessary repair. Don't even get started on lawyers; it will make your head spin. We don't understand the special language, so these and other professions can take advantage of us by hiding true intent in a cloud of words that may make us feel stupid and compliant. Am I being unfair to these professions?

Approximately 7.5 million surgeries are believed to be unnecessary procedures. Other estimates place the number at 60% of the total number of surgeries in the country, and that excludes cosmetic surgery **(36)**.

Hidden camera investigations of 90 auto repair chains in five countries, including the United States, revealed that over 40% of repairs were unnecessary **(37)**.

The number of frivolous lawsuits has become so excessive that government has had to make laws and levy fines to stop clogging courts with them. These cases wouldn't go to court if there weren't enough sophistic lawyers to plead them. For examples of such suits, see footnote (**38**).

Even **euphemisms,** literally "words of good omen," can interfere with a realistic perception of problems. A euphemism is a nice word used to conceal less pleasant reality. It can be harmless, like calling the garbage man "a sewage engineer," or calling a stewardess the less sexually biased term "flight attendant," or simply telling somebody in the wrong dress, "You look so yourself tonight." At this level, a euphemism may even be a normal courtesy. It's not always necessary for others to know our opinions.

However, euphemisms at the level of national politics may be weighted with more significance. ***Some euphemisms whitewash unsavory policy:***

- "The Final Solution" in Germany was what they called the ovens.
- In America, "separate but equal" meant "segregated schools."
- Firing people has become "downsizing."
- In Iraq, "collateral damage" means accidental civilian deaths.
- Military interventions have been called "reconnaissance in force."
- Torture has become "enhanced interrogation."

The Bush White House endorsed ***"preemptive strikes"*** to justify the invasion of Iraq. In plain language, the term says we can legitimately attack others before we've been attacked, much as we ourselves were attacked at Pearl Harbor in WWII. The Japanese also had a suspicion that the United States would enter the war against them, so they issued a preemptive strike. Yet few events have been more devastating to America than Pearl Harbor.

It's certainly uncomfortable to look at such parallels, isn't it? We want to believe that we're more righteous in performing the same acts that we condemn in others. Subtle twists in language can make it easier. Although two opponents may practice similar behavior, one side can call themselves "freedom fighters" while the other side calls them "insurrectionaries."

Repeated often enough, euphemisms can become deeply rooted among our social assumptions, numbing our awareness of harsh realities. So, when we use language in a reactionary or unconscious way, we should look carefully at what such words may conceal. The words we choose define the nature of the world. The more often we repeat certain kinds of phrases, the more habituated our world view may become.

The Institute for Propaganda Analysis suggested a number of *questions that people should ask themselves in the face of language abuses* (39):

- What does the virtue word (the glittering generality) really mean?
- Does the idea in question have a legitimate connection with the real meaning of the word?
- Is an idea that does not really serve my best interests being "sold" to me by the use of artificially positive language?
- Leaving the virtue word out of consideration, what are the merits of the idea itself?

CULTURAL CONDITIONING

Why do we get involved in poor attitudes and fallacies? We're sensible, rational people, aren't we? Much is due to our *cultural conditioning.* Values and principles are formed by input from others, as well as by the times and places in which we were raised. Personal experience, race, and nation are aspects of such conditioning. Often our cultural assumptions have simply been repeated to us so often by family, friends, and authority figures that we can't imagine thinking any other way **(40)**. Sometimes we merely repeat what we've heard often enough to make a subjective impression.

Sheer *force of repetition*, as the advertising community well knows, is persuasive though not necessarily accurate or responsible. In fact, there is a fallacy of appeal called **argumentum ad nauseum,** which is precisely translated as saying it over and over until we're sick of hearing it.

By the way, if you happen to be hot for the Latin names of these and other fallacies, see footnote **(41)**.

Advertisers are particularly adroit at exploiting repetition. For instance, I do a casual survey in every class that tests the force of repetition on name brand recognition. Students are asked to name the toothpaste that they prefer. The majority, as many as ninety percent, mention the number one and two advertisers, Colgate and Crest. Yet most can offer no evidence for the superiority of the product over Aquafresh, Tom's of Maine, Arm and Hammer, Mentadent Whitening, or any of the others commonly mentioned.

The truth about toothpaste is what? There are actually some good reasons for choosing Colgate "Total," the only toothpaste to contain triclosan, an anti-bacterial agent. It actually clings to your teeth providing an ongoing killing of bacteria. Otherwise, the only key ingredient for clinical effectiveness is fluoride. You might as well buy CVS generic tartar control toothpaste on the cheap. Whitening toothpastes are bogus, even the popular Crest 3D. They remove surface stains, but all toothpastes do that to one degree or another. Baking soda? Bogus. It has zero clinical effectiveness. It bubbles, though, and people seem to enjoy the effervescence (**42**). The point is not to be an ad for Colgate, but to point out that we act without really researching our actions, simply because we hear something often enough that it seems right.

It's not just advertising that wins through argumentum ad nauseum, though; it's our whole culture, country, race, and family who have us from a very early age. In our most impressionable years, our **hidden presumptions** are built for us, as Pink Floyd said in their album "The Wall," a brick at a time. Hidden presumptions are **beliefs taken so much as a matter of fact that we don't think they need to be proven.** And it can become a kind of a wall. We know so much that isn't so already that there's sometimes little room for the facts to work their way in. In a court, they may refer to hidden presumptions as "**assuming facts not in evidence.**" In our lives, that colors everything, how we think, talk, dress, vote, everything.

The various kinds of aggressiveness discussed earlier may be aggravated by **ethnocentric or socio-centric attitudes**. Respectively, these are the belief that our race or our society are automatically more normal or right somehow than others (**43**).

A humorous example is the father in the film "My Big Fat Greek Wedding" who insists that he can trace any word back to Greek. In fact, our alphabet is based upon that of the Greeks, but that is based on the Semitic alphabet that has influenced most of the world. The earliest stages of English were mostly influenced by Anglo-Saxons with substantial influences coming later from Latin and French. A lot of Latin is really "Latinized Greek," but it is hardly accurate to say that every word of English can be traced back to Greece. He just loves Greece so much that he can't imagine it any other way.

Historically, the effects of ethnocentrism and socio-centrism have been horrific. European Imperialism from the 16th century decimated third world peoples and has created terrible tensions between Euro-based cultures, including the United States, and the rest of the world. We can trace some of the roots of our problems with terrorism to effects of British colonialism in the oil-rich countries. Solving the problem is not only difficult because of what the west has done historically to Muslims, but their own tribalism divides them into substrata well beneath what we would consider a stable nation state. Perspective matters greatly, and ours is as far from theirs as it can be.

Our normal desire to keep conversation lively, as well as our need to be perceived positively by peers, may lead us to **exaggerations.** We say things are bigger in quantity than we really know to be true, and we assert wildly that something is so "most of the time," even "nine out of ten times," though we have no particular statistics on the matter. We use **words like "always" and "never,"** oversimplifying issues that could be quantified accurately with research. Exaggerations are insidious, though, because they lead to **stereotypes** about other societies and ethnicities. We begin to find it easier to make little jokes like, "A Muslim, a priest and a Jew go into a bar...."

These kinds of jokes may be intended good-naturedly but may also indicate serious prejudices. We stereotype classes of people who are different than we are, usually more out of frustration than actual knowledge, or even actual belief on the part of the speaker. We may use **ethnic slurs** against other drivers in the privacy of our car that we would never think to utter in a personal encounter. No harm, no foul? Consider what those kinds of repetitions are doing to your own mind. You're habituating yourself with certain kinds of reactions to groups without regard for the individual qualities of persons within the group.

Repeated often enough, even ridiculous rumors and stories can gain the momentum of truth. Consider this somewhat ethnocentric view of Afghans from an anonymous U.S. intelligence officer in a web chat room, paraphrased to leave out the harsher language:

These guys are savages. I can't even call them human. They have no respect for anything, not for each other or themselves, let alone people who are trying to help them. Their language is babble. They beat their women and force children into fights to defend family pride. Savages. Roaming packs of sub-human beasts. They should just kill each other off (**44**).

Anger is understandable when we're in conflict with vastly different cultures, but it is irrational to make other people less than human to justify our fear and hatred of them. That's precisely the purpose of this kind of ethnocentric speech; it's a way of focusing and expressing fear. We should, however, see this as a dangerous means of expression, allowing us to dehumanize other cultures and make killing them easier.

Nazi Germany, of course, became so wildly blinded by their socio-centrism that they thought they should rule the world and so overcome with their ethnocentrism that they committed genocide (**45**). By the way, not to say that Nazi genocide is a cliché, but this is a good example of one of those things we know that isn't so. I often hear that they were responsible for the greatest genocide in history, but is that factually correct? Using body count as a standard, Hitler ranks third having killed 12 million, behind Mao, who may have killed as many as 78 million, and Stalin, who ended 23 million lives counting his purges and his starving of the Ukraine (**46**). Pol Pot killed at least 2 million in relatively tiny Cambodia, one of the worst per capita acts of genocide.

Imperialism has lessened, but we still seem to feel that we have a right to the resources of other countries. Americans constitute 5% of the world's population but consume 24% of the world's energy. Each person in the industrialized world uses ten times as much commercial energy as a person in the developing world. The food we get in a given day amounts to 815 billion calories, at least 200 billion more than we really need and enough to feed about 80 million starving people. We throw out 200,000 tons of edible food daily (**47**). On a per capita basis, the United States is the second worst polluter in the world as measured by CO_2 emissions (**48**). Yet we probably don't get up every day thinking that we're greedy or wasteful. Why? We have developed a culture of consumption, and it is reinforced daily by the messages around us. Our folks lived that way, we live that way, and very few of us seem willing to make the changes necessary to be a more sustainable culture. Maybe that's something worth speaking about.

PROPAGANDA

When our cultural conditioning becomes overwhelming, it's more likely that we may be affected by propaganda. Propaganda is extreme persuasive practice using fallacies and stereotyped image to attack political opponents and unfairly manipulate public opinion. It employs intentional deceptions in speech and image to secure uncritical belief and compliant action (**49**).

Some of the **common tactics** include concepts we've already discussed but used to an extreme degree, such as appeal to fear, glittering generalities, and argumentum ad nauseum. Other important tactics are **disinformation, demonization, and "The Big Lie."**

Starting malicious rumors about opponents and enemies is the form of propaganda called "**disinformation**." Disinformation includes the intentional leaking or publication of lies to damage or confuse rivals, for instance, the distribution of forged documents, photographs, and fabricated intelligence (**50**).

During the House Un-American Activities Committee's persecution of people suspected of being communists, charismatic demagogue **Senator Joe McCarthy** made a famous speech, waving a nonexistent "secret" document, and saying "I have here in my hand a list of two hundred and five that were known to the Secretary of State as being members of the Communist Party and who nevertheless are still working and shaping the policy of the State Department." McCarthy also lied about his own military background, leading people to believe with a posed picture that he had been a tail gunner in a bomber. Tail gunning was a dangerous job, as the gun turrets would be targeted by attacking fighter planes. In truth, he was an intelligence officer who had merely ridden along as an observer. He also forged a letter from his commander to obtain a citation for a phony combat wound. Yet he was able to ruin many careers and even threaten the White House with fabrications until he was exposed (**51**).

Rumors were spread among Arabs abroad that Zionists were behind the **9/11** attacks, presumably to involve the United States against Muslims. There were rumors that 4000 Jewish workers stayed home from work near the Twin Towers on 9/11, and that Israeli spies videotaped the towers' collapse. Others in the bazaars of Pakistan spread rumors that the United States had attacked itself as an excuse to come after oil.

Disinformation about **Osama Bin Laden** included that he penned a memo to his cave mates, warning them to lay off his "Cheez-It" stash (**52**). The story has a purpose. At an obvious level, it has a humorous effect for the troops searching for him. It also demystifies someone who was a larger than life figure. It also makes a slightly more subtle point of propaganda: Even these rigid Muslim fundamentalists secretly like things American.

At an international level, disinformation leverages the self-interests of nations. At a national level, disinformation is used to distract a public from other truths propagandists wish you wouldn't notice. The outing of CIA agent **Valerie Plame** by Bush White House members was part of a campaign to support a lie about nuclear materials going into Iraq, an idea used to justify the war. The intelligence about the nuclear materials coming from Africa was itself disinformation. WMDs were never found in Iraq, though our government promised that they existed.

Another form of propaganda is "**demonization**," reducing opponents to stereotyped and unfairly negative images, an attempt to dehumanize them and make it easier to hate, oppose, and kill them.

In Nazi poster propaganda, stereotyped Jews with enormous noses were shown with Frankenstein green skin, never normal flesh color, usually clutching at money (**53**). These images are often attached to language that **scapegoats** the target and focuses the anger of the people on them, allowing your opposition of them to make you a hero. To this day, you may hear comments about the "international Jewish banker conspiracy."

In Iran and Iraq we have sometimes been called **"the Great Satan."** How much more demonized can you get than that? Yet we have also come to demonize terrorists so much that it has made it hard to think positively about any Muslim peoples. In fact, a common appeal of demonization is that we should suspend due process rights to stop the threat of the demonized.

Are some modern candidates in this country going beyond merely unfair or overeager campaign practices to demonize opponents? On a billboard ad in Colorado, President Obama was caricatured as a terrorist in Middle-Eastern garb strapped with dynamite, as a gangster in a pimp outfit, as a Mexican bandit, and as a flaming gay in a purple suit. Straining logic like a taffy pull, one could say that the board suggests that Obama is soft on terrorism, crime, illegal immigration, and gay rights, but the depictions are so profanely racist that the real message is louder.

How can anyone with an ounce of critical intelligence look at such a billboard and even think that it makes any sense? Both Democrats and Republicans agreed that the ad had to be taken down. A Tea Party group had planned to have a rally there but found themselves without a stage **(54).**

Finally, there is the concept of **"The Big Lie."** There's a principle in propaganda that the bigger the lie, the easier it is to sell. The idea was discussed in Chapter 10 of Adolph Hitler's *Mein Kampf*, as translated by James Murphy:

> All this was inspired by the principle—which is quite true within itself—that in the big lie there is always a certain force of credibility; because the broad masses of a nation are always more easily corrupted in the deeper strata of their emotional nature than consciously or voluntarily; and thus in the primitive simplicity of their minds they more readily fall victims to the big lie than the small lie, since they themselves often tell small lies in little matters but would be ashamed to resort to large-scale falsehoods. It would never come into their heads to fabricate colossal untruths, and they would not believe that others could have the impudence to distort the truth so infamously **(55):.**

This was how Hitler convinced Germany that Jews were responsible for them losing WWI. When this tactic is combined with forceful speaking from a charismatic person, the impact can be disastrous.

It is arguable that "The Big Lie" has been used by some banks during our mortgage crisis. The Bank of America, which bought paper from several troubled mortgage entities like Countrywide, have taken government money, promising to help homeowners with the Making Home Affordable program. They pledged to help lower mortgage rates, reduce total mortgage amounts, but only 3% of applicants have received help. Tactics have included entering people in the MHA program but delaying processing for a year to two years, during which time people have illegally lost their homes. There is continual loss of submitted documents followed by threat of forelosure. There is testimony that documents have been submitted and resubmitted multiple times, and the implication is that they have been intentionally lost to delay processing. Agents and even phone numbers for program access change frequently, making it hard for applicants to follow up with their requests. Freezes of evictions have been imposed, and recently, the states of Arizona and Nevada joined the ranks of others filing suit against the bank for dislocating families without proper review of forms, merely rubber stamping foreclosure notices without even reading them.

Yet, throughout the process, the bank has continued this mantra: "No one was wrongly thrown out of their home." All of this, and much of our economic problem, began with a huge lie that some people could afford homes with interest only and other kinds of tricky mortgages given to people who should never have qualified. In the meantime, the Bank of America and other banks hold money from the government, allowing it to collect interest while they disallow mortgage restructuring that would avoid evictions. They were also accused of lying about the loses of Merril Lynch in order to persuade stockholders during their acquisition of the company. Citibank and J.P. Morgan Chase have been similarly accused (**56**).

Here's one last historical example, ***The First Gulf War***, which occurred in Kuwait during the administration of George Bush, Sr. At the start of the war in 1990, I remember waking up on an August morning surprised to be at war. I was also impressed with video footage, narrated by Dick Cheney, showing how our missiles could do precise strikes, shoot right down into the top of a building containing enemy personnel, supposedly without harming the civilian population in the surrounding neighborhood. Later disproved in documentaries by Bill Moyers, who showed film of injured civilians, and by other reports of civilian damage, these videos were revealed to be ***disinformation.*** Estimates of civilian death have been controversial, ranging from 1000 to 3500. Certainly some civilian deaths occurred in spite of the video game illusion of absolute accuracy (**57**).

Also at the start of the war, three major news magazines—*Time, Newsweek,* and *U.S. News and World Report*—featured Saddam Hussein's face on the cover, painted green, that same ***demonization*** technique that Nazis used. We joined in a subjective repulsion tinged by ethnocentric fears. Afterwards, the American public was highly supportive of the invasion of Kuwait, then being held by Iraq. The president also changed his pronunciation of Saddam Hussein's name to "Sodom," with all its dark Biblical connotations.

The Big Lie was used before the current Gulf War when Iraq was incorrectly linked to 9/11 and reports of weapons of mass destruction proved false.

There is no question but that Saddam Hussein was a hated dictator who imprisoned and tortured his own people. There is also no question that it was the United States and our Arab allies who helped finance the rise of Hussein in Iraq out of fear of the more radical Muslim extremists in Iran. Part of our war goal in the Middle East is to clean up some problems we were at least partially involved in creating. There are photos of former Secretary of State Donald Rumsfeld shaking hands with Hussein. We also helped prop up Osama Bin Laden against Russians in Afghanistan (**58**).

And is the American public really illiterate and fearful enough to allow this kind of practice to determine the course of our lives. Let's ask ourselves that question again at the end of the course. At least people haven't gone quite as far as rhyming Osama with Obama, and there is no more cause for such a silly stunt, since it was Obama and Navy Seals under his command who got Osama.

IN SUM

Obviously, there's an ethical dimension to practicing good rhetoric and avoiding some of the poor practices discussed in this chapter. Rieke and Sillars mentioned some specific ethical responsibilities appropriate for argument in a classroom setting. Among them are these practical principles:

- Participants must not silence each other to prevent criticism.
- If you make a claim, you must be able to provide proof upon request.
- When you criticize an argument, you should be sure you're accurate in paraphrasing that argument.
- You should defend your claims only with relevant material.
- You should not falsely claim that others have argued something they have not, and you should be willing to admit to whatever you yourself have presumed.
- You should not say your claim has been established without proof
- You should stick to arguments that are logically defensible.
- Acknowledge it when you fail to establish your claims, or when your opponents have established theirs.
- Avoid being vague or ambiguous, and interpret the arguments of others clearly (**59**).

Here are a few ideas worth committing to memory:

- Arguments don't have to be quarrels.

- A single "argument as artifact" has a claim to be defended, a warrant that supports the claim with reason, and grounds that prove the claim.

- Don't claim what you can't prove and don't say that evidence says more than it really does.

- Rhetoric is the process of adapting arguments to particular audiences, at particular times and places.

- You're writing for the ear, not the eye.

- You can be argumentative without being aggressive.

- One basic pattern of critical thinking is "thesis, antithesis, synthesis." Offer your thesis, consider the other guy's viewpoint—your "imaginary opponent"—then generate a synthesis that accounts for the best of both sides.

- Watch your own hidden presumptions—or facts not in evidence— as well as cultural conditioning that can lead you to poor pre-critical thinking and the commitment of fallacies.

- Be aware that even "the good guys" commit fallacies and use propaganda.

VOCABULARY

I know. It's a lot of vocabulary, but argument is like getting off a plane in an exotic foreign country. You have to learn enough appropriate language to ask "where's the bathroom, " or express that you'd rather eat something other than iguana on a stick.

Argumentative vs. Aggressive

The Big Lie

    Cultural Conditioning

Demonization

Dialectial Thinking

Demonization

Disinformation

Ethnocentrism & Sociocentrism

Either Or Thinking

Eloquence

Euphemism

Fallacies of Appeal

    Ad Hominem

    Appeal to Humor

    Appeal to Ignorance

    Appeal to Novelty

    Appeal to the People (Bandwagon Argument)

    Appeal to Pity & Fear

    Appeal to Snobbery

    Appeal to Tradition

Fallacies of Language

    Argumentum ad Nauseum

    Emotive Language

    Equivocations

    Euphemisms

    Glittering Generalities

    Jargonese

    Jingoism

Hidden Presumption

Invention

Open Mindedness

Primary Certitude

Propaganda

Reaction Formation

Resistance to Change

Thesis/Antithesis/Synthesis

Tolerance of Ambiguity

REFERENCES

1) Kytle, R. Clear Thinking for Composition. Boston: McGraw-Hill. Martin, J.G. (1972)."The Tolerant Personality." Detroit: Wayne State University Press, 1987.

2) Sherrill, W.W. (2001). "Tolerance of Ambiguity Among MD/MBA Students: Implications for Management Potential." Journal of Continuing Education for Health Professions, Spring 21 (2001): 117–122.

3) Stoycheva, K., D. Stetinski, and K. Popova. Tolerance for Ambiguity. Bulgarian Academy of Sciences, 2003. http://mail.ipsyh.bas.bg//ipsych/projengkop.htm.

4) Barry, V.E. Invitation to Critical Thinking. New York: Holt, Rinehart, & Winston, 1984.

5) Festinger, L. A Theory of Cognitive Dissonance. Stanford, CA: Stanford University Press, 1957. Stamp, G.H., A.L. Vangelisti and J.A. Daly. "The Creation of Defensiveness in Social Interaction." Communication Quarterly 40 (1992): 177–190. http://changingminds.org/explanations/behaviors/coping/reaction_formation.htm.

6) "The Gay Anti-Gay Legislator," Los Angeles Times, March 10, 2010. http://articles.latimes.com/2010/mar/10/opinion/la-ed-ashburn10-2010mar10.

7) http://www.dailymail.co.uk/news/worldnews/article-1332314/Sarah-Palin-refuses-interview-journalist-Katie-Couric-following-2008-humiliation.html.

8) Colbert, K.E. "The Effects of Debate Participation on Argumentativeness and Verbal Aggression." Communication Education 42 (1993): 206–214.

   Infante, D.A. "Trait Argumentativeness as a Predictor of Communicative Behavior in Situations Requiring Argument." Central States Speech Journal 32 (1981): 265–272.

   Infante, D.A. "Argumentativeness: Its Effect in Group Decision Making and It's Role in Leadership Perception." Communication Education 31 (1982): 141–148.

   Infante, D.A. "Aggressiveness." In J.C. McCroskey and J.A. Daly (Eds.), Personality and Interpersonal Communication. Newbury Park, CA: Sage Publications, Inc., 1987: pp. 157–192.

   Shutz, B. "Argumentativeness: It's Effect In Group Decision-Making and It's Role in Leadership Perception." Communication Quarterly 30 (1982): 368–375.

9) Center for Disease Control website, July, 2006. CliffsNotes.com. Crimes against People. December 22, 2010. http://www.cliffsnotes.com/study_guide/topicArticleId-26957,articleId-26875.html.

10) http://blogs.telegraph.co.uk/news/tobyharnden/100061447/top-20-best-and-worst-political-ads-of-2010-us-elections-part-2/.

11) http://gawker.com/5670913/watch-animated-barney-frank-do-all-sorts-of-gay-dance-moves%20of%20a%20hip-swiveling.

12) http://www.examiner.com/libertarian-in-san-jose/jerry-brown-camp-calls-meg-whitman-a-whore.

13) "CBS Fires Don Imus Over Racial Slur." CBS News. http://www.cbsnews.com/stories/2007/04/12/national/main2675273.shtml.

14) "Of Mice & Men & Christine O'Donnel," Forbes, October 2, 2010. http://blogs.forbes.com/michaelfumento/2010/10/22/of-mice-and-men-and-christine-odonnell/.

15) "Fertility expert: 'I can clone a human being," The Independent, April 22, 2009. http://www.independent.co.uk/news/science/fertility-expert-i-can-clone-a-human-being-1672095.html.

16) "Sarah Palin versus Republican 'blue bloods,'" Christian Science Monitor, December 5, 2010. http://www.csmonitor.com/USA/Politics/The-Vote/2010/1205/Sarah-Palin-versus-Republican-blue-bloods.

17) Dowden, Bradley, The Internet Encyclopedia of Philosophy, January 31, 2010. http://www.iep.utm.edu/fallacy/#Appeal%20to%20Snobbery.

18) Mark Leibovich, "Being Glenn Beck," New York Times Magazine, October 3, 2010.

19) http://www.brainyquote.com/quotes/authors/r/rush_limbaugh.html.

20) http://www.brainyquote.com/quotes/authors/b/bill_maher_2.html.

21) http://www.deathandtaxesmag.com/35764/bill-maher-rips-stewart-colbert-rally-to-restore-sanity/ http://www.examiner.com/tv-in-national/jon-stewart-responds-to-rally-to-restore-sanity-criticism-creates-new-rally.

22) http://www.rateitall.com/t-20344-funny-quotes-from-politicians.aspx.

23) http://thinkexist.com/funny_politics_quotes/.

24) http://politicalhumor.about.com/od/barackobama/a/obama-quotes.htm.

25) http://www.innocentenglish.com/funny-bloopers-mistakes-quotes/famous-bloopers.html.

26) http://www.huffingtonpost.com/john-cusack/a-hollow-and-horrible-equ_b_203817.html.

27) http://feingold.senate.gov/issues_patriot.html.

28) Rieke, R.D. & M.O. Sillars. "Argumentation and Critical Decision Making." New York: Longman, 2001.

29) Seldes, G. (1985). The Great Thoughts. New York: Ballantine Books.

30) Leibovich, Mark, "Being Glenn Beck," New York Times Magazine, October 3, 2010.

31) "Palin calls Obama 'Barack Hussein,'" CBS News, September 23, 2010. http://politicalticker.blogs.cnn.com/2010/09/23/palin-calls-obama-barack-hussein/.

32) "Rumors Don't Worry Obama," Los Angeles Times, August 30, 2010.

33) "Man Up Gets Political," Visual Thesaurus, October 22, 2010. http://www.visualthesaurus.com/cm/wordroutes/2458/.

34) "Top 50 Most Sexist Quotes on the Campaign Trail," The Spin, http://thestir.cafemom.com/in_the_news/110242/top_50_most_sexist_quotes.

35) "Anchor Babies: Citizenship for Illegal Offspring," The Columbia Tribune, November 26, 2010. http://www.columbiatribune.com/news/ 2010/ nov/26/anchor-babies/.

36) Indiana Injury Law Blog, September 18, 2010. http://www.indianainjurylawblog.com/2010/09/some_facts_about_unnecessary_s.html.

37) http://www.carinfo.com/autorepair.html.

38) http://www.the-injury-lawyer-directory.com/ridiculouslawsuits.html.

39) aaron@propagandacritic.com.

40) Barry, V. E. (1984).

41) http://www.infidels.org/library/modern/mathew/logic.html.

42) http://www.consumersearch.com/toothpaste/colgate-total. http://www.slate.com/id/3604/.

43) Barry, V. E. (1984).

44) Los Angeles Times, April 4, 2002.

45) http://www.yourdictionary.com/grammar/examples/examples-of-ethnocentrism.html.

46) http://www.scaruffi.com/politics/dictat.html.

47) http://www.mindfully.org/Sustainability/Americans-Consume-24percent.htm.

48) http://www.thenewecologist.com/2009/10/the-worlds-biggest-polluters/.

49) Johnson, D. The Art and Science of Persuasion. Dubuque, IA: William C. Brown/Benchmark, 1994.

50) Various Web Dictionaries http://www.google.com/search?hl=en&defl=en&q=define:disinformation&sa=X&psj=1&ei=pWoXTZeFJIu6sAOlou3EAg&ved=0CBMQkAE.

51) http://www.people.ubr.com/political/by-first-name/j/joseph-mccarthy/joseph-mccarthy-quotes/i-have-here-in-my.aspx. http://www.wisconsinhistory.org/whi/fullRecord.asp?id=8005.

52) "Have You Heard The One About Osama's Cheez-It-Stash?" Los Angeles Times, March 24, 2002.

53) Gallo, M. The Poster in History. New York: W.W. Norton & Co, 2000.

54) http://www.msnbc.msn.com/id/39698327/ns/politics-decision_2010/.

55) http://gutenberg.net.au/ebooks02/0200601.txt and http://www.sourcewatch.org/index.php?title=Big_lie.

56) http://www.cnbc.com/id/34877347/Big_Banks_Accused_of_Short_Sale_Fraud.
http://www.usatoday.com/money/industries/banking/2010-02-04-bank-of-america-charged_N.htm.
http://www.ritholtz.com/blog/2010/10/the-big-lie-on-fraudclosure/.
http://www.credit.com/blog/2010/12/two-states-charge-bank-of-america-with-fraud/.

57) http://www.postgazette.com/nation/20030216casualty0216p5.asp.

58) http://www.gwu.edu/~nsarchiv/NSAEBB/NSAEBB82/.

59) Rieke, R.D., & M.O. Sillars. "Argumentation and Critical Decision Making." New York: Longman, 2001. Also, Brockriede, W. "Arguers as Lovers." In Philosophy & Rhetoric 5 (1972): 1–11.

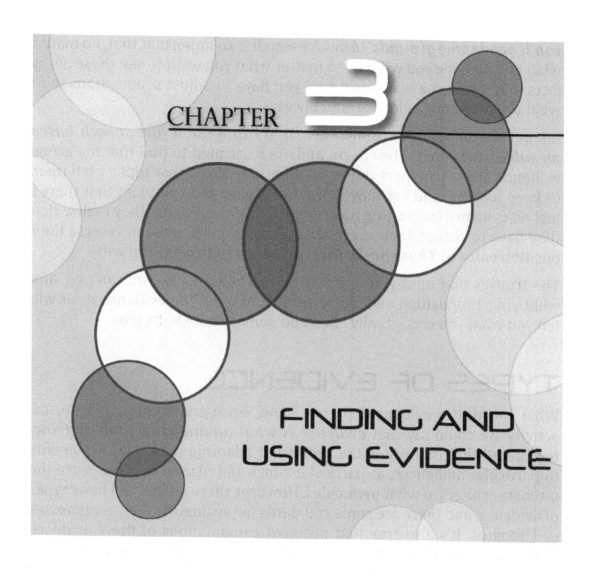

CHAPTER 3

FINDING AND USING EVIDENCE

"FACTS ARE STUBBORN THINGS; AND WHATEVER MAY BE OUR WISHES, OUR INCLINATIONS, OR THE DICTATES OF OUR PASSIONS, THEY CANNOT ALTER THE STATE OF FACTS AND EVIDENCE."

– JOHN ADAMS –

You've made up some propositions, probably discovering that there's an element of creativity in the process. You may even have generated some claims you think may work for arguments. Now for the process of argument invention to proceed, research is absolutely required. In Toulmin's terms, *you'll need some grounds.* In fact, research is so important that, no matter what you imagine you will say, no matter what you want to say, those pesky facts may get in the way. You'll find you have to adjust propositions to fit what the prevailing evidence actually says.

It's not uncommon that someone may try to write *a fact speech based on subjective belief.* They begin and are frustrated to find that the actual evidence doesn't support their presumptions about that topic. I tell them to keep looking, and yet they will return again and complain that there's just no evidence supporting their side of the issue. Finally, they realize that they have to change their original hypothesis, perhaps even reverse their position entirely. *Those pesky facts just keep getting in the way.*

The truth is that until you've really researched a topic, you can't be sure what your proposition and claims will be exactly. The evidence itself will tell you what you can actually state and demonstrate to be true.

TYPES OF EVIDENCE

What constitutes evidence? On one hand, since argument is a rhetorical activity, we could say that *evidence is what an audience finds convincing.* Recall that rhetoric is the process of adapting particular arguments to particular audiences, at particular times and places. Audiences are the ultimate arbiters of what persuades. However, there are certain basic types of evidence, and there are some standards for evaluating their weaknesses or strengths. It's also true that different combinations of these evidence types may be needed to achieve different purposes. There are *two general categories: evidence of fact and evidence of opinion* (1).

EVIDENCE OF FACT

This evidence primarily consists of three more specific types of material: *artifacts, examples, and figures or statistics.*

Artifacts are objects used to physically demonstrate a point. Don't confuse this with the term "argument as artifact," a single Toulmin argument. The word "artifact" in this case refers to individual physical items used as proof. In a court, for instance, lipstick prints on a glass, fingerprints from a crime scene, traces of clothing fiber, tire tracks, murder weapons, and traces of DNA can all be used to prove a point.

For an anthropologist, the skull of the "Java Man," once suspected to be the "missing link," was an important artifact, as would be aging pottery or art objects depicting the characteristics of another time for an archeologist.

In a sense, for a public speech, *a model* used to illustrate the dynamics of something could be considered evidence as artifact. A student explaining the BP oil spill might use a model to show how the accident occurred.

Even *a visual aid* — a map, a globe, or a statistical chart — could be considered a kind of artifact. These objects make the subject matter tangible and easier to visualize in an oral presentation. While you may have fewer opportunities to use this evidence type here, it remains a useful arrow in your quiver.

Examples are stories that illustrate and dramatize social issues. Examples consist of specific cases about the topic, short narratives that are literally true. They often dramatize something to create interest. Here's an example used to describe the fate of the rhinoceros being hunted into extinction.

> She has a bullet in her face, another in her leg, and every reason not to trust humans. But when Johannesburg Zoo rhino keeper Alice Masombuka calls her name, the wild black rhino flutters her ears delicately and stands alert, gazing in the direction of the voice. "Hey, Phila, Phila...!" Says Masombuka leaning against the fence, her sing-song voice floating irresistibly in Johannesburg's damp air. Phila takes a few steps, hesitates, stops, changes her mind, takes a few more steps and halts again fearfully....Then, as curious and brave as a foal, the rhino trots to the fence (**2**).

The strongest impact of examples may be that they create *"identification."* Identification means that we empathize with the persons in the story, perhaps even feel at one with them (**3**). Narratives with personal details are required to achieve that. If a news agency declares, "Six men died in an avalanche today," we may have more interest if we are climbers, or we know people who were in the mountains on that day. I once spent a New Year's Eve in the snow at the top of Mount San Gregornio, the tallest peak in Southern California. It was less fun than I thought it would be, even under a lovely full moon. The champagne froze in the snow bank. It was a three-dog night, as they say of cold evenings, and I only had two dogs. When I came down the next day, I discovered that six people had died within a quarter of a mile of where I'd been, each a separate incident, having fallen through the ice. Imagine the ferocity of my identification when I realized that, not only could it have happened to me, I was one of a lucky few in the area to come home safely.

Stories have a lot more impact with fuller depiction of the individual characters involved. If we know names and faces, their hobbies, their professions, their family relations, we might feel more for the personnel (**4**). Here's an extended example to make the point. A Reverend James Moran was making his rounds at a hospital when a patient bristled at the sight of his clerical collar, expressing disgust for the clergy's sex crimes:

> Moran, a beefy 60-year-old with an agonizing secret he had only recently started to let out, said: "I'm a victim of a priest myself." The patient stared at him from the bed. A question came, point-blank: "Then how can you be a priest?" It was time to leave, he decided after that conversation, and he arranged to retire on a medical disability. First, he wanted to let loose the whole secret—not just the abridged version. He wanted people to know that the fallout of clergy sex abuse is not over, even if it has waned from headlines.... He chose Holy Week. And that Tuesday, as about 20 hospital staff and patients' relatives filed into the chapel for Mass, Moran took a deep breath. Then he spoke about the whole story, right there in church during the most hallowed time of the Christian year.... The next day ... an archdiocese official called, telling him that the hospital thought his actions were inappropriate and that the church felt they were accusatory. His priestly credentials were being pulled immediately (**5**).

This example puts a human face on the problem, that of a priest torn between his desire to serve the church and his anger at being violated. We identify with him as a victim and as a priest trying to set things straight.

Examples often appear in lists with bullets.

While the city of Bell, California, has received a lot of attention for fattened salaries, Vernon next door is as bad.

- Eric T. Fresch was paid $1.65 million in salary and hourly billings in 2008 when he held jobs both as city administrator and deputy city attorney.

- Daniel O'Callaghan was paid nearly $785,000 as a city administrator and director of light and power.

- Former City Attorney Jeffrey A. Harrison earned $800,000.

- Finance Director Riordan Burnett made $570,000.

- Former City Administrator Bruce Malkenhorst made as much as $911,563.

- One ex-city administrator's pay topped $1 million in each of the last four years.

- Former Mayor Leonis Malburg, grandson of the city's founder, was ordered to pay back $500,000 in fines for fraud and conspiracy.

- Vernon City Council members are paid $68,052 a year, far more than other cities in the Los Angeles area. Over 99% of City managers make well below these kinds of salaries (6).

The logical process of generalization begins just this way, with lists of examples. When you hear enough stories about something, you begin to form an opinion that it happens regularly. Generalization is also called **"reasoning from example."** That's fine, especially if you have a lot of examples, though you'll require statistics for the soundest generalizations.

At the least, **examples catch our attention**, which is why they're often used as speech introductions and conclusions. Humans are natural storytellers. It's a basic source of community bonding, from campfire stories to sitting in a movie house together. We all love to hear a good tale.

Sometimes we use **hypothetical cases**, compilations of details from real cases that are representative of the situation you're discussing. "Let's join Officer Everyman on a typical day on the beat." Documented cases are preferable.

However, a few dramatic examples can't prove everything. They can show how issues may affect us, since the stories involve people who may be like us. **We see the quality of a social problem**. Yet examples can't answer the questions of how much, how long, or how many does this affect? We're attracted by stories, but a reasonable person has to ask how common these events are. To deal with issues of quantity, we need the use of numbers. **Figures and statistics "quantify" social phenomena (7).**

Numbers give us a sense of the larger social picture beyond individual experience. Numbers help us provide **more than "anecdotal evidence."** For instance, we're familiar with road rage at an incidental level, having seen it around us. Perhaps we've even being involved personally. We've read **road rage headlines** in the paper like:

> In Phoenix, "Man Killed in Apparent Road Rage Shooting"

> In Boston, "Mother and Son Shot by Driver Who Chased Them"

> In Seattle, "Maple Valley Man Charged with Two Felony Counts for Road Rage Incident"

Bulleted lists of examples certainly give us a sense that road rage exists, but just how pervasive is this behavior? 2010 research from the National **Highway Traffic Safety Administration** says that there has been a 51% increase in road rage incidents since 1990. They estimate that of the 20 million injuries on the road, 12,610 were caused by road rage. 37% of these involved the use of firearms, 28% other weapons, and 35% involved the use of a car as a weapon (**8**). Now that's a significantly clearer picture of the problem. This is not to say that numerical evidence is better than examples, but it's both necessary and complementary. Some of each will work well together.

Figures are derived from simple counting, as with the **U.S. Census**, during which time each household is checked to determine population and other demographic details. We can say with confidence, as of the 2010 census, that the population of the United States is 308 million. It grew at a rate of 9.7% since 2000, but that's the slowest rate since the Great Depression. By counting changes in state populations, we also know that the population concentration is shifting from the Midwest to states in the South and West.

So what? The figures mean that some states are going to lose representation in the House of Representatives and others are going to gain. The biggest gains have been in so-called Red States, those that tend to vote Republican. However, a lot of the increasing population in, for instance, Texas, consists of Hispanics who tend to vote Democratic. Thus, so simple a thing as the census can allow us to make inferences about future elections (**9**).

Statistics are a good deal trickier because we base them on figures but use various methods to infer more than the simple counting says. Sometimes even estimates of figures are used to speculate a statistic. In either case, figures are then applied across a population to achieve **percentages,** which may have more dramatic impact than figures.

> Smoking may cause long-term damage not just to the lungs but to the brain as well. In a study of more than 21,000 people who were followed for 23 years, those who smoked more than two packs of cigarettes a day in midlife were **157% more likely to develop Alzheimer's disease** and 172% more prone to vascular dementia in older age than nonsmokers The reason? Smoking impairs blood-vessel function, which may contribute to Alzheimer's **(10)**.

So statistics can be used both to make dramatic statements and help us predict the odds of something happening.

There are two functions of statistics. Some are meant **to describe.** A study of Californians age 40 and older, for instance, indicates that drug overdoses are twice as bad as the 1990 rate. The presumption would typically be that drugs are primarily a problem among the young. Yet, it's the baby-boomers who lead in drug deaths: "In 2003...the state of California had a record 3,691 drug user deaths among those over 40, up 73% since 1990. The total surpassed deaths from firearms, homicides, and AIDS **(11)**." Surprisingly, fatal overdoses among young people have declined, while the rate for older people has jumped from about eight to seventeen per hundred thousand. According to the FBI, arrests of Americans over 40 for drug offenses increased significantly from 22,000 in 1980 to 360,000 in 2006 **(12)**.

There are also statistics **to infer.** We observe specific portions of the population then generalize the characteristics of those samples to the population as a whole. Here is where things get tricky, because the **statistics are only as good as the research methods used to make the inference,** and the sampling of populations can be manipulated.

Simple **surveys** are like snapshots of a situation. "**Insta-polls,**" for instance, are common on television news. They simply open phone lines or email addresses for a particular period of time then post quotations from whoever happens to be watching at the time. **That's not scientific sampling.** As we'll see in the next chapter, television news audiences are segmented by partisan values, so two stations can achieve entirely different results from surveys taken on the same day. Besides, as we saw in the previous discussion of appeal to the people, the fact that something is popular doesn't necessarily mean that it's right or good.

The size and variety of the sample has everything to do with how credible it is. Our usual manner of achieving credibility is to **choose participants randomly.**

Say we're examining how many math classes have been taken on the average by graduating seniors at American colleges. There are thousands of colleges and universities, each enrolling many students. It would be impractical to examine the transcript of every college senior. Instead, we take a sample of college seniors and then make inferences to the entire population based on what we find. We might sample 100 students from each of the colleges with high enrollments. Yet we'd have to ask the question **is the sample representative of the population?** Perhaps we chose an overabundance of math majors, or chose too many technical institutions that have heavy math requirements. Bad sampling could make our statistics non-representative of "all seniors." **Being random and being representative requires a delicate balance.**

Longitudinal studies, which often take place over years, are more useful than surveys. Unlike snapshots, these more resemble film that looks at a research question over a long time period. **Research reviews**, which analyze, correlate, and synthesize the findings from various studies, offer a wider variety of perspectives on a research problem. They also let us know what hasn't been covered adequately on the topic yet.

For instance, many Americans have **a hidden presumption that college teachers are all liberals**, and some studies claim to have proved that this influences their grading. A review of eight of these studies on teacher bias was sponsored by the American Federation of Teachers. Two themes were common in the eight studies assessed: that faculty are liberal and that this inclination impacts assessment of student performance.

There is evidence for the first claim — around **70%** of college teachers are Democrats — but none for the second, the research review found. With regard to the first claim, however, the researcher found that there was no significant data on applicant pools for faculty positions, raising questions of whether or not Republicans tend to be as attracted to teaching jobs as Democrats. In other words, conservatives may be more inclined to jobs in the public sector rather than the service sector, accounting partially for the tilt. The primary and repeated concern in the review was that these eight studies asserted cause between the first idea and the second. "They're liberal, so they must reveal this bias in the classroom," the hidden presumption goes. Yet there was no concrete evidence in any of the eight studies that teachers allow their political attitudes to affect grades. Also, the eight studies tended to focus on top universities while using no particular data from community colleges or other institutions (**13**). In other words, *the methods* in the reviewed study tended to support what the experimenter expected to find, a phenomenon called *experimenter effects*, a kind of self-fulfilling prophecy. Most of the studies were conducted by *conservative think tanks.*

A problem student speakers commonly have with numbers occurs when they include words like *"more," "growing," "increasing"* in their propositions or claims. They'll give a number that may seem significant in itself, but in order to prove an increase in something *you need a baseline figure.* We need to know what the figure was before as opposed to what it has become.

Here is a study with sound methods.

> According to *The Journal of Pedriatics*, August 30, 2010, the number of children in the U.S. seeking treatment for concussions from sports more than doubled between 2000 and 2005.... Researchers tallied over half a million cases of minors visiting emergency rooms for concussions. About half were related to sports.... 40% of these sports related injuries were for children between 8 and 13. Statistics suggest a steady increase in such injuries. This becomes especially significant because there is a general decline in sports participation (**14**).

In other words, the injuries are increasing on *a per capita basis*, an important comparison because increases in phenomenon can often be accounted for as correlations to population growth. The study goes on to say that the trend seems to be continuing, and we've seen anecdotal evidence in college and professional sports that parallel the trend. There are an estimated 300,000 sports related concussions per year among college students (**15**).

As a cautionary note, Mark Twain once wrote that, "There are three kinds of lies, lies, damned lies, and statistics." *In a sense, figures are more "factual" than statistics*, as there is no abstraction or inference involved. Statistics are sometimes manipulated to create a one-sided view of a topic and are only as reliable as the methods used to gather and interpret them. We'll discuss more specific cautions when we look at tests of evidence.

Students should certainly not refer generally in the manner of *"studies say"* without citing the study specifically. Even more important, do not make up statistics of your own based on your personal opinion. I wish I had a dime for every time someone said, *"Well it's true 90% of the time."*

In sum, evidence of fact consists of artifacts, examples, and numbers.

EVIDENCE OF OPINION

The other kind of proof we use consists of *quotations* from various sources. We sometimes call it *source-based evidence.* Evidence of opinion is taken from two kinds of people, topic specific experts and the average Jack or Jill on the street.

Expert opinion is used to analyze and explain examples and statistics, as well as summarize conclusions. Examples rely on statistics to back them up, but statistics often require experts to sort out their significance. For instance, on the baby-boomer drug use issue:

> "Baby Boomers are the first generation that is facing a drug overdose epidemic in their middle age," said John Newmeyer, epidemiologist and drug researcher at the Haight-Ashbury Free Clinics in San Francisco, "They started using drugs recreationally or regularly over 20 years ago, and aren't really slowing down" (**16**).

Newmeyer provides **perspective** about the sociological causes of the raw statistics, and he has the credentials to make his assessment reasonably credible. He also gives us a **historical context** for the issue.

Expert testimony makes great introductions, transitions, and conclusions. Experts who are passionate about a topic are able to make pithy points about a subject that we ourselves are not trained to make, and they can sometimes summarize information in eloquent ways. They've simply spent more time and given more consideration to the issue than we have.

For instance, according to Dr. Mark L. Weiss, PhD in biology at the University of Pennsylvania, in spite of all the ethical controversy about stem cell research, it could be managed without use of the controversial fetus.

> Umbilical cord matrix cells could provide the scientific and medical research community with a non-controversial and easily attainable source of stem cells for developing treatments for Parkinson's disease, strokes, spinal cord injuries, cancers, and other conditions **(17).**

While others are locked in a value struggle of right and wrong, or the attendant political cautions, an expert can see new angles on issues that may offer more light than heat. Since the time of his prediction, specific research has advanced in using these cells to repair liver and retinal damage.

We have a serious problem with transplant donors. Wait lists have increased dramatically as the science has progressed and confidence has grown in the process. Yet experts at the University of San Francisco and elsewhere have produced a prototype of an implantable artificial kidney that could reduce, even eliminate that wait list problem **(18).**

Experts provide vision and perspective. If you don't have statistics or figures to give "a big picture" to complement the drama of examples, expert testimony may manage that for you. There are some ***important limitations***, though. Remember, this is evidence of opinion, and experts do differ. For every expert that says one thing, you can usually find others who disagree. You can't, for instance, make a sound speech of fact relying too much on what we call "***conclusionary evidence.***" An expert simply repeats the claim you've made – which is convenient - but we don't know how he got there.

He just says it's so. He's the expert, so we're supposed to buy what he says. Not so. We need to understand the facts he's using to infer, his analysis and his reasoning, or we've simply become passive messengers in the argument process. Indeed, that's the most slavish sort of critical thinking.

If the source is an everyday person, without particular expertise on the subject matter, we call it ***personal testimony.*** You simply share the common experience of everyday people through their quotations. You're all familiar with advertising testimonials.

"I used 'Colgate' toothpaste and had fewer cavities." (Smile for camera.)

Less facetiously: "I've had cancer for three years. This is what it's like."

We may not be experts in the sense that we've studied or have degrees, but first-hand experience can be very convincing. It's really much like an example spoken in first person in terms of its persuasive impact. That is, *it can create pathos and identification.*

For instance, I'm a three-time kidney transplant and have dealt with the issue of kidney failure since 1983. Having waited on donor lists, I could tell you in quite different ways from the researchers what an implantable artificial kidney could mean to the reduction of human suffering. If a person has some experience on the subject matter, their testimony may be considered more objective.

EVIDENCE AND PERSUASION

According to rhetorician John C. Reinhard in his review of fifty years of research on the effects of evidence, these are among the positive effects of using evidence (**19**):

1. Testimony seems to be consistently persuasive, as long as the source of the testimony is documented.

2. Factual information, such as reports of events or examples, seem to be persuasive, but specific facts are more effective than general ones.

3. In spite of the almost reverent attitude many people have toward statistical evidence, such evidence is not as persuasive as other factual evidence. However, when powerful, involving, and vivid examples are backed up by statistics that show them to be typical, the examples become more powerful.

4. Presenting audiences with evidence seems to "inoculate" or protect audiences against subsequent counter-persuasion.

5. Novel evidence is more persuasive than evidence the audience already knows.

6. Evidence is most effective with highly intelligent people who are concerned about getting the facts.

7. Evidence that reinforces the audience's beliefs is more persuasive than evidence that challenges it.

8. Good delivery enhances the effectiveness of evidence.

9. Evidence consistently increases speaker credibility.

10. A source's credibility has persuasive effects. That is, credible sources are more persuasive than less credible ones. This is one of the most consistent patterns identified by Reinhard.

Similar results were found by Rodney Reynolds and Michael Burgoon. They also mention **the importance of source citation in persuasiveness**. The clarity of evidence citations increases evaluations of the evidence and the advocate. That is, clear citation involves the audience more directly in the process of judgment.

The last two points by Reinhard emphasize the term **"speaker credibility,"** one of the most researched terms in speech-communication. Also, we mentioned the term briefly when discussing "ethos," one of Aristotle's three appeals, but what does credibility really mean?

CREDIBILITY

We say that certain speakers have "credibility," personal qualities that makes us want to believe and follow them. Some sources are more persuasive than others, too, and that's especially important when using source-based evidence. Here are some specific qualities associated with the term (**20**):

Attractiveness, in the sense of clothing, personality, and physical features

Character, behavior that measures up to the audience's ethical codes

Competence, the qualifications and ability to perform tasks well

Consistency, a sense of integrity among messages and behaviors

Dynamism, the ability to excite and activate audiences with your energy

Eloquence, using language well, saying the right thing at the right time

Good Will, genuine concern about what's best for the people

Honesty, telling the truth and being frank and open

Knowledge, both in the sense of study and experience

Wisdom, the ability of someone to use knowledge well

The first item, **attractiveness**, may be somewhat irritating, but it cannot be denied as a persuasive factor. Studies demonstrate that attractive people reading the same text as less attractive people achieve superior persuasive results. Across the board, people judged to be more attractive are generally evaluated as more persuasive as well.

The classic real world example is the presidential election between John F. Kennedy and Richard Nixon in 1960. Their televised debate was articulate, remarkably respectful by current standards, and well informed. Yet there was a distinct difference in the way Kennedy, a handsome fellow, was perceived on camera. Nixon, who was a debater for Whittier College, was judged by many in the live setting to have won, and that was the audience he focused on with his eye contact.. Yet due to close-up shots, Nixon was regarded as less attractive by people watching at home. He had a heavy 5 o'clock shadow, he had a tendency to sweat, and he was less comfortable with the camera than Kennedy.

This debate changed the face of politics forever. From that time forward, image, advertising, and focus groups became key to electoral success. T.H. White's book *The Making of a President, 1960* documented that shift.

Yet, even if you're no Sleeping Beauty or Prince Charming, you might at least be well groomed and appropriately dressed when speaking or giving reports. (Dude. Take off the backwards baseball cap and spit out the gum.)

Let's look at some **examples of public figures**, seeing if we can exemplify the above qualities of credibility. The first is a positive example:

> Though he is frail and bent by age, he sent a shudder through the dark heart of Big Tobacco the second he took the oath. Doll, an epidemiologist, spoke elegantly and with great modesty of the work for which he'd been knighted by the queen of England. Prodded by an attorney for a Newport Beach woman who is dying of lung cancer and has sued Philip Morris, he told a medical detective story that began in 1949.... Doll who had smoked for 20 years immediately quit and implored his wife to do the same. He also stepped up his research, and published a groundbreaking 1950 report contending that "smoking is a factor, and an important factor, in the production of lung cancer (**21**).

This is *a credible witness.* He presents a sympathetic image due to his frailty, a clear contrast to the strength of his *eloquence*. He has *competence* as a scientist. He's *consistent* in that his quitting smoking matches his words. His message reveals a real concern for the people, a sense of his *good will*. He has demonstrable *knowledge*, and his age confers a sense of *wisdom* to him. He's an actual knight, for heaven's sake, jousting with the tobacco dragon. Their very fear of him enhances his credibility.

Let's consider some less pristine examples of credibility. Here are some cases in which *credibility may be mixed, or non-existent.*

How would you like to be told you have *cancer* when you don't? Would you go back to that doctor? *The Arizona Daily Star*, June 25, 2006, reported that circumstance for Janice Lomen. After living in the shadow of fatal cancer for years, she discovered that she'd been misdiagnosed by her doctors. She was told she had myeloma, an incurable cancer of the plasma cells in bone marrow. Several experts have now confirmed that not only has she never had the disease, but that the chemotherapy has left her at high risk for leukemia. Also, the osteoporosis that was really the problem had gone untreated. Certainly *competence* would come into question here.

It was revealed that *Richard Grasso*, head of the New York Stock Exchange, had received an extraordinary deferred pay package of $140 million. The amount was jaw dropping, especially since the hand-picked compensation committee consisted mainly of representatives from companies listed on the NYSE over which Grasso had regulatory control. Grasso was sued by the State of New York for return of his ill-gotten gains, Grasso counter-sued, and all claims against him were dismissed by the New York Court of Appeals in 2008. Grasso repeatedly invoked Fifth Amendment rights, refusing to speak about his part in the investigation of improper behavior by exchange firms (22). His refusal to testify and his use of influence over his salary bring issues of *honesty* into question.

The Lehman Brothers investment firm was responsible for the biggest bankruptcy in U.S. history. A March 2010 report by the court-appointed examiner indicated that Lehman executives regularly used cosmetic accounting gimmicks at the end of each quarter to make its finances appear less shaky than they really were. In brief, while there were accusations that they were short-selling stock, they continued to lead investors along to give a false appearance of stability (**23**). One can hardly credit them with **good will** for their investors nor with **honesty**.

EVIDENCE AND APPEALS SELECTION

These types of evidence in grounds are not the only ways to convince an audience. There are also appeals, using persuasive language and referring to popular imagery to motivate an audience. If your evidence search doesn't cover a vital topic, an appeal may be all you have to sway your public, of course, avoiding the fallacies of appeal mentioned previously.

Aristotle, the fifth century Greek philosopher and father of rhetorical study, observed that there were **three ways to appeal to an audience** (**24**):

> **LOGOS** - appealing to an audience's sense of logic and reason
>
> **PATHOS** - appealing to an audience's sense of emotion
>
> **ETHOS** – the character of the speaker

In a loose way, you can also think of ethos as making moral and ethical appeals, though this was not specifically Aristotle's use of the word. He focuses on the credibility of the speaker himself. Yet it's not a bad idea to remind an audience that something you oppose is immoral or unethical on the face of it.

In a sense, all three appeals flow from the speaker. A good speaker needs ethos, pathos, and logos. The ethos is his moral character, the source of his ability to persuade. Pathos is his ability to touch feelings, to move people emotionally. Logos is in his ability to give solid reasons for an action, to move people intellectually. So, it wouldn't be incorrect to say that a speaker himself is a kind of proof from an audience viewpoint.

We can also try to make appeals in other ways than the implicit nature of our own characteristics. Appeals may occur as **a matter of persuasive language**. In other words, explicit appeals can appear in claims, warrants, introductions, transitions, and conclusions:

As sensible people, we reject the illogical point made by my opponent. Can't we feel some pity for these children abandoned by the system? Come on, folks, we must know that this is just wrong on the face of it.

Appeals may also be evoked by evidence. It's possible that a single piece of really great evidence might touch an audience in "mind, heart, and spirit." Yet we can be aware that some kinds of evidence are more likely to achieve one or another appeal.

Logos can be imbedded in our use of statistics and figures. Logos is also available, however, in descriptions of scientific process, manufacturing or medical process, describing how something is discovered or made. Organization is an aspect of logos.

Try some example or personal testimony to evoke pathos. As Aristotle said in "The Poetics," a tract about Greek drama and how it exerts influence on an audience, "We feel pity and fear for one who is like ourselves." In other words, we relate to, we identify with people in stories.

To suggest ethos, use testimony from upright and credible people. Boost your own credibility by associating yourself with the best and the brightest.

It's wise to balance your use of evidence and appeals. You wouldn't want a text that was all examples, as your audience would have no sense if these moving stories were really typical, or an exception to the rules. If we ***pair examples with statistics,*** though, we'll have a good sense of perspective on the issue at hand. When statistics are not available, use expert testimony to back up your examples with a sense of perspective. If you don't have examples, put some personal testimony with statistics for a similar 1–2 combination punch. Yes. That's right. You can think of evidence selection like ***combination punching in the boxing ring.*** If all you have is a roundhouse right and no jab, you may be the one who kisses the canvas.

For another example, think of evidence selection ***like directing a movie.*** What would you think of a film with nothing but close-ups? That's what a speech with all examples would be like. You'd have no sense of place or the social dynamics around the characters. Adding statistics would be like pulling back for a wide shot, a look at the big picture.

Imagine a speech of all statistics. Apart from putting people to sleep with all those numbers, it would be like a film with nothing but wide shots. With no close-ups there would be no sense of individuality among the characters. You'd never get involved. Also, it's difficult for an audience to absorb lots of statistics at once, unless they're intermittently illustrated or exemplified.

Imagine a speech of all testimony. It would be like a film without dynamic visuals, just dialogue upon dialogue. Blah, blah, blah. Zzzzzz.

Though this is no guarantee, there is a good chance of imbedding ethos in quotations, pathos in examples, and logos in figures and statistics. If you balance your types of evidence, it's possible that your appeals may be more likely to balance as well. Of course, a single good piece of evidence may have the qualities of all three appeals, as may a single good speaker.

EVIDENCE TESTS

A debate may come down to the strength of each side's grounds. This is not just a matter of having more evidence, but of having better evidence. These tests can help us to compare the quality of competing evidence. That's **useful both in choosing which evidence to use in building arguments and later as a tool for counter-argument** (25). We'll focus on seven tests in alphabetical order.

Accuracy—Are the details of the story reported without error? During research, check the accuracy of stories by looking at several versions of the account from different sources. Determine which is most credible and consistent with other accounts. *Directly quote evidence rather than paraphrasing it.*

Some reports are more accurate because they're *firsthand accounts.* A fair number of newspaper and magazine reports are written from AP releases by people who are nowhere near the events in question. CNN created itself, with a lot of help from British news agencies, by being right on the spot for the bombing of Baghdad in the first Gulf War.

The farther one is from the primary source, the more subjective filters there are to the information. The more error-prone technology and bias-ridden bureaucracy the information passes through, the less pristine it may be. In a court of law, *we don't allow hearsay testimony*, only eyewitness testimony that is a first hand account.

Bias—Are the authors of the evidence being objective? Are there reasons to believe that they have a skewed perspective? Are they influenced, by some self-interest they can gain from your acceptance of their claim?

Bias is important in all matters of source-based proof. Even scientific study should be observed carefully for bias. A researcher working with a grant might exaggerate results to preserve the financing that the grant offers. Recall the great "cold fusion" boondoggle. Utah researchers claimed to have harnessed fusion power in a water glass. There was lots of buzz about the glass, along with some grant money, but no nuclear "fizz" in it. Also, a source may be ***invested emotionally*** because it's their idea. This can lead to experimenter effects.

Another example is the use of ***expert witnesses in trials***. While they are experts, they are also paid. In fact, for some, that's a primary source of income. The opposing attorney would typically point this out as a factor to consider when looking at their testimony. Are they "guns for hire" with a predisposition to favor those who pay them?

Also, realize that ***publications and news agencies have bias***. There are liberal and conservative publications. There are magazines designed to inform, but many are designed to entertain, leading them to focus on only the most sensational details. We'll examine this in detail in Chapter 4.

Consistency—Is evidence inconsistent with other evidence in the speech?

It's a fairly common novice error to be inconsistent in early talks because you're initially focused on building individual arguments. You may grab a piece of evidence that makes one point without considering its impact on other arguments. It's possible to prove two individual points that disprove each other. If you contradict yourself, you don't get to choose which point you want. You simply lose both, along with the trust of the audience.

Recency—Is this the most current evidence available? The most current data is generally preferable, though that depends on the subject matter at hand. Some scientific and medical theory changes very rapidly. Something not possible last week may suddenly become plausible today, even likely, with the announcement of a new discovery. Other older data, like an established and still useful theory, the rhetorical traditions discussed here, historical examples, or quotations from famous figures of the past, may still be useful. Ultimately, if new knowledge is available, you'd best know what it is, or your opponent may demonstrate that your viewpoint is obsolete.

Relevance—Does the evidence used really apply to your specific claim? Make sure the data clearly relates to "the fort" that you've chosen to defend. ***Your evidence choice may be relevant to the topic in general yet not fit the individual argument.*** For instance, if the topic focus is within American borders, then introducing evidence about Europe wouldn't work for you. If your topic is confined by a state border, then nationwide statistics would not be relevant either.

In practical terms, make sure your grounds directly support your claim. ***This is as much a matter of proper claim phrasing as it is finding evidence.*** If you are accurately summarizing what the evidence actually says rather than what you wish it would say, your grounds and claims will relate.

Representativeness—Is the evidence representative of the general condition? When you choose that great example, make sure that it is the typical, not the exceptional, case. With inferential statistics, ask what the characteristics of the sample population are? Who did they sample? Where? Under what conditions? Was the number sampled sufficient, or were too few people included? If you're combining or comparing different statistics, are they working with similar definitions of the field of study? If comparisons are made by statistic, are the units compared alike?

Consider ***exit polls*** at an election, sometimes conducted with random samples of people leaving polls after voting. We know not to rely too much on this kind of quick survey. In a given county, we may have both very liberal neighborhoods and very conservative neighborhoods. Focusing on unbalanced samples of a neighborhood could easily (and unfairly) distort the results.

Source Qualifications—What credentials does the source possess that make his or her observations credible? This is especially important for testimonial evidence. What is the source's connection with the issue? Do they have educational degrees or certification directly relevant to the issue? A general practitioner is not a specialist on hearts, kidneys, or any other particular organ. Any scrupulous medical generalist would send you on to a specialist to treat diseases of a singular organ.

Sufficiency—Is the evidence enough to prove the full extent of the claim? In other words, does it meet your burden of proof? A common novice error is to exaggerate the impact of the available evidence. Your claim should say no more than you can prove.

For instance, let's say that your claim is: "Most Americans oppose gay marriage." This is an issue of fact, but you use a quotation to support it, which says: "Nobody I know supports gay marriage," or even, "Research shows that there is strong opposition in Mid-Western states." Would either be sufficient to prove the point? No. The point you're making has a qualifier that calls for quantifiable evidence, "most Americans." We have to have a national statistic. According to a 2004 CNN poll, 62% of **87.**

Americans opposed gay marriage, though many of those supported civil unions for gays. However, a 2010 Pew Poll found that 42% support gay marriage while 48% oppose it. This is the first time since Pew began researching the issue that fewer than half of Americans opposed same sex marriage (**26**).

The key point is that you have to *watch what qualifiers you choose for your claims and relate them specifically to your evidence.*

Also, remind yourself of a rule we mentioned earlier: Don't claim more than you can actually prove.

Verifiability—Can you confirm your findings? Can you locate them in more than one news source, or is this a rumor? Does the field of opinion show some coherent viewpoint, or are you basing your claim on exceptional evidence or eccentric perspective?

RESEARCH

Now that you know the basic types of evidence and ways to explore evidence quality, let's discuss how to find the evidence. The primary goal of research is to find the best approximate truth about the issue studied. It's not to prove a preconceived point of belief at the expense of the truth.

Approach the defense of your proposition with an open mind. You may find evidence that forces you to qualify or change your opinion.

Explore the topic from multiple points of view, or you might be tempted to gather only information that supports your idea, without exploring the other side through the eyes of an imaginary opponent.

Use a wide variety of sources, both the web and from library sources, periodicals, magazines, journals, and newspapers.

Depth of research will vary with the complexity of the topic. There's really no specific number as to how many sources is enough. As a beginner's rule of thumb, though, *use at least one source for every minute of speaking* that you do. If I read a typewritten page without any source citations, I'm likely to think that student research is light. For longer and more serious projects, like a term paper length assignment, there is what may be called *a research baseline.* There tend to be particularly seminal sources on a given topic, a couple of people who are continually cited by others talking about it. If those names keep coming up, read their work. Then you may have discovered the research baseline.

If your teacher assigns a speech with a specific number of required sources then be wary of committing *an ethical breach called "source splitting."* That is, you read one article with many citations in it, but you quote those pre-cited sources as though each was an article you'd read yourself. You can certainly go to those cited articles individually to enhance your research, but you can't claim them as original research when you've only read the compilation. That may also lead you to fail at least one of the tests of evidence, bias, as you're only looking at the facts through one author's eyes.

Most students are probably accustomed to *using the web* for almost all of their research. It has the advantage of being quick. A single search can yield a wide variety of materials that you can bookmark on your computer. You can then *copy and paste examples, statistics, and quotations*, and put them on an organization page. That is, you can just grab the information as it comes then go back later and *sort it into categories*. The categories should be *the stock issues* of the particular kind of speech you're doing. So divide your first research task on facts into causes and results. Then build your arguments from the best bits of evidence.

If you're using a library or school computer, you may want to download the source list right then. If you have the internet at home, you can easily duplicate and bookmark the material itself from the public computer, read it more carefully, highlight the key evidence, then recopy it into the text.

The web is just the start of a good research process, though. As vast as it is, the net has less "quality control" than other sources. The WWW could easily stand for "the wild, wild west," instead of world wide web. You can find excellent sources there, and exploring a topic search can either broaden or focus your brainstorming. Yet anybody with the resources to put up a website can say just about anything they want. There are undocumented assertions out there, as well as many self-proclaimed experts. Apply the same tests that you would for any evidence to separate wheat from chaff.

Journalistic sources are nearly as convenient as the web, as they contain *condensed* information, and that information is *current*. Scanning newspaper files is time consuming, but with local topics not covered by national magazines they may be your best available source. Sometimes it's hard to find enough for local topics. In such cases, you may have to expand the size of your "fort" to the state or national level. Newspapers may also recopy recent articles for a fee and send them to you, but *don't rely on the mail for research*, or you may miss your assignment deadline.

Books are only occasionally useful because they take longer to absorb and editing useful information is time-consuming. They also tend to be less recent, as it takes awhile to build a book and get it published, let alone to get it into your library.

Reference *books in your local library are useful: dictionaries, encyclopedias, and statistical abstracts.* Statistical abstracts may be a good source of figures and statistics. *The Statistical Abstracts of the United States,* for instance, includes annual figures from the U.S. Government Printing Office about everything from how much oil we imported, how many crimes there were, to how much corn we grew. A *"Who's Who"* can be a way of finding the qualifications of experts you quote.

If all of this is new to you, arrange a conversation with *your local librarian* about what reference sources are available to you, including internet search services like *LexisNexis*. Librarians don't just tend books. They are experts at using the sources and can teach you. Your instructor may include a library tour as an aspect of the course. So don't just sit at home staring at your computer. It's a start, not an end to your research. To the extent that you do rely on the web, remember to vary your search language to ask specific questions. Don't just put a general topic up and give up.

It's OK to edit the information you collect for focus and brevity, but do not exclude qualifiers, significant exceptions, or internal contradictions. In fact, you may find that you have to trim evidence to fairly short paragraphs for the average audience member to hear and absorb.

Do not commit the very dangerous ethical breach of plagiarism. It's very easy to do, even by accident. I notice that student punctuation errors are pretty pervasive. If you do so little a thing as use language from an article without surrounding it with *quotation marks*, or you paraphrase language from the article too closely, that would be considered plagiarism. In many colleges, even a first offense could get you expelled. You can also avoid this by proper documentation.

DOCUMENTATION

Whatever materials you use, it's important that you document them with a source citation. You're doing speeches, so we're talking about oral citations. *Your audience has a right to know where you got your material.* They should be able to replicate your research and examine the sources themselves. It's simply not enough to report that you "got it in the library," or "in a magazine," or "a book." *The audience cannot hear a bibliography*, though your teacher will certainly expect that one be attached as well, probably in the style of the Modern Language Association.

What information do you need to refer to in your texts? The minimum requirement for source citation to be credible to an audience and fair to your opponents would be:

> *Source Name*
> *Source Qualifications*
> *Article Title*
> *Publication Title*
> *Publication Date*

This information is required to make inquiry into the quality of sources anyway, so you ought to have it. If it is not expert testimony, you may get by with *the minimum, article, publication, and the date*. There is no need to re-do a complete citation every time you use that source. If you cite a source more than once, you can simply cite the article or the person who wrote it. "Again, from the Jones article" may do. If you find yourself using one source more than two or three times, you're not diversifying your research enough.

Web sources may be particularly obscure. There should be some notation about the source and the last date at which the website was updated at the bottom of page. Know who is offering the information from dot.com websites. "According to the website of the FBI on such and such a date" may be appropriate. Otherwise, you'd best find another source that verifies the information provided. ***Do not quote web addresses as your oral citation***. Apart from being ungainly speech, they're not the source; they're only the address of the source. If you were quoting me, would you use my home address as the citation? No, you would use my name and my qualifications, where I wrote the quotation, and the date of the publication.

URGENT: Be careful about documenting the information you acquire as you go, not later. Develop a careful note-taking habit when you examine research materials. If you're going to copy information as you find it in the library, keep a brief list of sources that you can later turn into a bibliography. If you cut and paste web sources, be sure to attach the documentation as well. The evidence tests of accuracy and verifiability will depend on this careful scholarship. It's much easier than you may think to forget where you got information. I make the point firmly because this is one of the main errors that students seem to make today. Your teacher will probably want to see your sources from the start when you submit sample arguments. Proper documentation is a matter of following a process from the start, not looping back later. ***Dealing with the tedium of citation as you go is actually easier and faster than looping back later to find a source.***

Finally, please, do not refer to "this quote" when using source-based evidence. "Quote" is a verb as in "I now quote the previous source." ***The noun is "quotation,"*** though it is commonly misprinted as "quote" on the web.

BACK TO TOULMIN

Our discussion about propositions in the last chapter bears upon "claims." You'll have, as in most texts, an overarching proposition, which is your thesis, plus at least two arguments, each with a claim supporting the thesis,

FIGURE 3-1.

The real truth is that we **build your arguments from the "grounds" up.** That is, we make a general hypothesis about our proposition and our c laims, but we have to let the evidence itself tell us what we can actually, justifiably say to be true. How do we go about building something in an architectural sense? We start with a vision, a plan about what the building will look like. Then we build a foundation from which the structure rises. The same is true of successful argument building. Your foundation is the grounds, the evidence that you find about that issue. To understand, think in terms of **an analogy from architecture, the pyramid** (Figure 2):

Like a pyramid, the reason and the conclusion you draw from it, begin with the foundation of grounds.

Start with some rudimentary arguments consisting of a claim supported by some grounds. We'll build warrants where necessary as we go. You probably won't understand warrants fully, even after reading about the patterns of reasoning in Chapter 5. That's O.K. It's a learning process that will unfold over time. For now, concentrate on evidence and building argument from "the grounds up."

Here are some examples of rudimentary arguments. They're also arguments on issues of fact, your first assignment.

Let's say that my initial proposition of fact is that **"the challenged economy is hurting the gambling industry."** Notice that I've included both the cause and the effect in the proposition, the two stock issues involved in the fact speech. We'll do at least one supporting argument on each stock issue.

Claim A: Nevada gambling is doing poorly.

Grounds A1: According to an October 3, 2010, *New York Times* article entitled "Vegas Faces It's Deepest Slide," "Las Vegas is in the deepest economic dive since casinos started in the 1940s. There is a recession accompanied by the decline of the construction industry, the second economic pillar of Nevada. Unemployment is 14.4% in the state. It's even higher in Las Vegas where gaming revenues have declined." One sign of this is that, "while there were more people coming to Las Vegas in recent months, gambling receipts have been stagnant.... Nevada has led the nation in foreclosures for the 44th straight month. Gaming revenues have steadily declined for 3 straight years (**27**).

Grounds A2: In the same issue of *The New York Times*, there is another article called "For Nevada Casinos, Threats in California." It documents problems in Reno as well. "In Reno, gambling receipts are down by 25% and has declined 30 of the last 37 months (**28**)."

There are also some more specific causes other than the generally lousy economy. According to the first article, "Gambling by Nevadans has fallen off as a result of the unemployment. Baby Boomers are less likely to gamble, worried about their retirement years."

O.K. So far so good, but the article goes on to say, "Internet gambling appeals more to gambling addicts than the casino experience, so that doesn't help. "And the second article states that Native American gambling is directly blamed for this by members of the Nevada Gaming Control Board for the decline in Reno. Native Americans have built more elaborate casinos on major California highways leading from the Bay Area and from Central California over the Sierra Nevada. undercutting Reno with greater convenience.

So, now what do I do? My proposition suggests that gambling everywhere is doing worse, but the evidence says that both internet and Indian gambling in California is doing well at the expense of Nevada, With a little further research, therefore, I'll have to adjust my proposition by decreasing the argumentative ground to "The economy and other factors are hurting Nevada gambling." The additional evidence on Native American casinos and internet gambling can be used to build a second argument on the stock issue of "cause."

Then we'll have **two arguments built from the grounds up**. With further research, two sources being too few, we can even say that we've built **a prima facie case**.

A LAST WORD ON RELEVANCE: FALLACIES OF EVASION

All of the evidence tests are important during the research process, but the test of relevance brings up **another class of fallacies**. We're not just learning to build arguments but also how to oppose arguments in an ethical way. Once an advocate creates his "fort," his argumentative ground, opponents are ethically obligated to respond in a relevant manner. When in a debate, **research should clash directly with what the advocate** says, not what an opponent wants him to say or assumes he will say. These are some **common ways of avoiding direct clash (29).**

Simple avoidance is refusing to talk about an argumentative challenge at all. My wife has perfected this method: I ask her how much money she's spent, but she ignores me and goes on to a different subject. This is the **"no comment"** response we often see from public figures, or "I don't recall" when questioned before judges or congressional committees.

Seizing on a trivial point is focusing on a picky detail that isn't the main thrust of your opponent's argument. For instance, your opponent reads a piece of evidence that defeats your position, but you notice that there's a clerical error on the date of the magazine cited. So, you say, "that was printed on the 15th not the 16th!" True, it is sloppy scholarship, and you should try to keep the original materials you quote available. Yet the point of the evidence remains the same. Also, the opponent has just admitted that the evidence exists.

Red herring, a deliberately misleading argument, is used commonly by politicians. A red herring is a fish with a pungent odor that was often spread across a trail by poachers to mislead tracking dogs (30). "Red Herring" has also been popularized in mystery stories as false clues that lead the detective astray from the real crook. In the context of argument, the term refers to raising a point not directly relevant to the advocate's argument because it's easier to oppose. One then issues arguments against a point the advocate never really made. The key to a Red Herring set-up is **misrepresentation,** giving an inaccurate or exaggerated version of your opponent's position. The goal is **distraction**, sounding good while arguing against a point the advocate never made. For instance, the attack on what's been called "Obamacare"

- though the details of the plan are a congressional invention - uses several key misrepresentations, according to *FactCheck.org* (**31**):

Some ads go so far as to claim (falsely) that the law would cause Medicare patients to lose their doctors, or (also falsely) that Democrats favored giving Viagra to sex offenders, or (false again) that typical families will pay $2,100 more in premiums. A common theme is that the law contains a $500 billion Medicare "cut" that will translate into less benefits, but that's misleading. The law calls for reducing the future growth of Medicare spending over the next 10 years by about 7 percent. Plus, the law stipulates that guaranteed Medicare benefits won't be reduced, and it adds some new benefits, such as improved coverage for pharmaceuticals.

Shifting ground is another way to avoid an issue that you have difficulty arguing. ***Advocates***, who might also commit any of the other fallacies of evasion, ***are particularly vulnerable*** to this mistake. Let's say that you're the opponent laying siege upon your adversary's fort. You've cornered him in a weak position for which he has no answer, so he shifts to a different one. He might either retreat to a tighter position in the fort, abandoning a portion of his burden of proof, or he may leave the fort entirely and pretend that his position is closer to yours than it initially was. Doing either, he will hope that you don't notice that he's altered the original proposition. You'll watch for that, however, and hold him to his original ground.

One reason that Senator John Kerry's 2004 presidential campaign failed was that he voted for the Iraq invasion, admittedly for reasons including false data, but he then became critical of the war. He said, "I actually did vote for the $87 billion before I voted against it." At the same time that he argued we should stay the course, just do it better. As a result, he was successfully labeled "a waffler" with an unclear position. Equivocation commonly accompanies shifts of ground (**32**).

These fallacies of evasion will become more important in a debate, but even as we offer critique and counter-argument after speeches, let's be aware of these fallacies as a potential problem in research.

IN SUM

Go directly to the library and begin research NOW, if you haven't already done so. Do not pass "go." Do not collect $200. Just do it! If possible, start research on all three of the topics you've chosen for your fact, value, and policy texts. Focus on your library time early in the semester, so you can study the material carefully. You should have a clear sense of what your proposition of fact is in the next week of research. You should also have samples of the various types of evidence, all relevant to your proposition of fact. Finally, you should be building rudimentary arguments consisting of a claim and some grounds to support it.

VOCABULARY

Appeals: Ethos, Pathos, Logos
Artifacts
Assertion
Citation
Conclusionary Evidence
Credibility
      Attractiveness
      Competence
      Consistency
      Dynamism
      Eloquence
      Good Will
      Honesty
      Knowledge
      Moral Character
      Wisdom
Documentation
Evidence of Fact
Evidence of Opinion
Examples
Expert Testimony
Fallacies of Evasion

Simple Avoidance

Seizing on a Trivial Point

Red Herring

Shifting Ground

Figures & Statistics

Identification

Inference

Multiple Viewpoints

Quantify

Relevance

Representative

Sample Population

Source-Based Evidence

Source Splitting

Sufficiency

Tests of Evidence

Accuracy

Bias

Consistency

Recency

Relevance

Representativeness

Source Qualification

Verifiability

REFERENCES

1) Perelman, C., and L. Olbrechts-Tyteca. The New Rhetoric. Notre Dame, IN: Univ. of Notre Dame, 1969. Willebrand, M. L., and R.D. Rieke. "Strategies of Reasoning In Spontaneous Discourse." Communication Yearbook. Ed. Anderson, James A. Newbury Park, CA: Sage (1991): 414–440.

2) "Rhino left with no place to hide," Los Angeles Times, November 24, 2010.

3) Burke, K. (1950). "The Range of Rhetoric." A Rhetoric of Motives. Berkeley: University of California Press: 3–46.

4) Fisher, W.R. "Narration as a Human Communication Paradigm: The Case of Moral Argument." Communication Monographs 51 (1984): 1–22.
    McDonald, K., and J.W. Jarman). "Getting the Story Right: The Role of Narrative Academic Debate." Rostrum 72 (1998).

5) "Finding Little Solace in Sharing of Long-Guarded Secret Catholic Priest Who Was Victim of Sex Abuse Draws Fire After Speaking Out," The Washington Post, April 27, 2006.

6) "Hefty Paychecks for Vernon Officials Rival Those in Bell," Los Angeles Times, August 20, 2010.

7) Brownlee, Don (1982). "The Consequences of Quantification." CEDA Yearbook 3, 29-31.
    Spiker, B. K., T. D. Daniels, and L. Bernabo. "The Quantitative Quandary in Forensics: The Uses and Abuses of Statistical Evidence." Argumentation and Advocacy 19 (1982): 87–96.

8) "Road Rage: A Culturally Acquired Habit," April 15, 2010. http://www.suite101.com/content/road-rage-a-culturally-acquired-habit-a225769

9) "Census Winners and Losers," December 22, 2010. http://www.newsy.com/videos/census-winners-and-losers/?gclid=CPnTrM7sj6YCFQdMgwodgzyeoA

10) "Lab Report," Time, November 8, 2010.

11) "Boomers Overdose Deaths Up," Los Angeles Times, October 10, 2005.

12) "Bad Ass Baby Boomers," The Book of Odds. April 22, 2010. http://www.bookofodds.com/Daily-Life-Activities/Articles/ A0713-Badass-Baby-Boomers.

13) "Bias seen in bias studies," Inside Higher Ed, January 22, 2007. http://www.insidehighered.com/news/2007/01/22/bias

14) "Concussions in Child Athletes Soar," Los Angeles Times, August 30, 2010.

15) The American Academy of Pediatrics, "Recurrent Concussions in College Football," AAP Rounds. http://aapgrandrounds.aappublications.org/cgi/content/extract/11/2/16

16) Los Angeles Times, October 10, 2005.

17) http://www.biocompare.com/ProductDetails/2162671/Human-Mesenchymal-Stem-Cells-from-Umbilical-Cord-Matrix.html
    http://www.ncbi.nlm.nih.gov/pubmed/18243183
    https://www.lablife.org/g?a=pubs_ll_no_user&id=19285791

18) "Researchers Announce First Artificial Kidney Prototype," Popular Science, September 3, 2010.

19) Reinhard, J.C. "The Empirical Study of the Persuasive Effects of Evidence: The Status After Fifty Years of Research." Human Communication Research, 15 (1988): 3–59.

20) Baudhin, S., and M. Davis. "Scales for the Measurement of Ethos: Another Attempt." Speech Monographs 39 (1972): 296–301.

21) "Big Tobacco Curses the Day Expert Witness Took the Oath," Los Angeles Times, August 25, 2002.

22) Richard A. Grasso, The New York Times, December 29, 2010.

23) Trumbull, Mark, "Lehman Bros. used accounting trick amid financial crisis," The Christian Science Monitor. March 12, 2010.

24) Solmsen, F. "The Rhetoric and Poetics of Aristotle." New York: Random House, 1954.

25) Dahnke, G.L., and G.W. Clatterbuck. Human Communication: Theory and Research. Belmont, CA: Wadsworth, 1990.
Capaldi, Nicholas. The Art of Deception. Buffalo, NY: Prometheus Books, 1975.

26) "Fewer than half of Americans oppose gay marriage," CNN, October 6, 2010. http://articles.cnn.com/2010-10-06/us/poll.gay. marriage_1_gay-marriage-americans-favor-new-poll?_s=PM:US

27) "Las Vegas Faces Its Deepest Slide Since the 1940s," The New York Times, October 3, 2010.

28) "For Nevada Casinos, Threats in California," The New York Times, October 3, 2010.

29) Rybacki, K.C., and D. J. Rybacki. Advocacy and Opposition: An Introduction to Argumentation (3rd edition). Boston, MA: Allyn & Bacon, 2004.

30) The 365 Dogs Calendar. New York: Workman Publishing, 2003.

31) Whoppers of Campaign 2010," FactCheck.org, October 26, 2010. http://factcheck.org/2010/10/whoppers-of-campaign-2010/

32) http://www.cbsnews.com/stories/2004/09/29/politics/main 646435.shtml

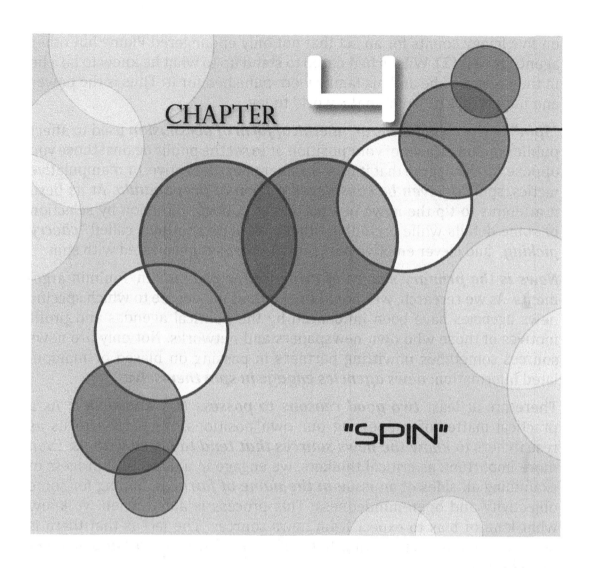

CHAPTER 4

"SPIN"

"THE SPIN OVERWHELMED THE SUBSTANCE."

So said Joseph C. Wilson, foreign service diplomat in Africa and famous author of the article "What I Didn't Find in Africa," posted in *The New York Times* after the invasion of Iraq. In the article, he noted that there was no solid evidence of nuclear materials being sent to Iraq and that the Bush administration had exaggerated facts to justify the invasion (1). A week after the article was published, his wife, Valerie Plame, was revealed to be a CIA agent through a leak to the *Washington Post* from the White House. Lewis Libby, Chief of Staff to Vice President Dick Cheney, was convicted on five felony counts for an act that not only endangered Plame but other agents as well **(2)**. Wilson had dared to stand up to what he knew to be a lie in the press, and he and his family were punished for it. Thus is the power and importance of "spin" in the world today.

"Spin" can be classified as ***an unethical form of persuasion*** used to affect public opinion in favor of your position or to set the public against those you oppose. To the degree that it uses disingenuous, deceptive, or manipulative tactics, spin ***can even be considered a form of propaganda***. At its best, it attempts to tip the news in a particular political direction by selection of some details while excluding others, an act sometimes called *"**cherry picking**,"* and clever emotive phrasing **(3)**. News is permeated with spin.

News is the primary source of evidence for grounds in Toulmin arguments. As we research, we should understand the degree to which specific news agencies have been influenced by the political agendas and profit motives of those who own newspapers and networks. Not only are news sources sometimes unwitting partners in passing on biased or manipulated information; ***news agencies engage in spin themselves.***

There are at least ***two good reasons to possess this knowledge***: As a practical matter of supporting our own positions, it's helpful to us as researchers to ***know the news sources that tend to agree with us***. Even more important, as critical thinkers, we engage in a dialectical process of examining all sides of an issue ***in the name of fairness***, hoping for some objectivity and open-mindedness. This process is aided when we know what kind of bias to expect from news sources. The fact is that there is news bias in today's reporting, both left and right. ***None will be spared in this chapter***.

MEDIA BIAS DOES EXIST

Several reports and studies about media bias exist. The 2008 Presidential election inspired several.

The Project for Excellence in Journalism published, "The Invisible Primary—Invisible No Longer" after the 2008 election. They found that there was *"**measurably more favorable coverage**"* early in the campaign for both ***Barack Obama and Fred Thompson***—attorney, Republican Tennessee senator, and an actor frequently playing government figures—than other primary candidates. **Both Hillary Clinton and John McCain received far more negative reporting** than their opponents. Democrats generally received more favorable coverage than Republicans (49% positive to 31% negative). 63% of the coverage focused on political and tactical aspects of the campaign, four times the number about candidate background (17%) or ideas and policies (15%). A mere 1% of stories looked at candidate records or past performance. This was based on an analysis of 1742 stories (**4**).

The study authors commented on **a kind of selective perception**: The journalists "didn't have a bias as the term is normally used.... They just appeared to think they knew the subject well enough, or had a set of enough ideas in their heads as to what this kind of story was about, that they pursued only the lines of questioning necessary to fill in the blanks of that presumed story line."

Some of these studies themselves, however, show bias. In the *Columbia Daily Tribune,* September 12, 2010, banking and investment executive Bob Roper wrote "Liberal bias is real, revealing." He discusses **"the liberal bias"** **of "mainstream media"** or MSM, which he defines as *The New York Times, The Washington Post, ABC, NBC, CBS, NPR, Time, Newsweek,* and CNN. He does not include *The Wall Street Journal* or Fox News.

Roper mentions **a Rasmussen poll** that said 55 percent of voters believe MSM bias is a bigger problem than big campaign contributions. Another poll showed that 77 percent of Republicans and 47 percent of Democrats believe there is a liberal bias in MSM. This is significant since 42 percent of Americans identify themselves as conservative; only 20 percent identify as liberals (**5**).

Could this have something to do with the polarizing language of pundits, that people who don't identify themselves as liberals are called same? Where does the word "centrist" appear in the current equation of cable news banter? Of course, the term "liberal" has become a kind of dirty word. Karl Rove is fond of the notion that his candidates can "tar them with the liberal brush."

Also, though Roper mentions that **"study after study"** reveals these conclusions, he names only The Rasmussen Poll. The Rasumusson Poll is particularly interested in providing numbers for Republican talking points, and it tends to ask Republicans exclusively for their opinions. There are explicit defenses of Sarah Palin in their comments (6).

In fairness, the Roper article does discourage using the extreme labels of "archconservative" and "archliberal." Yet not only are "the facts" that reporters share often a matter of spin, even studies about their bias are, too.

WHY IS THERE BIAS IN NEWS?

Many of you don't recall a time when there really was such a thing as a relatively straight news report, followed briefly by "commentary" that used to be clearly labeled as opinion.

Now, television news allows *the newsreader*—frequently one with little or no actual reporting experience but with appealing looks or personality—the *freedom to offer editorial side comments without noting it as opinion.* Comments are asserted confidently, accompanied by dramatic phrasing, knowing glances among reporters, and "Boy, I did that well" winks into the camera, as though the reader's own reflections constituted expert opinion. Those who are most effective at this gather followings that create good ratings further motivating loose self-assertion by these spontaneous pundits.

News has been *drifting toward a lack of objectivity for a long time*, probably before many of us were born. News has always been limited in objectivity by staff editorial opinions. The choice of what you include and exclude even in frank and honest news stories is a form of subjectivity.

In fact, there has always been some bias in news since at least the 1880s, including intense periods of what's been called "*yellow journalism*." The Spanish American War was driven by sensational reporting. Newspaper owners William Randolph Hurst and Joseph Pulitzer sometimes fabricated or romanticized dramatic events and used hyperbole to sell newspapers (7).

Yet the drift from center seems to be *accelerating for several reasons* including:

- The collapse of news divisions into the entertainment divisions of networks creating "infotainment" and personality based news.

- National departure from The Fairness Doctrine in the late 1980s.
- The concentration of news ownership into the hands of powerful corporations with political agenda.

THE END OF NEWS DIVISIONS

An Academy Award winning film called *Network*, made in 1976, written by American playwright Paddy Chayevsky and directed by Sidney Lumet, created a farseeing portrait of what would happen to reporting once entertainment divisions absorbed news divisions. A mad reporter at "UBS-TV" is exploited by his network and portrayed as a prophet when he has seizures and awakens raving about his personal frustrations. "I'm mad as hell, and I'm not going to take it anymore," he screams, boosting ratings immensely. ("UBS." Not very subtle, is it?)

The real message of *Network*, however, is contained in a speech by the station owner reprimanding his reporter for daring to believe his own prophecies. The owner scolds him for even thinking that there is such a thing as nations or peoples, asserting that they don't exist anymore:

> There is only one holistic system of systems, one vast and immense, interwoven, interacting, multivariate, multinational dominion of dollars ... one vast and ecumenical holding company, for whom all men will work ... in which all men will hold a share of stock, all necessities provided, all anxieties tranquilized, all boredom amused **(8)**

The full speech is much better, and the film is worth viewing. The climax is an announcement that the news division at UBS is dead, absorbed by the entertainment division, heralding the beginning of "infotainment."

THE FAIRNESS DOCTRINE & "SHOCK JOCKS"

The Fairness Doctrine was a United States Federal Communications Commission policy that attempted ***to ensure that all coverage of controversial issues by a broadcast station be balanced and fair.***

The Fox news motto of "Fair and Balanced" is a clear reference to that goal. **The FCC thought of station licensees as "public trustees"** who had an obligation to offer contrasting views on controversial issues. It was not uncommon after their 1949 ruling that a minute was offered, even to private citizens, to comment on network editorials. Congress attempted to pass the doctrine into law, but it was *vetoed* by President Reagan in 1987 in keeping with his general policy of deregulation (**9**).

This combined with an earlier switch to FM bandwidths in broadcasting to open a sizeable new territory of easily purchased radio time, filled by *"a vast meritocracy of talent: thousands of pundits, working for hundreds of stations,"* competing for shares of the global broadcasting market. Thus, the 90s brought about the rise of the "shock jock," mostly Republican men willing to push the edge of issues for shock value and good ratings (**10**).

INFOTAINMENT & PERSONALITY BASED NEWS

Infotainment is "information-based media content or programming that also *includes entertainment content in an effort to enhance popularity* with audiences and consumers (**11**)."

One natural corollary of infotainment is the increase of *personality oriented news rather than what one might call "hard news,"* the kind of detailed reporting that doesn't have time for quite so many "human interest stories" or tolerance for random editorial comment.

There have often been beloved news figures. *Walter Cronkite*, the CBS news anchor who covered the civil rights movement, the assassination of President Kennedy, and landmarks of the space program, was more trusted than most presidents that he covered, but it wasn't for his antagonisms, interruptions, or self-righteous judgments of political figures. It was for being truly "fair and balanced (**12**)."

Now, however, not only have we come to accept personality news as the norm, there are *three other important accompanying phenomena:*

A) Since the media itself has changed, offering something for virtually every niche of television consciousness, *cable news makes it possible* *to watch only those with whom you already agree* and who reinforce your personal and cultural prejudices. This would tend to eliminate dialectical thinking in steady viewers.

B) *A process of continual involvement and loyalty* is encouraged by allowing viewers to post their opinions through *instant polls*, nothing statistical, just quick quotations from viewers at an anecdotal level. MSNBC's "Gut Check" would be one example, but "insta-polls" are almost universal in news. The primary effect is not to improve the accuracy of facts, but to reinforce the attitude of the station and its "niche" viewers.

C) Further, these news personalities operate in *the atmosphere of so-called "reality television," which encourages conflict and personal "meltdowns"* on air for the amusement of viewers. Cable news seems to have adopted a parallel course whereby *interrupting and baiting interview guests constitutes "hard hitting reporting."* Rather than rational discourse, some news seems to be closer to gladiatorial combat with a distinctly partisan flavor. Nancy Grace of CNN or Sean Hannity at Fox, discussed in more detail later, are examples of personality news gone too personal.

A glaring example of personality news at its worst is *Rick Sanchez.* In writing this chapter, I have sat and watched hour upon hour of news at each station, sometimes amused, sometimes disgusted, sometimes surprised at the lack of basic broadcasting competence. Rick Sanchez had a CNN show that included *"Rick's List: The List You Don't Want to Be On."* His grammar was poor, he often stumbled over text, but he seemed so pleased with himself at the same time. He once called Obama "the cotton-picking president" and got away with it.

I was not surprised that he was released by CNN, especially after he called comedian Jon Stewart a "bigot" and suggested that the media are run by Jews. Instead of quietly going away—and this is typical of personality news ego—he went on *"The Rick Sanchez Apology Tour."* He said, "Despite what my mangled and tired words might have implied, they were never intended to suggest any sort of narrow mindedness and should never have been made. " He then *plugs his own book*—a seemingly inevitable exercise among even the least of newsmen today—"Conventional Idiocy" twice. (This is not his autobiography, by the way.)

"I just realized something," Stewart jabbed back. "Rick Sanchez delivers the news like a guy at a party who's doing a lot of coke and traps you in a corner and explains really intensely how an ant is the strongest animal on Earth."

Sanchez also said that he'd be happy to return to CNN if they asked (**13**).

WHO OWNS THE NEWS

A natural requirement of the growth of infotainment is **the need to satisfy sponsors in the private sector**. To measure the objectivity of a news source, one might follow the advice of any good detective, "You follow the money." According to the Los Angeles Independent Media Center website these are the owners of the news.

General Electric, a million dollar donor to the 2000 campaign of George W. Bush, owns **NBC** through 13 stations that reach 28% of households. NBC has included such deans of the reporting world as Tom Brokaw, as well as "The Today Show" and "Meet the Press." Universal Studios is also a part of this communication conglomerate. GE co-holds **MSNBC** with NBC and Microsoft. The "MS" in MSNBC refers to Microsoft, which gave $2.4 million to help George W. Bush's campaign, which is interesting given the station's liberal reputation. GE is a vast conglomerate with holdings in everything from health care to oil. Vivendi, a French multimedia corporation, also has major holdings.

Westinghouse, which is responsible for much of our nuclear energy, owned **CBS**, including "60 Minutes" and "CBS Evening News." Westinghouse was then owned by *Toshiba*, a Japanese company invested in nuclear energy in this country. Presently, the owner is billionaire **Sumner Redstone** through National Amusements. He also owns Viacom, Paramount Pictures, and DreamWorks film studios, a formidable communication network.

ABC is co-owned by a Las Vegas company, Citadel Broadcasting, after merging with primary shareholder Walt Disney Company. Citadel was the first news organization to give money to the Environmental Protection Agency's "Green Power Partnership Program." However, this group has recently been cash poor. Bankruptcy filings have been discussed.

Time-Warner, who donated 1.6 million to George W. Bush's 2000 campaign, owns CNN, as well as TBS, HBO, and 33 magazines including *Time*.

Thus, news is business. While one may be surprised that the owners of NBC were big Republican contributors, while ABC is an EPA supporter, news makes appeals to us in a manner much like advertisers urging us to "just stay tuned in" to the next dramatic or amusing anecdote. News is a cash cow, and businesses may be fed in ways we little understand or appreciate **(14).**

BIAS IN SPECIFIC NEWS SOURCES

Whether we call it bias, spin, or tone, subjective reporting seems to have intensified in this century, especially since the 2008 presidential election. News seems less and less objective, almost defiantly so, leaving us with a serious research problem: ***Who can we trust for the facts?***

It's a challenging question, especially since ***news pundits aren't always or even usually right.*** U.C. Berkeley professor Philip Tetlock questioned 284 people who made their living in commentary to make predictions about future events. After analysis of 82,000 predictions, he found that a mere 33% of them were correct. Tetlock argued that the problem was certainty, indeed, hubris among commentators **(15).**

To answer this question, we'll discuss various news media but will focus especially on cable, the primary means by which most people get news, not newspapers, not news magazines, not even your local news, but cable.

We'll examine MSNBC, Fox, and CNN. We will also examine radio and print news that students should be reading for a more detailed look at world events, as well as the "think tanks" that often provide philosophical frameworks and information for news agencies and politicians. We will include some foreign news services, which are useful measures of how objectively we look at ourselves.

My distinct prejudice was well-expressed by the George Washington University pollsters. "It becomes increasingly important for viewers to ***sample multiple sources*** in order to best understand the issues."

CABLE NEWS

A George Washington University poll released on September 20, 2010, found that *81% get the news from cable channels*, like Fox News, CNN, MSNBC, or their websites. 71% watched national network news channels, such as ABC, NBC, or CBS. Fox was viewed by 42% of 1000 likely voters responding, 30% watched CNN, and 12% viewed MSNBC.

In other words, to the degree that one assumes CNN and MSNBC to be more liberal than Fox, there's *an even 42% split between conservative and liberal viewers.* What these statistics don't account for are people who may be watching the news from both sides, which could demonstrate good critical thinking. It's possible that either "side's" statistics could be inflated by multi-source viewing. It's certain that we slip into *either/or thinking when we stereotype news sources as solely and distinctly conservative or liberal.* There are many points along the scale including relatively moderate or centrist news sources, as represented on the chart in this chapter.

What is most disturbing is that George Washington University pollsters say voters turn to "media sources that reinforce their own worldviews rather than those that present more objective reporting that might challenge voter assumptions (**16**)."

We'll examine each station in the order of their ratings. We'll start with CNN because it has the highest global ratings, broadcasting to over 200 countries. Also, they are arguably the most centrist in their reporting (**17**).

CNN

Founded by *Ted Turner*, CNN was the first 24-hour news channel. Its growth was fueled by its reporting of the Challenger shuttle disaster and the first Gulf War. To the extent that it is a *Time-Warner* company, it shares a loosely similar editorial style with *Time* magazine. It also has international programming available in most countries, giving it the largest worldwide audience of the big three cable news shows. Fox rules U.S. ratings. CNN rules the globe (**18**).

CNN has been accused of perpetrating bias for both conservative and liberal agenda based on previous incidents (**19**). Accuracy in Media and the Media Research Center claim that CNN's reporting contains liberal editorializing within news stories. In a joint study by the Joan Shorenstein Center on Press, Politics and Public Policy at Harvard University and the Project for Excellence in Journalism, the authors found disparate treatment of Republican and Democratic candidates during the earliest five months of presidential primaries in 2007: "The CNN programming studied tended to cast a negative light on Republican candidates by a margin of three-to-one."

These are the key news personnel.

WOLF BLITZER

Wolf Blitzer is the anchor of CNN's "The Situation Room," CNN's political news program airing every weekday and in an hour-long format on Saturday evenings.

In addition to politics, Blitzer is also known for his *in-depth reporting on international news.* In 2003, Blitzer reported on the Iraq war from the Persian Gulf region. In 2005, he was the only American news anchor to cover the terrorist attack on the U.S.S. Cole on the ground in Dubai. He reported from Israel in the midst of the war with Hezbollah during the summer of 2006.

Blitzer is the recipient of an Emmy Award from The National Academy of Television Arts and Sciences for his 1996 coverage of the Oklahoma City bombing and a Golden Cable ACE from the National Academy of Cable Programming for his and CNN's coverage of the Persian Gulf War. He anchored CNN's Emmy-award winning live coverage of the 2006 Election Day. He was also among the teams awarded a George Foster Peabody award for Hurricane Katrina coverage; an Alfred I. DuPont Award for coverage of the tsunami disaster in Southeast Asia; and an Edward R. Murrow Award for CNN's coverage of the Sept. 11 terrorist attacks in 2001 (**20**).

He is known for confronting George W. Bush on the lack of federal action in the Hurricane Katrina disaster. "Mr. President, haven't you been watching the news? Katrina hit New Orleans five days ago. The city is flooded. Many people are homeless, desperate for food and water. They're wondering why it's taking so long for the government to send help (**21**)."

However, while generally fair-minded, Wolf Blitzer lost his cool during the 2004 presidential election. He was visibly upset that early returns showed Bush beating Kerry, and he continually asserted that there was still a chance for Kerry to win. He was among a very few who took that position. Blitzer registers as an independent to avoid charges of bias.

Anderson Cooper

Anderson Cooper is a graduate of Yale. He joins Wolf Blitzer as someone who *has actually done some reporting*. He is essentially "the bread and butter" of CNN's primetime line-up with "Anderson Cooper 360." His own station says of him, "Anderson Cooper is *the standard bearer for the type of journalism that CNN has become famous for* and that we want to continue to be known for." His coverage of the recent disastrous Haiti earthquake may well have been the best of any reporter on any channel. Yet his ratings are often below those of his primetime competitors (**22**). It may be that audiences find his appropriately mild demeanor more boring than the shock jocks that he competes with, but he is an authentic investigative reporter.

He is generally professional in demeanor, but while covering Hurricane Katrina, he confronted Senator Mary Landrieu of Louisiana. Cooper boiled over. "I got to tell you," he said, "there are a lot of people here who are very upset, and very angry, and very frustrated. And when they hear politicians ... thanking one another, it just, you know, it kind of cuts them the wrong way right now. Because literally there was a body on the streets of this town yesterday being eaten by rats, because this woman had been laying in the street for 48 hours. And there are not enough facilities to take her up. Do you get the anger that is out here?"

Cooper said later, "Yeah, I would prefer not to be emotional and I would prefer not to get upset, but it's hard not to when you're surrounded by brave people who are suffering and in need."[As *Broadcasting & Cable* magazine noted, "In its aftermath, Hurricane Katrina served to usher in a new breed of *emo-journalism*, skyrocketing CNN's Anderson Cooper to superstardom as CNN's golden boy (**23**)."

* * * * *

Until 2011, CNN also featured the very popular *"Larry King Show,"* which featured interviews on a variety of political and social topics. A moderate conservative, Mr. King was always a courteous gentleman with his guests. CNN continues to host the intelligent and fair-minded conservative **David Gergen** as a guest commentator.

The station, aware that it's losing the ratings war with Fox, seems to be **searching for a more controversial and stimulating programming edge**. They brought disgraced New York governor **Eliot Spitzer** on as a commentator for a round-table discussion format.

They've introduced **"Piers Morgan Tonight"** with shameless self-promotion by Morgan himself. His ads say, "the best television is theater," "I want every night to be an event," and "I want to interview the most important people in the world and have everybody in America the next day saying, 'Did you see that?'" Yet Morgan has delivered an often entertaining and informative celebrity interview show. Among the first was an informal, candid, and humanizing interview with Condoleezza Rice, former Secretary of State. His ratings have raised CNN over MSNBC at the same hour, though they remain behind Sean Hannity at Fox.

FOX NEWS

Fox is owned by **Rupert Murdoch,** a naturalized Australian billionaire, even richer than Sumner Redstone. Murdoch also owns broadcasting companies in Great Britain, Germany, Latin America, and Asia. His holdings include *The London Times* and *The New York Post*, commonly a conservative counterpoint to *The New York Times*. He owns 25 magazines, including *The Weekly Standard*, a conservative magazine critical of progressive policies.

This is the only cable channel that is consistently regarded as right of center, though they themselves urgently deny any such claim. Murdoch himself says, "I challenge anybody to show me an example of biased reporting in Fox News Channel." Fox seems to say that we're so saturated in liberal news that they only look conservative in comparison. In fact, they **see themselves as the center.**

Yet on this date of October 26, 2010, I'm watching a Fox reporter minimize a beating taken by a female, liberal MoveOn.org demonstrator trying to get close to Republican Candidate Rand Paul in Kentucky. While the film shows male Rand supporters forcing her to the ground, holding her down on the curb with the foot on her back and neck, even kicking at her head, the Fox reporter emphasized that "she wasn't injured" and commented not at all on the behavior of those assaulting her (**24**).

Fox personnel includes *founder and president Roger Ailes*, a pugnacious veteran of the Nixon and Reagan presidential campaigns. Ailes is described by colleague Lee Atwater as having two speeds "attack and destroy." He is fond of calling Clinton "the hippie president" and has lashed out at "liberal bigots." This is not atypical of the *emotive language* used by Fox reporters.

The number of conservative reporters at Fox may not be an accident. Andrew Kirtzman, a respected cable newsman from New York, applied for a job at Fox. When asked what his political party was, Kirtzman refused to say, and the interview was terminated.

More typical of the Fox staff is *Britt Hume*, chief political analyst for the station. While his commentary is consistently conservative, his demeanor is reserved and somber, maybe even world-weary, but his *"Special Report with Brit Hume" little resembles the "shock jocks"* that dominate their most highly rated programming. Hume was a respected reporter with ABC for many years.

When liberals are brought on Fox, though, it sometimes seems like *a "red herring" set-up*. Pundits will paraphrase an extreme version of the liberal viewpoint under debate then mostly ineffective liberal pundits take the bait and struggle against the tide.

The *"Hannity & Colmes"* show was one example. Alan Colmes is less telegenic than Sean Hannity and barely representative of mainstream Democratic thinking. He didn't last very long, though Hannity continues to thrive. The working title for the program was "Hannity & Liberal to Be Determined?" There is no prominent liberal reporter at Fox today.

There was even a time that "claques" were used on Fox shows to boo visiting liberals and vigorously applaud the conservative host. A claque is "a group of people hired to applaud (**25**)."

Further, Fox is *not always kind to Republicans* whom they consider not conservative enough. They have been critical of GOP party leader Tony Snow, and they were extremely critical of President Bush being conciliatory with China when a downed U.S. spy plane was being held.

None of this is to say that it isn't valuable to have a conservative news outlet, but it tends to oversimplify and discredit almost everyone to the left of them as "liberals," even "socialists," *seldom recognizing a center in American thinking.*

According to FAIR, "Fox could potentially represent a valuable contribution to the journalistic mix if it admitted it had a conservative point of view, if it beefed up its hard news and investigative coverage (and cut back on the tabloid sensationalism), and if there were only an openly left-leaning TV news channel capable of balancing both Fox's conservatism and CNN's centrism (**26**)." FAIR said this before MSNBC went further left.

The three most highly rated of the Fox News headliners are Bill O'Reilly, Sean Hannity, and Glenn Beck"

Bill O'Reilly

It's at least a little ironic that O'Reilly's program is called *"The No Spin Zone,"* because it is a primary bastion of conservative analysis. O'Reilly often gives the appearance of being *aggressive,* if not downright angry. He and MSNBC's Keith Olbermann have engaged in a number of furious media exchanges. Neither is one to shrink from offering his opinion.

O'Reilly is interruptive with liberal guests. He has no qualms at all about *telling people to "shut up"* (**27**). Yet O'Reilly is good-natured enough to appear on liberal comedian Bill Maher's show by satellite hookup sporting a knowing wink. It's safe to say that O'Reilly remains *an iconoclast but a well-educated one* with a B.A. from Boston College and a Masters of Public Administration, from Harvard. He's a *generous charitable contributor* to "Habitats for Humanity," heavily supported by ex-Democratic President Jimmy Carter, which seems surprising when you look at the incendiary nature of O'Reilly's statements (**28**).

On weapons of mass destruction: "If the Americans go in and overthrow Saddam Hussein and it's clean, he has nothing, I will apologize to the nation, and I will not trust the Bush Administration again, all right?" Bill O'Reilly, March 18, 2003 (**29**). No apology is as yet forthcoming.

On the UN: "I just wish Katrina had only hit the United Nations building, nothing else, just had flooded them out, and I wouldn't have rescued them." Bill O'Reilly, September 14, 2005 (**30**).

On race: "I couldn't get over the fact that there was no difference between Sylvia's restaurant and any other restaurant in New York City. I mean, it was exactly the same, even though it's run by blacks." Bill O'Reilly, September 21, 2007 (**31**).

In spite of his fierce right-leaning commentary, "The O'Reilly Factor" has *the highest watcher ratings of any single news show* on the air today with a peak of 3.1 million viewers on any given night (**32**).

Sean Hannity

Hannity ranks close behind Bill O'Reilly in viewership with *an audience of up to 15 million a week.* He is not as well-educated, having attended two colleges but finished neither. He has *a propensity for provocative incidents*.

According to IMBD, the Internet Movie Database that provides biographical information for media personnel, Hannity, "*was fired from his first radio job*, on a college station in Santa Barbara for an incident in which a guest on his show, an avowed white supremacist, made a string of inflammatory racial remarks, which the station said Hannity encouraged." He then went to a radio station in Huntsville, Alabama, where his ultra-conservative political views found favor, and he eventually got a national show on WABC/770 in New York (**33**).

Hannity *has misrepresented public figures* he criticizes. He said on January 30, 2004, "If he (John Kerry) had his way the CIA would almost be nonexistent." The truth is that John Kerry had supported $200 billion in intelligence funding over the past seven years a 50 percent increase since 1996 (**34**).

Hannity shared *"disturbing reports,"* we know not from whom, about the transition into the Bush presidency in 2001, saying that exiting White House staff had looted the building and Air Force One. He asserted that $200,000 in furniture was removed and that pornographic materials were left on printers and voice mails. The "reports" were debunked by the G.A.O.

Hannity asserted in his book, *Let Freedom Ring*, that "liberal Democrats showed little interest in investigating the intelligence failures of 9/11." It was, in fact, Bush who resisted the creation of a special commission to examine these failures for over a year (**35**).

Hannity insisted no less than twenty times during 2003 and 2004 that George W. Bush inherited a recession from William Clinton, **never once recognizing the surplus Bush actually started with**, and insisting that Bush ended the recession that actually began after he took office and persisted until a year ago.

According to BBC news online, January 15, 2001. "President Clinton will leave office with the longest boom in U.S. history still intact.... Mr. Clinton also leaves the legacy of a huge and growing budget surplus...." Their estimate was that the economy expanded "50% in real terms" and that the gross national product grew to one quarter of the entire world economic output. The unemployment rate he inherited from George Bush, Sr., dropped by half to 4%, a forty-year low, and 15 million jobs were created. The stock market grew by three times. The very surplus, however, inspired tax cuts that rebuilt the national debt over the Bush years. Clinton was criticized for leaving the international trading system with problems to solve.

Hannity also claimed on August 5, 2003, that there is no mention of the separation of church and state in the Constitution, ignoring the phrase "Congress shall make no law respecting the establishment of religion, or prohibition the free exercise thereof." *"It doesn't say anywhere in the constitution this idea of the separation of church and state (36)."*

He called the torture practice of waterboarding "dunking" on April 4, 2009, *"I am for enhanced interrogation. I don't believe water boarding is torture... I'll do it. I'll do it for charity."* Hannity evaded an agreement to undergo water boarding to prove that the practice doesn't amount to torture. In fact, the U.S. prosecuted Japanese for the practice after WWII as a war crime. It was also used by the dictatorial Khmer Rouge regime of Pol Pot during the Cambodian genocide after the Vietnam War (**37**).

Glenn Beck

"This is Beck land where things tend to be black and white. Abortion is bad; God is good. Gays are 'faggots,' torture is 'enhanced interrogation,' public healthcare should actually be called socialized medicine.... Global warming, of course, is a myth cooked up by left wing scientists in a conspiracy to prevent Americans from fulfilling their patriotic duty to guzzle gas. He is, of course, the consummate showman." So wrote *The Independent* (**38**).

His career has skyrocketed. In the first four months of his career at Fox, Beck's time slot increased by 150% to 2.3 million regular viewers. Mr. Beck *has a high school degree but did not attend college*. Yet he is worth around 32 million dollars. He gives twenty live stage shows a year and *wears bulletproof vests* to public engagements. He confesses to being a "recovering dirt bag" suffering from *alcoholism and marijuana addiction*. He calls his own book collection, "the library of a serial killer." He thinks out loud then reverses himself often. His rhetoric is *divisive and polarizing*. That is, he tends to divide "us" from "them" with the extremity of his assertions. *Yet he doesn't have an angry bearing* like Bill O'Reilly often does. While he speaks at Tea Party Rallies and is a key figurehead for them, he says he's "not involved with the Tea Party (39)."

Glenn Beck is *vocal about his dislike for progressives* and frequently utters how much he hates Woodrow Wilson, President from 1913 to 1921, whom he perceives as inventor of "the progressive era." His involvement in the Treaty of Versailles and The League of Nations heralded principles that later lead to the United Nations, another hate object for Tea Party members.

Progressives are interested in using federal authority to enforce civil rights and to regulate state or business autonomy when it damages such rights or the general welfare. It concentrates more authority in the hands of the federal government as a result of instituting programs such as FDR's "New Deal," including Social Security, up through Kennedy's "New Frontier," which brought about the Civil Rights Act, and Lyndon Johnson's "Great Society." The movement was not merely a matter of Democrats versus Republicans, though. Progressivism is a philosophy of government that actually originated with Republican President Theodore Roosevelt, who used federal power to create the National Parks system. Yet progressivism is cast today as a radical "liberal" movement and is compared to Bolshevik and Marxist philosophy by Tea Party members (40).

Beck even goes so far as to say, "We've lost our way since Andrew Jackson (41)." (I'll refrain from jokes about coonskin caps as appropriate attire for Beck fans.... Oops. Too late.)

He often breaks down and cries in the passion of his oratory. In fact, there are *openly religious moments* during his show with an almost evangelical style. He also recommends a book written by an ultraconservative Mormon,

Beck's own faith, who argued the divine origin of the Constitution, a book that the Mormon church itself has disavowed. Like Hannity, Beck asserts that President Georgh W. Bush inherited a recession (**42**). These are among Beck's personal quotations:

On climate: "If you believe the mainstream media hype, you'd think that every time you drive your SUV, the Earth's temperature rises six degrees."

On politics: "Good for you, you have a heart, you can be a liberal. Now, couple your heart with your brain, and you can be a conservative (**43**)."

"God's finger wrote the constitution (**44**)." Yet he argues for the repeal of the fourteenth and seventeenth amendments.

As of Wednesday, April 4, 2011, it was announced that the Glenn Beck Show would cease production. About half of the headlines said Beck was fired. Four hundred sponsors asked that their commercials not be aired on his show, according to the *Today Television* website of April 6, after his comment that President Obama had a deep-seated hatred of whites. Yet Roger Ailes, President of Fox, and Beck himself say that they will continue to work together on other projects for Fox. At his departure, Beck still had the third highest rated show on cable news. One suspects he will resurface with a modified format.

MSNBC

While MSNBC has the lowest viewership of the major cable news shows, station ratings seemed to surge during the years leading up to the 2008 presidential election. Directly related to NBC, MSNBC is distinctly more liberal in its evening line-up than its parent network. The analysis, however, is sharp and pairs off somewhat evenly to either side of the center against the evening line-up of Fox (**45**). In November 2007, a *New York Times* article stated that MSNBC's prime time lineup was tilting more to the left.

Washington Post and CNN media analyst Howard Kurtz stated that the channel's evening lineup "has clearly gravitated to the left in recent years and often seems to regard itself as the antithesis of Fox News (**46**)."

"Hardball" with Chris Matthews and "Countdown" with Keith Olbermann lead the evening lineup. Rachel Maddow follows Olbermann. Former Republican representative Joe Scarborough is popular in the morning.

Chris Matthews

Matthews is another real reporter. He worked in print news for fifteen years before going to television. *His "Hardball" lives up to its name.* Matthews is aggressive, even brash, cruelly witty, and he does not suffer fools. He may interrupt a guest like Bill O'Reilly in the pursuit of a point, though he doesn't say "shut up." His comments on Tea Party gaffs have been fierce and frequently funny. Yet, despite having worked for Democrats, Matthews has said, "I'm more conservative than people think I am.... *I voted for George W. in 2000* (47)." One wonders if anyone at Fox voted for Al Gore.

Matthews has been *accused of having panels of guests that skew to the right* by liberal media watchdogs and of supporting Republicans in his questions and comments (48). Conversely, he is also often *criticized by conservatives for his opposition to the Iraq War* among other stances he took against the Bush administration. There have been rumors of political ambitions (49). Whether one sees him as right or left, or, God forbid, as an intelligent centrist, these are some of his quotations:

"I know one thing: There are a billion Islamic people in the world today, and there will be about 2 billion by the time we're dead. They're not going to give up their religion."

"Sarah Palin—now don't laugh—is writing a book. Not just reading a book, writing a book. Actually, in the word of the publisher, she's 'collaborating' on a book. What an embarrassment!"

"I think my numbers would be a lot higher if I were out there beating the drum for this war. In fact, I don't think it. I know it. But I can't be for the war (50)."

This is a position, by the way, that puts him in league with Ron Paul, the only congressman, Republican or otherwise, not to vote for the Iraq War. Paul also has the most conservative voting record of anyone in Congress. In brief, we should check our stereotypes when listening to Matthews.

Keith Olbermann

He is hardly timid in his partisanship. His positions are *unapologetically liberal.* He is unremittingly critical of conservatives and sometimes hilarious in a sharp and sarcastic way, almost like comedian Bill Maher.

However, he is *as aggressive from the left as the Fox headliners are from the right.* If Chris Matthews doesn't suffer fools, Olbermann has a mission to hunt them down no matter where they hide and destroy them. I confess to calling him "Keith Doberman," and that was when he was just a sportscaster. When he was a sportscaster, he said, "Even on the greatest teams, there's always one role player." One may sometimes get the impression that Olbermann has cast himself in that role.

He has a section of his show called "*The Worst Person in the World*," inevitably a conservative of one kind or another. Bill O'Reilly has made that list, and the two have been ordered by their stations to minimize their public interchange. Howard Kurtz wrote that Olbermann was *"positioning his program as an increasingly liberal alternative to The O'Reilly Factor."* Both men's comments are often blunt (**51**). Olbermann quotations include very partisan exclamations, many targeting conservative pundits and icons:

"Fox News is hated because they're elitists, and the worst winners television's ever seen."

Regarding conservative radio host Rush Limbaugh's public responses to his drug arrest: " I guess the painkillers wipe out your memory along with your ethics (**52**)."

"Reagan's dead, and he was a lousy President."

When President Bush commuted the sentence of Scooter Libby, Cheney's aide who outed CIA operative Valerie Plame, Olbermann called for the resignation of both Bush and Cheney (**53**).

He was criticized by fellow reporter Joe Scarborough about an outburst in which he called Massachusetts Senator Scott Brown "an irresponsible, homophobic, racist, reactionary, ex-nude model, Tea Bagging supporter of violence against women." Brown had said that President Obama was not a U.S. citizen, refused to give aid to state Red Cross workers who helped with the 9/11 rescue, and he supported a constitutional amendment against gay marriage. It had also been alleged that Brown had tolerated a comment from a supporter that someone should "shove a curling iron" up the backside of his female opponent in the last election. The nude model comment referred to a layout Brown had done when, before his political career, when he had been voted *Cosmo* magazine's sexiest man

(54). "How reckless and how sad," Joe Scarborough said of Olbermann's ranting.

Olbermann was **briefly suspended** by MSNBC for making political contributions to three Democrats in the 2010 elections, but the news of his return may have reached some before they knew he had been gone. Basically, he was given a long weekend **(55).** However, he was fired on a permanent basis in January of 2011. He was given a job at Current TV, but has been cautioned to lean more toward the center. Mr. Olbermann has a B.S. degree from Cornell.

Rachel Maddow

Rachel Maddow has a lower profile than other evening MSNBC personnel. Yet she is **as incisive as any without being quite as divisive or derisive** as Olbermann. She is biting but has a slightly quieter satirical voice. She has a BA in public policy from Stanford and a PhD in political science from Oxford, which she attended as a Rhodes scholar. "The Rachel Maddow Show" had **the most successful launch of any MSNBC show**, and she has been praised by *The Washington Post* and *The Los Angeles Times* as one of the best reporters of the last decade **(56).**

Joe Scarborough

Mr. Scarborough is a former Republican representative from Florida, **a competent conservative who helps to balance out the station's viewpoint.** He has a BA from the University of Alabama and a law degree from the University of Florida College of Law. He conducted a famous defense of David Gunn who killed an abortion doctor. He had a well-regarded primetime radio show called "Scarborough Country."

He once said the word "fuck" on air, not cursing, but contrasting the transition team of Obama to that of Clinton. "These were decent steady men who don't go around flipping people off or screaming 'fuck you' at the top of their lungs **(57).**" Otherwise, he was relatively controversy free until he was slapped on the wrist in November 2010 with **a short suspension** for donating money to conservative candidates within his own family.

He takes a moderate Republican point of view and suggests the need to fill an empty space for an intelligent liberal in the Fox lineup. In October,

2010, Scarborough called the former Speaker of the House Newt Gingrich "cartoonish" and said that Gingrich engages in "hate speech **(58)**." Other quotations include:

"We're going to look awfully stupid if we give income tax relief to people who do not pay income taxes."

"This is all about a media war that continues to rage between the old and new media. Unfortunately for our soldiers, these brave Americans are caught in the crossfire **(59)**."

CABLE NEWS IN SUM: THE TRUST FACTOR

Regardless of what scientific study may yield, recent polls regarding trust of news heavily favor the station many believe to be the most biased source of cable news, Fox. A Public Policy nationwide poll of 1151 registered voters found that 37% said they didn't trust Fox, but that was the lowest level of distrust for any agency polled.

49% of the population trusted Fox 10% more than other networks. CNN was the second most trusted network with 39%. Each of the three major networks received less than 40% trust. 44% did not trust NBC when combined with its affiliate MSNBC. There was a strong partisan split, with 74% of Republicans registering trust for Fox against 30% of Democrats, emphasizing just how partisan and non-objective our response to news has become. There are concerns about the statistical sample: besides being fairly small, the sample appears to favor Republican respondents.

However, the poll does make an important point, that these are **terribly partisan times**. In the words of Public Policy Polling president Dean Debnam, "A generation ago you would have expected Americans to place their trust in the most neutral and unbiased purveyors of news. But the media landscape has really changed, and now they're turning more toward the outlets that tell them what they really want to hear **(60)**."

Worse than that, in my estimation, is that **cable news is becoming an example of poor critical thinking habits and fallacies** discussed in this book. It is also contributing a tone of divisiveness to news watched by an already divided nation.

THE SURVIVING DEANS OF NETWORK NEWS

Dan Rather, formerly of CBS, and Tom Brokaw of NBC outlived ABC's Peter Jennings to become the elder statesmen of network evening news.

Dan Rather is a multiple Peabody award winner and reported many of the same events that Walter Cronkite did, the Kennedy assassination and Watergate among them. He is far more controversial than Brokaw, having been both more **partisan and prone to gaffs.** He allows his personality to become a part of the mix. His "**Ratherisms**" are sometimes pithy and funny and at other times curious metaphors:

"This race is hotter than a Times Square Rolex."

"This situation in Ohio would give an aspirin a headache."

"In southern states they beat him like a rented mule (61)."

Rather launched **a news story questioning President Bush's National Guard service** during his last week on "60 Minutes," unwittingly using falsified documents to support the story. Rather was informed of this by the secretary to Bush's former squadron commander who was the supposed source of documents indicating that Bush had evaded some duty, but she did say that they reflect the commander's belief that Bush received preferential treatment to escape some of his commitments. Rather sued CBS for removing him from "CBS Evening News" saying that they tried to make him a scapegoat for the miscued story (62).

Rather committed an astonishing gaff regarding Obama during an interview with Chris Matthews on MSNBC, in which he was trying to say that Obama would be mugged by the ad hominem attacks of the right wing. What came out was, "Listen, he's a nice person, he's very articulate. This is what's going to be used against him. But, he couldn't sell watermelons if you gave him the state troopers to flag down the traffic." The oblique racism of the watermelon comment drew much criticism (63).

He is now hosting his own news magazine on HDNet TV "Dan Rather Reports," which is a credible and well-done show.

Tom Brokaw is the only person to host all three of ABC's major shows, "The Today Show," "The NBC Nightly News," and "Meet the Press." The author of a very highly regarded book about the WWII generation, *The Greatest Generation*, he has been the **recipient of many awards and has honorary degrees at over twenty universities.** He appears for special reports and election coverage, but is seen less often with time.

By the end of his stay as the "NBC Nightly News" anchor, he came to be **regarded as the most popular news entity in the country**. In contrast to more personality-based newsmen, he ended his stay with a simple, " That's Nightly News for this Wednesday night. I'm Tom Brokaw. You'll see Brian Williams here tomorrow night; and I'll see you along the way (**64**)."

Peter Jennings, a Canadian-American **high school dropout**, made himself into **one of American television's most distinguished and polished reporters.** Among his best-known credits are being at the Berlin Wall both when it went up in the 60s and when it came down in the 90s. He hosted ABC's "World News Tonight." He died of lung cancer and complications of leukemia (**65**).

As for **the best female reporters**, a power list of media personalities by *Business Insider* placed the following women among the top ten most important media influences: **The women of "The View,"** which has included the distinguished interviewer **Barbara Walters**, were eighth. CNN's **Candy Crowley** and ABC News' **Christiane Amanpour** tied for tenth place. Fox President Roger Ailes was number one (**66**).

Amanpour is particularly noteworthy. She spent 27 years as the chief international correspondent for CNN. Another real reporter, she was on the scene for many of the most tense and dangerous of Middle-East events. She actually parachuted into the Gulf War to report. She was respected enough to be the first international reporter to interview British Prime Minister Tony Blair and French President Jacques Chirac. Now the anchor of ABC-TV's "This Week," she is an informal advisor to Secretary of State Hillary Clinton. Yet she has low ratings with ABC (**67**).

Immediately after the death of the great Walter Cronkite, *Time* magazine took an online poll to determine who was now "America's most trusted newscaster." Seven percent of those responding named **Katie Couric.** Couric is known for disassembling a poorly prepared Sarah Palin in an interview. Palin says she will not see Couric again (**68**).

RADIO NEWS

Cable channels participate in radio broadcasts as well. While the editorial policies remain similar, Fox news is notably more centrist on radio than on television, except when the evening lineup shows up for comment. I often prefer Fox while driving to the more personality oriented and human interest driven CNN radio news. Two entities have to mentioned here, and they represent opposite ends of the political spectrum: NPR and Rush Limbaugh.

NPR

NPR, an acronym for **National Public Broadcasting**, is a non profit station that distributes both news and cultural programs. There are a lot of reports about the arts, and national subgroups of all kinds are given attention. A 2005 study conducted by UCLA and the University of Missouri found that "Morning Edition" leans left. "Morning Edition" was found to have a bias comparable to *The Washington Post* and "The CBS Morning Show." NPR was found to be only slightly more liberal than *Time, Newsweek*, and *U.S. News and World Report*. In spite of comments about them being a leftist station, the study found NPR to be more liberal than the average U.S. Republican yet **more conservative than the average U.S. Democrat**. Fairness and Accuracy in Reporting, a progressive media watchdog group, disputes the claim of an NPR liberal bias **(69)**.

NPR is not without controversy. In 1995, **Nina Totenberg** commented that if there was **"retributive justice,"** former Sen. Jesse Helms would **"get AIDS from a transfusion, or one of his grandchildren will get it."** Helms had strongly opposed funding for AIDS research and treatment, saying that "deliberate, disgusting, revolting conduct" was to blame for the disease. He also attempted a 16-day filibuster to prevent the enactment of Martin Luther King day. NPR took no action over Totenberg's remarks. The statement seem **atypical of what is mostly a civilized and surprisingly centrist conversation** for a station with such a liberal reputation **(70)**.

NPR fired news analyst Juan Williams for saying in an interview with Bill O'Reilly that, "If I see people who are in Muslim garb and I think, you know, they are identifying themselves first and foremost as Muslims, I get worried." O'Reilly accused the station of bias in the firing. Sen. Jim DeMint (R-S.C.) announced plans to argue for defunding PBS and NPR. Williams has also been a Fox news contributor since1997 (**71**).

Rush Limbaugh

While only 58% of respondents to a UCLA poll say that they listen to radio for news, Rush Limbaugh carries a huge audience. *He pulls up to 20 million listeners a week,* only marginally less than "American Idol." In 2008, he was given an eight year $400 million dollar contract for the syndication firm Clear Channel. Yet he remains reluctant to feature himself on television.

An indication of Limbaugh's influence occurred when Michael Steele, chairman of the Republican National Committee, attempted to distance the party from Limbaugh on CNN, calling him *"an incendiary figure who should not be taken seriously since 'his whole thing is entertainment.'"* Within 48 hours he was pressured to issue an apology to Limbaugh, though Steele is elected and Limbaugh is not.

Limbaugh teed off on Clinton's failure to serve in Vietnam, though he himself had received a deferment for a boil on his buttocks (**72**).

He called President Obama "the magic negro" and played a song by that title to the tune of "Puff the Magic Dragon." "We are being told that we have to hope he succeeds... because his father was black (**73**)."

On immigration, he said: "You don't have the right to protest. You're allowed no demonstrations, no foreign flag waving, no political organizing... you're a foreigner, shut your mouth or get out (**74**)."

Among Limbaugh's most controversial gaffs was a *claim that Michael J. Fox exaggerated the effects of his Parkinson's Disease during a commercial* "moving around and shaking and it's purely an act." Michael Fox later told Katy Couric that Limbaugh was "dyskinesic," meaning overmedicated.

Limbaugh turned himself in to police *on a prescription fraud charge.* Yet he continues to top radio talk show hosts (**75**).

"I'm a businessman," he told *Newsweek.* "My first goal is to attract the largest possible audience so I can charge confiscatory ad rates. I happen to have great entertainment skills, but that enables me to sell airtime." In other words, while Limbaugh is incendiary, he seems to be purposefully so and is aware of himself as an entertainer. When asked if he would consider a career in politics, he said, "I couldn't take the cut in pay (**76**)."

PRINT NEWS

Students simply don't read as much as they used to or should. I am making **an urgent appeal** to you to reconsider, at least for the time that they are taking this class. Go beyond your normal practices of relying entirely on the web, **go to the library, go to a bookstore and look at magazines** discussing today's real world issues. This section on print news will help you **understand which publications are closest to your viewpoints** and which may challenge you to take new perspectives.

CONSERVATIVE MAGAZINES

The American Conservative, The American Spectator, The National Review, and *The Weekly Standard* are the most widely read conservative magazines. Like cable, they have online entities that you can use for research (**77**).

The American Conservative

This is the magazine for more **traditional Republicans** who may feel disenfranchised from neo-conservatives and especially the Tea Party. They are not for gay marriage, but they think the right is making the wrong fear-based arguments to keep that from happening. In "Divorced from Reality," Stephen Baskerville makes a rational, non religious argument (**78**):

> With conservatives as prominent as Glenn Beck and Ann Coulter joining those "influential Americans," in the words of the *National Review,* who "have been coming increasingly to regard opposition to same-sex marriage as irrational at best and bigoted at worst," we can no longer rely on vague assertions that homosexual marriage weakens true marriage in some way—which in itself, actually, it does not…. Marriage exists primarily to cement the father to the family. This fact is politically incorrect but undeniable. The breakdown of marriage produces widespread fatherlessness, not motherlessness. As Margaret Mead pointed out long ago—yes, leftist Margaret Mead was correct about

this—motherhood is a biological certainty whereas fatherhood is socially constructed. The father is the weakest link in the family bond, and without the institution of marriage he is easily discarded.... Even the conservative argument that marriage exists to rear children is too imprecise: marriage creates fatherhood. No marriage, no fathers. Once this principle is recognized, same-sex marriage makes no sense.

They praise President Obama for making inroads with Asian allies, which they claim Bush forgot, except to try enrolling them in his war on terror **(79)**. In the same issue, they offer a balanced analysis of the controversial Arizona "Krentz Law" that requires proof of citizenship upon determination of probable cause for any crime. They note that we don't want to alienate Mexicans who frequently find work and fit in well, largely indistinguishable from native Mexican-Americans, but argue that liberals can't forget that we need adequate law enforcement.

This is a rational, thorough, and well-written conservative magazine.

The American Spectator

Recall that this magazine is owned by **Rupert Murdoch** of Fox news, and its positions are similar, complete with the free use of **emotive language.**

"There is now a class of people in this country who at every turn seek to increase the power of government at the expense of the people's freedom, who in practice have largely inverted the meaning of the Constitution and hold in contempt the beliefs on which the country was founded **(80)**."

So begins a pro-gun article written by Dan Peterson. The article discusses a Supreme Court case, MacDonald v. City of Chicago, in which the court held that the Second Amendment protects the right to bear arms not only from intrusions by federal authority but also by states and localities. Two main devices for limiting arms ownership have existed: the notion that the Second Amendment is a collective right to maintain militias, and the idea that state authority could more specifically limit gun rights. This case challenges both standards. Many positions held by The American Spectator are pro states rights, except when they limit individual liberties.

In the same issue, "How Enviros Obstruct the Border Patrol," Tom Bethell argues that **"almost all"** of the migrant and drug smugglers come across federal lands protected by stringent wilderness designations or endangered species rules. He claims that **"almost all"** of Arizona is protected federal land and that **"greenies"** supporting environmental causes are inhibiting border protection (**81**). **There is no solid use of statistics.**

The article is **factually incorrect.** I have a home in Arizona, work with local environmental groups, and am familiar with this issue. Only 48.1% of Arizona land is owned by the federal government according to the Bureau of Land Management, and a significant portion of the land, including border land, is owned by Native Americans.

There's a further assertion that **"the mainstream media won't report"** that stringent environmental law is encouraging illegal immigration. There is not a single mention of a particular law that hurts border patrol, nor a single specific instance of said interference on federal lands. In fact, the only example given is the shooting of a rancher by drug smugglers on privately owned land, which seems to contradict the author's own assertion. Yet there are frequent allusion to "enviros." He even specifically says that there's **a war on property ownership by communists, and their allies "greens, socialists, and American liberals,"** an extraordinary oversimplification.

I wrote to Mr. Bethell, telling him that I admired his article, but would like to know the specific federal laws to which he was referring. I have not received a response.

In "Caught In the Crossfire" in the same issue, James Antle argues that the NRA's leadership has become part of the gun law problem: "There are few organizations purportedly on the side of freedom that aggravate me more than the NRA. The NRA—a 4 million-member, $307 million organization— has become too pragmatic, too willing to compromise with Democrats, too cautious in its approach to Second Amendment legislation." In other words, **the NRA simply isn't conservative enough.**

The National Review

This magazine was **founded by one of the most eloquent of conservatives,** the now deceased **William F. Buckley**. Compared to *The American Standard*, this is an intelligent magazine that uses facts and analysis in a rational way. They have a distinctly conservative agenda, but it's much better written than *The American Spectator* and less likely to be quite so jingoistic. However, they are certainly critical of the Obama healthcare plan, saying that it, "exemplifies everything voters dislike about the reigning party: its zeal for government, its subordination of economic to ideological objectives, its conviction that it knows better than the voters who balk at the imposition of sweeping and ill-considered change."

There are **ads for "The Conservative Book Club"** featuring titles like "Culture or Corruption" with Obama on the cover, or "Liberty and Tyranny." The extreme dichotomies of such titles are worth noting as either/or thinking, but there are also ads for green-oriented industry like Westinghouse with its "release zero greenhouse gases while producing electricity," or the American Clear Skies Foundation advocating that natural gas can produce jobs.

Constitutional issues are central, and they are intelligently discussed with specific cases. The National Review argument that there is no need nor foundation for **gay marriag**e is not just fear-ridden propaganda. While they see value in the mutual care of any partners, "Marriage exists to solve a problem that arises from sex between men and women, but not from sex between partners of the same gender: what to do about generativity," or the care of children. "Let individuals make whatever contracts they want and receive the blessings of whatever church agrees with it, but confine the government's role to enforcing contracts." *There is no real moral judgment about coupling of any kind. They just want government out of it.*

This is not your Tea Party magazine, though it is more right-wing than *The American Conservative.* You don't find a lot of compliments for President Obama. In fact, the November 29, 2010, issue features a caricature of Obama making the "L" for loser sign on his own forehead. It's entitled the "Special Post-Shellacking Issue" (**82**).

The Weekly Standard

This magazine was founded by **William Kristol**, a Harvard graduate and sometimes commentator on Fox news. He was a vocal opponent of President Clinton's health plan and an earnest advocate for the Iraq war (**83**).

On the controversial issue of the Supreme Court decision in *Citizens United v. FEC*—which holds that corporate funding of independent political broadcasts in candidate elections cannot be limited under the First Amendment—**The Weekly Standard** supported the decision vigorously and decried President Obama for spreading untruths about it. The criticism is that this decision allows corporations and unions to contribute huge amounts of money to ads outside of campaign approval without identifying where the funds came from, some under the cover name of "Citizens United."

> **Myth 1: 'Citizens United' overturned 100 years of law prohibiting corporations from spending money in elections.** President Obama has been the most notable proponent of this myth. In the State of the Union he said that *Citizen United* "reversed a century of law that I believe will open the floodgates for special interests to spend without limit in our elections...." While federal law has indeed prohibited corporations from directly contributing to federal candidates since 1907, that portion of the law was not at issue in *Citizens United*. It remains the law of the land. Direct corporate contributions to candidates are still banned **(84)**.

However, practically, the change does allow indirect and secret campaign contributions by corporations at the state level without identifying themselves. This allows significant influence on the make-up of congress, and it gives lobbyists a powerful tool: "We have got a million we can spend advertising for you or against you—whichever one you want,'" a lobbyist can tell lawmakers, said Lawrence M. Noble, a lawyer in Washington and former general counsel of the Federal Election Commission **(85)**.

Like almost all conservative news sources, they are critical of what they call "Obama-care." Caricatures of political figures abound in artwork, including *"the official Obama head,"* which features hugely exaggerated ears.

Among their regular columnists is **Anne Coulter,** Ann Coulter has described herself as a *"polemicist"* who likes to *"stir up the pot"* and doesn't "pretend to be impartial or balanced, as broadcasters do" She has also said that **women shouldn't vote** since every Republican presidential candidate since Barry Goldwater would have won without them **(86)**.

The magazine was a big Sarah Palin supporter, but they've grown increasingly critical of her, in Karl Rove's words, lack of "gravitas."

LIBERAL MAGAZINES

Liberal magazines include *The American Prospect*, *The Atlantic Monthly*, *Harpers*, *The Nation*, and *The New Republic*, and *Mother Jones*.

The American Prospect

This magazine has **a progressive political commitment**. They have pro-labor articles like "Labor's New Globalism" and pro-ecology positions like "Where Are the Green Jobs (**87**)?"

In "Destroying the Village," **they ask how far Republicans will go to oppose Obama, even if it means hurting America**. Eager to beat Obama in 2012, they note that Republicans even used the rejection of his bid for the 2016 Olympics as a talking point. *The American Prospect* reports that "cheers erupted" in the office of *The Weekly Standard* when it was announced that we lost the bid. They say, "Republican Senate Leader Mitch McConnell put things so plainly when he said in October, *'The single most important thing we want to achieve is for President Obama to be a one-term president.'* No policy goals, no improvement in Americans' lives—just get Obama out and their guy in." *The American Prospect* speculated that the new Republican dominated House could shut down the government if they put out a budget that the Senate can't accept. "No matter what Republicans do, Sean Hannity and Rush Limbaugh will have their backs (**88**)."

In "Why we are angry at the TSA," they discuss the new scan or grope security policy at airports.

> The conservative, torture-friendly *Washington Times* declared that "a balance must be struck between reasonable security measures and the maintenance of a free society." Abu Ghraib was a fraternity prank, but getting frisked at the airport is a sign of, to quote the *Times*, "Big Sister's police state." Hatred of the TSA makes for strange bedfellows, with some conservatives now sounding like **card-carrying members of the American Civil Liberties Union** (**89**).

The term "card carrying members of X" goes back to the House Un-American Activities Committee and was used to suggest disloyalty to the country. It's a fairly standard conservative jab, but liberals play emotive language games, too, and this magazine sometimes does.

The Atlantic Monthly

Usually simply called *The Atlantic*, this Boston publication has been around and respected since 1857. **They were around to do interviews with the first progressives**, Theodore Roosevelt and Woodrow Wilson. They are known as much for fiction and comments on cultural issues as they are for political comment. **It is well-written, balanced, and moderately liberal** (**90**).

In "83% of Congressional Districts went Republican in 2010," they discuss the gravity of the mid-term election swing to the right. They call it "the whiplash" election as opposed to the commonly used Republican term "tsunami," later reduced to "wave" (**91**).

While analyzing the new TSA security measures, they argue that there's an **important distinction between doing what must be done in the case of a direct threat and trying to stop all future terrorism.** "People who study terrorism—or crime, or natural disasters—also generally conclude that after a certain point, it's better to work on ways to recover from an attack, or limit its damage, rather than spend limitlessly toward the impossible end of reducing the risk to zero." They refer to the 3000 dead from 9/11, which was done "on the cheap," as opposed to our response of **trillions of dollars that have yet to make us safe**. They argue that, while we think of acceptable levels of risk in matters like driving cars, which kill 30,000 people a year, we allow politicians to spend and attack our privacy over terrorism as if they could achieve zero-risk, which is simply impossible (**92**).

Harpers

Like *The Atlantic, Harpers* is a literary magazine with a broad spectrum of social and political topics. They have in-depth reporting in sometimes long articles. It's not liberal in a Marxist sense. Their editorial policy suggests a **Jeffersonian Liberalism**. They write intelligent book reviews. Though usually extremely tasteful, they often offer controversial items. They used a cartoon that calls TSA "tits, schlong, and ass" on November 23, 2010, poking fun at the new, more intimate search procedures.

In "The Guantanamo 'Suicides,'" **they play whistle-blower** over a military cover-up of what may really have been murders of terrorist suspects. They don't pull any punches on Bush or Obama on the matter. "New evidence now emerging may entangle Obama's young administration with crimes that occurred during the George W. Bush presidency, evidence that suggests the current administration failed to investigate seriously—and may even have continued—a cover-up of the possible homicides of three prisoners at Guantánamo in 2006." None of the men, one a 17 year old, had been charged with a crime, though they had participated in a hunger strike. The prisoners had supposedly hung themselves from steel mesh ceilings eight feet up, having somehow managed to tie their own hands and stuff rags down their own throats **(93)**.

The Nation

This magazine is far from a centrist vision of the country, nor is it a mouthpiece for Democrats. **It is a distinctly progressive magazine**. In "Our Iraq Debacle," posted in their September 20, 2010, issue, they call the U.S. invasion of Iraq "one of the worst foreign policy disasters in decades" and claim that it will take at least two generations to repair. They are very critical of Obama's message that we have met our responsibility there, noting 100,000 Iraqi deaths, millions of traumatized Iraqi children, and the squandering of trillions of dollars.

They are critical of Wall Street and corporate America. In "Layoff Kings," they refer to a recent study from the Institute of Policy Studies, one of the oldest progressive policy think tanks, saying that **fifty CEOs of the firms that laid off the most workers during the recession received 42% more pay**. Those who laid off the most received $12 million in salaries compared to peers on the Standard and Poor's 500 who averaged $8.5 million. Among those mentioned was a Johnson & Johnson executive who cut 9000 jobs and made over $25 million and a Hewlitt-Packard CEO who laid off 6400 and took home $28 million on top of a bonus of over $24 million.

After months of Glenn Beck denouncing healthcare reform "as the beginning of reparations" and Rush Limbaugh accusing Obama of inflicting economic pain as a form of "payback" against whites, it is clear to this publication that there is an attempt to use racism against the incumbent president. "As one Tea Party blogger put it, 'Next Stop Zimbawbe" **(94)**.

The New Republic

This is **a reasonable mirror from the left for The National Review**. One could do worse than to have these two thorough and well-written magazines for a dialectic view of the world. *The National Review* says of **Afghanistan** that it "is the graveyard of empires," while *The New Republic* provides historical analysis that it is "the revolving door of empires," arguing that nobody stayed because there wasn't that much to be had and that even the Russians never sent their best troops in to tame this rocky terrain. Both reveal doubt about our efforts there. *The National Review* would blame Obama. *The New Republic* argues that this was Bush's initial and more popular war effort, though it was less popular with conservatives than Iraq. Both would note that Afghanistan was a relatively neutral country in the twentieth century until the invasion of Russia (**95**). *The New Republic* says our goals are not necessarily close to those of the country. In a combined BBC and ABC poll there, one third said their biggest concern was unemployment and poverty; another third said that violence and insecurity were primary; only 14% said that corruption and bad government, our concerns, were a problem, and only 2% mentioned the drug trade at all. Yet 70% agree with us that the Taliban is a serious problem.

The New Republic focuses more on **social concerns like rebuilding infrastructure and pollution**, noting that fecal matter in water is a serious threat to U.S. soldiers and that air pollution, a byproduct of fighting, could kill as many as 3000 citizens of Kabul a year. **They present both sides of the argument in two articles, "Get Out Yesterday" and "Stay Forever."** In fact, there is a wide variety of opinions, not just a doctrinaire or ideologue view. So, far from being a knee-jerk pro-liberal magazine, **it does use facts in an objective and thorough way.**

They do focus on improvements made during the war. With regard to schools, less than a million were enrolled before, none of them girls; now there are more than 6 million, a third of them girls. Nine percent had access to healthcare before; now 85% have at least some access. There are 68 times the free radio channels and TV stations now than under the Taliban. However, the death rate for children remains exactly the same, and the **average life expectancy has declined during our occupancy from 47 to 44 years, fourth worst in the world.**

Mother Jones

This magazine, named for a community labor organizer, is *a long standing stalwart of the far left.* They are not specifically or even often proDemocrat, often attacking the party for not being left enough. In one issue, they focused on *"BP's Deep Secrets,"* attacking the company for having much greater liability for eco-damage than the public seems to realize. In typical *expose style*, the cover reads "The truth is down there" a la "X-Files." They refer to BP's "laughable Gulf oil spill plan," a document featuring wildly inaccurate wildlife assessments," including walrus and other creatures that don't even inhabit the Gulf. The plan includes *"an on call expert" who has been dead for some time.* They also criticize environmental groups and the Minerals Management service for not noticing a preview of the Gulf event at the West Atlas oil rig off Australia, another deep oil rig disaster that took 74 days to contain. "Their reckless quest has endangered and perhaps condemned, not just the Gulf Coast, but the largest, richest, most pristine, most biologically important, and last completely unprotected ecosystem left on earth: the deep ocean."

The language is emotive, but the reporting is thorough. They enumerate more specific damage to the Gulf than other publications, a timeline of BP lies, and inept U.S. attempts to control them. They mention Rep. Joe Barton's apology to BP for the government's "shakedown" and the fact that Barton has received $15 million in the last decade from oil interests. BP CEO Tony Hayward, who fought vigorously against having film of the spill made public, resigned with nearly a million dollars a year in pension. They enumerate 33,000 miles of pipeline and thousands of abandoned rigs along the Gulf coast, calling them the "other time bombs."

In *"Who Owns Congress,"* *Mother Jones* relates major contributors to congressional figures. After recent difficulties with the economy spurred by irresponsible and unrestrained banking practices, it may be little surprise that the *finance and insurance industries are the largest contributors at $2.4 billion*. It's also small wonder that it takes so much to get a healthcare package through congress; the third largest identifiable contributor is the health industry. *Individuals of both parties are skewered equally for their acceptance of contributions*:

Democrat Harry Reid of Nevada has accepted more than $1.7 million from gambling; Senator Mitch McConnel of Kentucky raised $37 million from smokeless tobacco industries and the makers of Jack Daniels; Democratic Representative Nancy Pelosi has received millions from the Gallo Brothers wine company; and Ron Paul, Texas Representative, received the majority of his over $50 million, somewhat surprisingly, from military sources. Ron Paul ran on a libertarian perspective that we had no business being in the war. Nonetheless, *Mother Jones* reports where the money came from and who took it.

The November, 2010, issue portrays Sarah Palin on the cover as the main character from a 1950's sci-fi film, "Attack of the 50-Foot Woman." She's crouching over and looting middle-class homes. The relevant article is called "Attack on the Middle Class." Included is a line that might have been used on the movie poster: "They say they're taking back America, but really they're taking your money **(96)**!!!" That's rather emotive language.

CENTRIST MAGAZINES

The most centrist magazines include *The Economist, Time, Newsweek, and U.S. News and World Report.*

The Economist

A British publication, this is *as fair-minded a news source as one can find.* They are objective, thorough, and far-reaching in their global analysis. They seem to *see us better at times than we see ourselves*.

For instance, in "Are We There Yet," September 18–24, 2010, they discuss the potential for economic recovery in the U.S. and are *fair to both American political parties, their typical tendency toward dialectical thinking.* On one hand, they acknowledge that the recession ended a year ago and that, while Republicans argue that Obama's shift to "big government" explains economic weakness, most of the growth is temporary and necessary and reflects the policies of both Bush and Obama. They also argue against the Republican position that our stubborn unemployment rate, roughly one in ten, does not prove that the stimulus package, again something that reflects the policy of both Bush and Obama, has failed. Indeed, they argue that the recession would have been much worse without it.

They then argue that the Democrats are also playing the blame game when they say that it's all about tax cuts to the rich. They suggest that all of the

Bush tax cuts should be extended because cutting them could tip the weak economies back into recession. They say that this should be temporary and that not even middle-tax cuts should be permanent, which Obama proposes. The key way to solve the economic problem is to reign in budget growth and encourage more write-downs of mortgage debt, as a quarter of Americans owe more on their homes than they're worth. Cleaning up the housing market would cut unemployment by making it easier to move to better jobs. It's a very balanced and sensible analysis that cuts across our party rhetoric.

Time

In spite of a liberal reputation, this is *a reasonably centrist magazine* that focuses on a broad range of political, scientific, and popular culture events.

In the September 27, 2010, issue, they devote an entire pre-election issue to the Tea Party. The cover features a teacup with an elephant, the traditional symbol of the GOP, barely peeking out of the cup. They do note some of the more obvious mistakes of members, like Christine O'Donnell's witchcraft dabbling, but doesn't spend time mocking the party like more liberal magazines. The articles focuses on the growing power of the party and predicts its potential for political influence:

> Not since Barry Goldwater thumbed his nose at country-club Republicans in 1964 has a rebel movement created such a crisis of legitimacy among the GOP establishment. And like that rebel movement, this one may spur an evolutionary change in the party that could last a generation. At a time of historic economic insecurity, the Tea Party movement has stolen the hearts of conservatives.

Time describes their movement as a backlash against elites, note the reservations of centrist Republicans, and correctly predicts at least some success in the upcoming midterm elections.

Time is in the top 25 most popular U.S. magazines at number ten (**97**).

Newsweek

Newsweek is the only other magazine of all discussed to be in the top 25 most popular magazines in the country (**98**).

Like *Time*, this is ***a centrist "coffee table" magazine*** that we can find easily to keep abreast of the news and a wide variety of political, scientific, and popular culture topics. It is the second most widely read newsmagazine after *Time*. It is owned by *The Washington Post*, yet it would probably be perceived as less liberal. However, conservative critics have associated with them liberal bias. Though one wouldn't associate controversy with them, they were the first magazine to break the Monica Lewinsky/Clinton scandal. They were criticized for what was seen as a sexist Sarah Palin cover, depicting her in a tight, short skirt, a red top, and tennis shoes with an American flag. The cover said, "How Do You Solve a Problem Like Sarah?"

The October 25, 2010, issue discusses "***Pot and the GOP***," an article suggesting that the libertarian lean of the party is causing them to change their minds about legalizing pot. It is a moderate and sensible analysis of the issue. They use the example of Ann Lee, a Catholic and a conservative Texas Republican, who thought pot was a refreshment from the devil. When her son had a serious spinal injury, however, she changed her mind and even supports her son's marijuana business, which has made him a millionaire.

As the Tea Party's slash-the-budget message penetrates the party, it has become harder to justify the immense costs of drug interdiction, over $41 billion a year, or ignore a potential "capitalist" profit in sales and tax of a $14 billion a year crop. The more one argues for individual liberty and freedom from government, the harder it is to seem disingenuous in using so much government energy to stop pot. In fact, there's a popular joke in the party, **"A libertarian is a Republican who smokes pot."**

Less funny, they argue, is the fact that the war on drugs has gotten more violent with 28,000 killed in Mexico since more fervent crackdowns on cartels responsible for most of our pot. Thus, it makes a certain sense that conservative thinkers as varied as Milton Friedman, Pat Buchanan, and William F. Buckley have argued for legalization.

They published their first annual issue of "***The Power 50***" on November 8, 2010. The issue ranks the highest paid news pundits and politicos. Among pundits discussed in this chapter, some of the rankings were.

1. Rush Limbaugh: $58.7 million

2. Glenn Beck: $33 million

3. Sean Hannity: $22 million

4. Bill O'Reilly: $20 million

5. Jon Stewart: $15 million

7. Don Imus: $11 million

9. Keith Olbermann: $7.5 million

15. Ariana Huffington: $5 million

17. Chris Matthews: $4.5 million

19. Bill Maher: $4 million

22. Joe Scarborough: $3.5 million

32. Rachel Maddow: $2 million

The method of simply listing the income of the pundits/entertainers is inherently objective (**99**).

U.S. News & World Report

They were traditionally slightly more rightist than the other two most common coffee table news magazines, *Newsweek* and *Time*, and they tend to publish fewer popular culture articles. Yet their former focus on military and foreign policy issues has shifted. Most recently, they've been known for their ranking issues of colleges, hospitals, etc. Their reporting is fact-based and even more moderately conservative than in past days.

NEWSPAPERS

The George Washington University study cited earlier indicated that, while cable is the number one news source and while newspaper circulation has declined steadily over the last decade, *72% of respondents still turn to newspapers* and websites associated with them (**100**).

Newspapers have declined in circulation and readership as cable news has come on strong. It went down 8.74% this year. *The Wall Street Journal* has the country's largest circulation at over 2 million. *USA Today*, once taunted for its "factoid" approach to news, has 1.8 million. *The New York Times* has just under a million, while the *Los Angeles Times* has over 600,000. *The Washington Post* rounds out the top five.

The New York Daily News and *The New York Post*, which counter the liberal tendencies of *The New York Times*, are a close 6 and 7 at over half a million. *The Chicago Tribune*, another well-respected paper weighs in at 450,000, ninth on the list. Most of these papers, with the exception of *USA Today*, have won multiple Pulitzer Prizes. *The New York Times*, which also publishes the respected *Boston Globe*, would top that list with 104 prizes.

The only major newspapers commonly perceived to be conservative are *The Wall Street Journal*, mainly due to their editorials, and *The New York Post*. *The Christian Science Monitor*, a well-written newspaper, is also perceived as conservative, yet it is also NPR-like humanist. *The Washington Post's* liberalism is also countered by *The Washington Times* (**101**).

THINK TANKS

A 2006 think tank analysis of over 27,000 citations from the 25 most often quoted groups showed a 4% decline in citations. However, progressive or left-leaning think tanks upped their exposure by 11%. Of course, this paralleled the enthusiasm of people interested in moving away from the policies of President Bush.

Overall, however, centrist and right-leaning think tanks remained the most cited. Centrist tanks were cited 45% of the time, right leaning ones 40%, a drop of 6% and 7%. The progressive increase only showed a total of 16%.

The centrist **Brookings Institution** was the most widely cited think tank. **The Heritage Foundation** and **The American Enterprise Institute** were among the most widely cited conservative groups. **The Center for American Progress** and the **Economic Policy Institute** were the two progressive think tanks in the top ten most cited.

The Iraq War seems to have been an important contributing factor. **The Cato Institute**, often higher in the rankings, has a position that we should leave Iraq. They remained, however, in the top ten most cited think tanks (**102**).

WWW

Many online sources are aggregates of news posted elsewhere and they constitute difficult citation problems. Again, I caution against relying on websites that are not associated with specific, identifiable organizations or do not post updates containing specific months and years.

Moveon.org is one of the most liberal online sources. Readers of *Mother Jones* would be comfortable there. *The Huffington Post* is another **(103)**.

Among the most widely read conservative online sources is **The Drudge Report**, which has been criticized for some "exclusives" that turned out to be shaky in fact. The classic example of this is the case of Ashley Todd, the McCain campaign volunteer in the Pittsburgh area who Drudge attempted to depict as a white martyr to candidate Obama's ways. Weeks before the November 2008 presidential election, Todd told police that she had been mugged by a black man who carved a "B" for Barack Obama into her face. Of course, she made the whole thing up, and had actually carved the 'B' into her own face, backwards, one might add **(104)**.

SO, WHO IS FAIR AND BALANCED?

The most credible and comprehensive study of media bias was conducted by Tim Groseclose, a UCLA political scientist, and Jeffrey Milyo of the economics department at the University of Missouri at Columbia. It was posted in the *Quarterly Journal of Economics* in December, 2005. *Unlike most studies, which had subjective measures of what constituted liberal or conservative, this study used votes of the national legislature as a comparative standard.*

Americans for Democratic Action traced the percentage of times each lawmaker votes on the liberal side of an issue then assigns numerical value, for which 100 is the most liberal. They adjusted this to compensate for disproportionate representation that the Senate gives to states with low population. They assumed that legislative votes would reflect those of American voters. They also employed an equal number of Democrats and

THE POLITICAL SPECTRUM OF NEWS SOURCES

LEFT (Liberal)	CENTER	RIGHT (Conservative)
		FOX-TV
		Rush Limbaugh
		American Spectator
	National Review	
	Weekly Standard	
MSNBC	The American Conservative	
CNN		
CBS	Fox Radio	
NBC		
ABC		
	The Economist	
		NY Post
		Wall St. Journal (Editorial)
		Washington Times
		American Enterprise Inst.
		Heritage Foundation
		The Drudge Report
	Time	
	Newsweek	
	U.S. News & World Report	
	The Brookings Institution	
NPR		
	Atlantic	
	Harpers	
American Prospect		
The Nation		
The New Republic		
	Boston Globe	
	Chicago Tribune	
	LA Times	
	NY Times	
	Wall St Journal (Reporting)	
	Washington Post	
Mother Jones		
Center for American Progress		
Economic Policy Institute		
MoveOn.Org		

Republicans as research assistants. The average score was 50.1. They then compared 20 news outlets and found that they were moderate compared to members of Congress but there was a quantifiable tendency to lean to the left. *Yet many of the specific results were surprising.*

- Of the 20 major media agencies, 18 scored left of center.

- "CBS Evening News," *The New York Times*, and the *Los Angeles Times* ranked second, third, and fourth to the liberal side.

- Surprisingly, the most liberal reporting occurred in the stories of *The Wall Street Journal*. It scored a little to the left of the average voting Democrat. It was the editorial page of that paper that scored on the right of center.

- Otherwise, only Fox News and *The Washington Times* scored right of the average legislator or American voter.

- Even *The Drudge Report*, a common source for Fox News, was seen as left of center voters.

However, the majority of reports are not from the notably conservative leader of that group, Matt Drudge himself. Also, the study excluded all editorials, which might have sent several of these findings farther left or right, for instance, *The Wall Street Journal*.

- Also surprising was that National Public Radio, commonly viewed as leftist, was considered relatively centrist.

- The most centrist outlets were the Jim Lehrer News Hour, CNN's "Newsnight," and ABC's "Good Morning America." Also ranking high was *USA Today*.

- Fox's Special Report with Brit Hume was the fourth most centrist news.

- Most news media were less liberal than Senator Joe Lieberman of Connecticut with an ADA score of 74.

The authors found the centrist results credible because three of the four moderators of the Presidential debates came from these shows. Had any of them leaned too far in either direction, one campaign or the other would have objected. *The authors concluded that watching Fox " Special*

Report," ABC's "World News," and NBC's " Nightly News" would give a nearly perfect balance version of what was going on (105).

My coffee table would also include the following *print news*—if I could afford all the subscriptions—as a means of viewing all sides of an issue from the most literate print news. The Sunday editions of *The New York Times* and/or *The Los Angeles Times*, *The Washington Post*, *The Wall Street Journal*, and *The Christian Science Monitor*. Along with the usual coffee table magazines, I would certainly include *The Economist*, *The New Republic*, and the *National Review*. I would continue to watch all three major cable networks, and I would switch back and forth on my car radio from Fox to NPR.

IN SUM

The chart on the previous page is an approximation of the political viewpoint of various news sources. It is based on my own analysis and the various studies posted thus far about bias in the news. Hopefully, it will help you in two ways. You can locate news sources that are close to the positions you intend to advocate, but I also hope that you will open your mind to sources all along the political spectrum.

It should matter less what our political philosophies are than how we express them. We live in a free society, and there's room for all ways of thinking. Those ways are subdivided into far less simple categories than conservative and liberal. When we degenerate into divisive, hostile, and alienating means of expressing our viewpoints, it is my testimony that the Republic itself is lessened as its people become more hateful and divided. That's not my vision of what it means to be an American.

VOCABULARY

Cherry Picking
Emo-journalism
Infotainment
Spin
Yellow Journalism

REFERENCES

1) Wilson IV, Joseph C, "What I Didn't Find in Africa", The New York Times. July 6, 2003.

2) http://www.msnbc.msn.com/id/17479718/ns/politics/

3) Safire, William. "The Spinner Spun," New York Times. December 22, 1996.

4) "Liberal bias is real, revealing," Columbia Daily Tribune, September 12, 2010. http://www.columbiatri-bune.com/news/2010/sep/12/liberal-media-bias-is-revealing/.

5) http://www.rasmussenreports.com/public_content/politics/obama_administration/daily_presiden-tial_tracking_poll and http://mediamatters.org/blog/200907070015.

6) Ibid.

7) PBS, "Crucible of Empire: The Spanish American War" http://www.pbs.org/crucible/frames/_journal-ism.html.

8) "Network," Metro-Goldwyn-Mayer (MGM) & United Artists. 1976.

9) Streeter, T. "Beyond Freedom of Speech and the Public Interest: The Relevance of Critical Legal Studies to Communications Policy." Journal of Communication (New York), Spring, 1990. "The Fairness Doctrine," The Museum of Broadcast Communications. http://www.museum.tv/eotvsection.php?entrycode=fairnessdoct

10) "Shock Jocks: The Voice of Unreason," The Independent, May 28, 2009. http://www.independent.co.uk/news/world/americas/shock-jocks-voice-of-unreason-1691792.html.

11) Demers, David, "Dictionary of Mass Communication and Media Research: A guide for students, scholars and professionals," Marquette, 2005, p.143.

12) http://www.museum.tv/eotvsection.php?entrycode=cronkite walter. http://www.washingtonpost.com/wp-dyn/content/article/2009/07/17/ AR2009071703350.html.

13) "Rick Sanchez fired after explosive interview..." The Washington Post, October 2, 2010. "Fired Anchor Rick Sanchez undertakes contrition tour," The Washington Post, October 12, 2010.

14) Los Angeles Independent Media Center website, April 9, 2003. http://la.indymedia.org/news/2003/04/47530.php. Also confirmed by other current sources, including company promotion pages.

15) "Liberal bias is real, revealing," Columbia Daily Tribune, September 12, 2010. http://www.columbiatri-bune.com/news/2010/sep/12/ liberal-media-bias-is-revealing/.

16) "Bill O'Reilly is popular...," Politico, September 26, 2010. http://www.politico.com/news/stories/0910/42738.html#ixzz12vf0Ro8M.

17) "CNN is Viewers Cable Network of Choice for National Convention Coverage," Timewarner.com. 2000-08-18. http://www.timewarner.com/corp/newsroom/pr/0,20812,667801,00.html.

18) Kiesewetter, John (May 28, 2000). "In 20 years, CNN has changed the way we view the news". Cincinnati Enquirer. http://www.enquirer.com/editions/2000/05/28 /lockiesewetter.html. "This date in deal history: CNN begins broadcasting". The Deal Magazine. May 31, 2006.

19) "CNN and the Liberal Propaganda Machine," Media Research Center CyberAlert—17 February 1999— slant of CNN's Tuesday night town meeting. http://www.hks.harvard.edu/presspol/publications/reports/invisibleprimary_ invisible_no_longer.pdf.

20) http://edition.cnn.com/CNN/anchors_reporters/blitzer. wolf.html.

21) http://thinkexist.com/quotes/wolf_blitzer/.

22) http://edition.cnn.com/CNN/anchors_reporters/cooper.anderson.html.

23) Van Meter, Jonathan, "Unanchored," New York, September 19, 2005.

24) http://bluegrasspolitics.bloginky.com/2010/10/25/moveonorg-activist-involved-in-incident-at-paul-conway-debate/.

25) http://www.thefreedictionary.com/claques.

26) "The Most Biased Name in News, "FAIR, July/August 2001. http://www.fair.org/index.php?page=1067.

27) http://www.slate.com/id/2200298/.

28) "Poll: Bill O'Reilly is popular..." *Politico*, September 26, 2010.

29) http://www.quotesstar.com/quotes/i/if-the-americans-go-in-29355.html.

30) http://politicalhumor.about.com/od/billoreilly/a/oreillyquotes.htm.

31) "Shock Jocks: The Voice of Unreason," The Independent.

32) http://mediamatters.org/research/200709210007.

33) "Sean Hannity," IMBD biography. http://www.imdb.com/name/nm0360458/.

34) Center for American Progress.
    http://www.americanprogress.org/aboutus.
    Kerry votes supporting intelligence funding were as follows:
    FY03 Intel Authorization $39.3–$41.3 Billion.
    [2002, Unanimous Senate Voice Vote 9/25/02].
    FY02 Intel Authorization $33 Billion.
    [2001, Unanimous Senate Voice Vote 12/13/01].
    FY01 Intel Authorization $29.5–$31.5 Billion.
    [2000, Unanimous Senate Voice Vote 12/6/00].
    FY00 Intel Authorization $29–$30 Billion.
    [1999, Unanimous Senate Voice Vote 11/19/1999].
    FY99 Intel Authorization $29.0 Billion.
    [1998, Unanimous Senate Voice Vote 10/8/98].
    FY98 Intel Authorization $26.7 Billion.
    [1997, Senate Roll Call Vote #109].
    FY97 Intel Authorization $26.6 Billion.
    [1996, Unanimous Senate Voice Vote 9/25/96].

35) Hannity, Sean. Let Freedom Ring. Harper, 2004.

36) The Sean Hannity Show, August 5, 2003.

37) "Shock Jocks: The Voice of Unreason."

38) Lebovich, M. "Being Glenn Beck," New York Times Magazine.

39) "Shock Jocks: The Voice of Unreason."

40) http://www.u-s-history.com/pages/h1061.html
    http://www.digitalhistory.uh.edu/modules/progressivism/index.cfm

41) "The Revisionaries," *The New Republic*, September 23, 2010.

42) Leibovich, M.

43) "Shock Jocks: The Voice of Unreason."

44) "The Revisionaries."

45) Cable Channel Nods to Ratings and Leans Left. *New York Times*. November 6, 2007.

46) Kurtz, Howard, "MSNBC leaning left and getting flak from both sides," *The Washington Post*, May 28, 2008. http://www.washingtonpost.com/wp-dyn/content/article/2008/05/27/AR2008052703047. html.

47) October 3, 2003, and February 23, 2004, editions of Hardball.

48) (2005-05-31). "Matthews's statements defy conservatives' claims that he is a "liberal Democrat." *Media Matters for America*. http://mediamatters.org/items/200505310005.

49) Gitlen, Todd. "The Harder He Blows." *The American Prospect*. March 3, 2006. http://www.prospect.org/web/page.ww?section=root&name=ViewWeb&articleId=11345. Retrieved 2008-04-23.
B, J (2006-01-06). "Matthews trumpeted comparatively small Abramoff client donations to Sen. Clinton, virtually ignoring larger donations given to Bush, Hastert". *Media Matters for America*. http://mediamatters.org/items/200601070003.

50) http://www.brainyquote.com/quotes/authors/c/chris _matthews.html.

51) Kurtz, Howard. "Bill O'Reilly and NBC, Shouting to Make Themselves Seen?". The Washington Post. January 15, 2007. http://www.washingtonpost.com/wp-dyn/content/article/2007/01/14/AR2007-011401124.html.

52) http://www.brainyquote.com/quotes/authors/k/keith_ olbermann.html.

53) "Olbermann: Bush, Cheney should resign". Msnbc.msn.com. July 3, 2007. http://www.msnbc.msn.com/id/19588942/.

54) "Scarborough Slams Keith Olbermann's Rant...." Politik Ditto, January 19, 2010. http://www.politik-ditto.com/2010/01/joe-scarborough-slams-keith-olbermanns.html.

55) http://news.yahoo.com/s/yblog_upshot/20101108/cm_yblog_upshot/keith-olbermann-returns-to-msnbc-on-Tuesday.
http://www.talkradionews.com/news/2010/11/8/sanders-olbermannsuspension-highlights-need-to-block-nbc-co.html.

56) http://www.msnbc.msn.com/id/26318771/ns/msnbc_tv-rachel_maddow_show/.

57) Greenwald, Glenn (November 10, 2008). "Joe Scarborough: Hoisted by his own sanctimonious petard". Salon. http://www.salon.com/opinion/greenwald/2008/11/10/scarborough/.

58) Scarborough, Joe (2010-10-12). "Gingrich's rhetoric will backfire". Politico. http://dyn.politico.com/printstory.cfm?uuid= 9DAC34BD-F904-0596-4D112EAA3E8832A1.

59) http://www.brainyquote.com/quotes/authors/j/joe_ scarborough.html.

60) "Fox most trusted name in news," Politico, January 27, 2010. http://www.politico.com/news/stories/0110/32039.html.

61) http://politicalhumor.about.com/library/blratherisms.htm.

62) "Dan Rather Concedes Papers are Suspect," *Washington Post*, September 16, 2004. http://www.washingtonpost.com/wp-dyn/articles/A24633-2004Sep15.html.
"Dan Rather Sues CBS for $70 million ," Fox News, September 20, 2007. http://abcnews.go.com/Business/story?id=3625465&page=1.

63) http://www.foxnews.com/politics/2010/03/08/dan-makes-watermelon-quip-depicting-gop-attacks-obama/.

64) "Tom Brokaw: U.S. Broadcast Journalist," Museum of Broadcast Communications. http://www.museum.tv/eotvsection.php?entrycode= brokawtom.

65) "Peter Jennings dies at 67," ABC-TV News, August 7, 2005. http://abcnews.go.com/US/story?id=1015438&page=1.

66) http://www.businessinsider.com/10-most-powerful-in-tv-news-2010-4.

67) "Christine Amanapour to join ABC News, August 7. 2005. http://news.blogs.cnn.com/2010/03/18/christiane-amanpour-to-join-abc-news/?hpt=T2.
"This Weak: Christiane Amanpour Leads ABC To Worst Ratings Since 2003." September, 2010 - | url = http://www.mediaite.com/tv/this-weak-amanpour-leads-abc-to-worst-ratings-since-2003/.

68) *The Atlantic Monthly*, October 2009. http://www.theatlantic.com/magazine/archive/2009/10/cheap-laughs/7650/.

69) Groseclose, T. "Media Bias Is Real, Find UCLA Political Scientist." UCLA. December 14, 2005. http://www.newsroom.ucla.edu/page.asp?RelNum=6664.
Steve Rendall; Daniel Butterworth (June 2004). "How Public is Public Radio?". Extra!. http://www.fair.org/index.php?page=1180.

70) Fox News Channel. 21 October 2010. http://www.foxnews.com/politics/2010/10/21/brief-history-nprs-intolerance-imbalance.
Rainey, James (21 October 2010). "On the Media: Juan Williams' firing is hard to justify". The Los Angeles Times. http://www.latimes.com/entertainment/news/la-et-onthemedia-20101021,0,6731954.column.

71) http://www.businessinsider.com/npr-fires-juan williams2010-10.

72) http://www.askmen.com/entertainment/special_feature_300/344b_rush-limbaugh-5-things-you-didnt-know.htm.

73) http://www.brainyquote.com.

74) "Shock Jocks: The Voice of Unreason," The Independent, March,28, 2009. http://www.independent.co.uk/news/world/americas/shock-jocks-voice-of-unreason-1691792.html.

75) "Rush Limbaugh Turns Himself in on Fraud Charge in Rx Probe," The Washington Post, April 29, 2006.

76) "The Power 50," Newsweek, November 8, 2010.

77) http://usconservatives.about.com/od/gettinginvolved/tp/Top ConservativeMagazines.htm.

78) "Divorced from Reality," The American Conservative, November 22, 2010. http://www.amconmag.com/blog/divorced_from_reality/.

79) "Obama Remembers Asian Allies," The American Conservative, November 22, 2010. http://www.amconmag.com/blog/obama-remembers-asian-allies/.

80) Peterson, Dan, "A Splendid, Precarious Victory," The American Spectator, September 2010.

81) Bethell, Tom, "How Enviros Obstruct Border Patrol," The American Spectator, September 2010.

82) The National Review, September 20, 2010.

83) http://www.newamericancentury.org/iraqclintonletter.htm. "frontline: the war behind closed doors: interviews: william kristol". PBS. http://www.pbs.org/wgbh/pages/frontline/shows/iraq/i nterviews/kristol.html. Newamericancentury.org. 1998-01-26.

84) Roper, William, "Campaign Finance Myths," The Weekly Standard, November 20, 2010. http://www.weeklystandard.com/articles/campaign-finance-myths_518387.html.

85)   "Lobbyists Get Potent Weapon in Campaign Ruling," New York Times," January 21, 2010. http://www.nytimes.com/2010/01/22/us/politics/22donate.html.

86)   Aloi, Daniel. "Conservative pundit Ann Coulter '84 to speak May 7". Cornell University. 3April 17, 2006. http://www.news.cornell.edu/stories/April06/coulter.pre.dea.html.Freedland,Jonathan."Anappalling magic". The Guardian. May 17, 2003. http://www.guardian.co.uk/media/2003/may/17/pressandpublishing.usnews.

87)   The American Prospect, December, 2010.

88)   The American Prospect, November 23, 2010. http://www.prospect.org/cs/articles?article=destroying _the_village.

89)   The American Prospect, November 18, 2010. http://www.prospect.org/cs/articles?article=why_we _are_angry_at_the_tsa.

90)   The Atlantic. http://www.theatlantic.com/a/masthead.mhtml.

91)   "The Whiplash Election," The Atlantic Monthly, November 24, 2010.

92)   "Like a Full-Body Massage: Thinking About TSA," The Atlantic Monthly, November 23, 2010. http://www.theatlantic.com/national/archive/2010/11/like-a-full-body-massage-thinking-about-the-tsa/66923/.

93)   http://harpers.org/archive/2010/03/0082865.

94)   The Atlantic. August 16, 2010, edition "Getting Out of Afghanistan."

95)   "Afghanistan Special Issue," The New Republic, August 12, 2010.

96)   Mother Jones, October, 2010.

97)   http://www.magazinecost.com/popular-magazines/.

98)   Ibid.

99)   "The Power 50," Newsweek, November 8, 2010.

100) "Bill O'Reilly is popular...."

101) http://www.physorg.com/news191505381.html http://www.mondonewspapers.com/circulation/ usatop100.html.
      "Scandalous scoop breaks online". BBC. 25 January 1998. http://www.thedailybeast.com/blogs-and-stories/2010-08-03/newsweek-losses-revealed/.
      http://www.thedailybeast.com/blogs-and-stories/2010-08-03/newsweek-losses-revealed/.
      Brody, David. "Newsweek Photo of Palin Shows Media Bias and Sexism." CBN News. November 16, 2009.
      Pérez-Peña, Richard. "The Times Wins 5 Pulitzer Prizes." The New York Times. April 21, 2009. http://www.nytimes.com/2009/04/21/business/media/21pulitzer.html?hp.

102) "Think Tank Sources Fall, but Left Gains Slightly," Fair, March/April 2007.

103) http://www.moveon.org/ and http://www.huffingtonpost.com/.

104) http://www.drudgereport.com/.
      http://trueslant.com/level/2010/03/09/why-are-the-drudge-reports-exclusives-so-often-completely-false/

105) Vivian B. Martin, "Media Bias: Going beyond Fair and Balanced," Scientific American, September 26, 2008. Meg Sullivan, "Media Bias is Real, Finds UCLA Political Scientist," UCLA Newsroom, October 2, 2010.

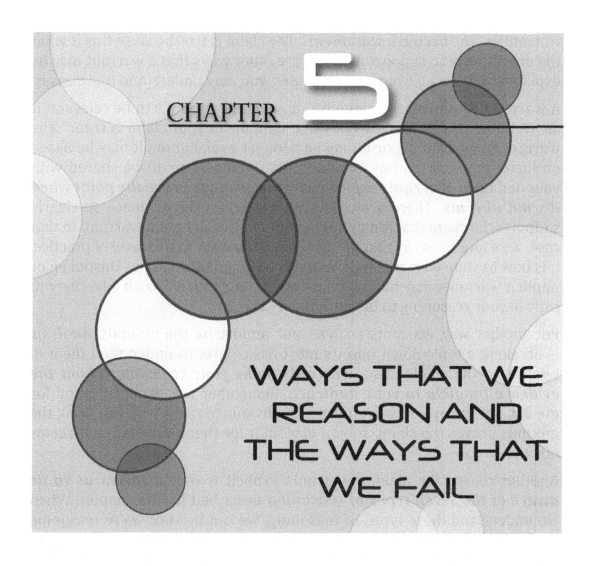

CHAPTER 5

WAYS THAT WE REASON AND THE WAYS THAT WE FAIL

"MAN IS A REASONING, RATHER THAN A REASONABLE ANIMAL."

- ALEXANDER HAMILTON -

We've discussed propositions in the first chapter, including Toulmin's claims, and we've looked at evidence, Toulmin's grounds, in the third. What about Toulmin's warrants? How do we understand and manage the patterns of reasoning that relate grounds to claims?

That's one simple definition for a **warrant**, that it links the grounds to the claim. If you struggle with this chapter, and you might for a bit, think of the warrant as "**the because statement.**" The claim is true because this is what the grounds say to support it. There are other ways that a warrant may be explained. Observed from several angles, you may understand more easily.

A warrant legitimizes the claim by showing the grounds to be relevant. It answers the question "Why does that data mean your claim is true?" The warrant may be simple or it may be a longer explanation. It may be based on logos, ethos, or pathos, or values that you assume to be shared with your audience. **Warrants explain why the grounds prove the point when it's not obvious.** There are circumstances when the evidence so clearly supports the claim that it may seem unnecessary to have a warrant. In that case, we sometimes say that the warrant is **implied**. At this level of practice, it is best to state warrants in an **explicit** way, however simply. Unspoken or implicit warrants may be hidden presumptions that allow an adversary to expose your reasoning to be unfounded (**1**).

Put another way, warrants analyze and summarize the grounds. **Analysis** is breaking a topic down into its most basic parts to understand them in relation to the whole. Also, **warrants make your reasoning about the evidence tangible to your audience.** Remember that you're writing for the ear, not the eye. It won't always be obvious to them why you think the grounds proves the claim, so you explain it for them, even when it seems obvious to you.

Another reason for making warrants explicit is that it **forces us to be aware of the seven types of reasoning** described in this chapter. When we understand these types of reasoning, we can be sure we're reasoning correctly and **avoid the logical fallacies related to each type of reasoning.** Also, when students aren't confident about their warrants, there's a strong temptation to call everything implied or obvious, even when it's not.

You should already have built some **rudimentary arguments** for your fact speech that look like this example:

Claim: The earth's temperature is rising.

Grounds: According to reports from British scientists published in *The Guardian* on July 28, 2010, "Global temperatures in the first half of the year were the hottest since records began more than a century ago, according to two of the world's leading climate research centers. Scientists have also released what they described as the 'best evidence yet' of rising long-term temperatures.... Publishing the newly collated data in London, Peter Stott, the head of climate modeling at the UK Met Office, said despite variations between individual years, the evidence was unequivocal: 'When you follow those decade-to-decade trends then you see clearly and unmistakably signs of a warming world (2).'"

Good. Great start. But is that enough? Unfortunately, it isn't. This is what we called **conclusionary evidence**, a tidy bit of expert testimony that says something is so without explaining why. The expert seems to have some appropriate credentials, but how did he arrive at his claim? If we supplied a warrant to this argument, it would be something like "British scientists say it's true." That would be the simplest pattern of reason called *"reasoning from authority."* The arguer pleads the claim to be true based on his own credentials or the expertise of others. No more critical thinking is involved than that of a primitive tribesman believing something because his chief says, "The great god Gajubu declares it."

There are certainly uses for reasoning by authority. When Stephen Hawking speaks of space and physics, I listen carefully because he's so far ahead of me that I can't possibly challenge his thinking. Yet on social issues, we must be able to understand the reasoning of our "tribal chiefs" before we comply.

Also, **experts disagree**. There is a contingent of scientists and politicians who believe that global warming is a myth and that what we're seeing is normal from the perspective of geological time (3). Ice ages and periods of heat come and go naturally, and we're still here. 1998 was the hottest year on record, and we've actually seen cooling, they say, and some months are cooler rather than there being a steadily growing trend. There are groups like The Global Climate Coalition, The George Marshall Institute, The Oregon Institute of Science and Medicine, The Science and Environmental Policy Project (SEPP), and the Center for the Study of Carbon Dioxide and Global Change, all of which say that global warming is being exaggerated.

When we throw the credentials of authorities around, it sounds impressive, but what do we do in public debate? Do we simply weigh my authorities on a scale against yours? We can and should do that in the case of expert testimony. For instance, if you did a little research, you'd discover that most of the above groups include scientists **employed by oil companies**, suggesting that they fail the **bias** test of evidence. Tobacco companies have long trotted out a cavalcade of scientists minimizing smoking effects.

Wouldn't it be better to know the actual reasoning used by authorities before we simply believe them based on their titles?

For instance, what if we continued our global warming argument by looking at the actual methods used by the British scientists? They developed an entirely new model for evaluating global warming. Skeptics challenged the former model saying that, if it worked, earth should be even hotter. The British report was the first to correlate "11 different indicators," from air and sea temperatures, each based on three to seven data sets dating back to between 1850 and the 1970s to the present. This would be ***"reasoning from sign,"*** observing clues or "indicators" of changing phenomena.

Claim: The earth's temperature is rising.

Warrant: We know this because of a wide variety of signs or indicators carefully observed in the most recent scientific studies.

Grounds 1: "Currently 1998 is the hottest year on record. Two combined land and sea surface temperature records from NASA's Goddard Institute for Space Studies (GISS) and the U.S. National Climatic Data Centre (NCDC) both calculate that the first six months of 2010 were the hottest on record. According to GISS, four of the six months also individually showed record highs."

Grounds 2: "Seven of the indicators rose over the last few decades, indicating 'clear warming trends.' One of these was air temperature over land—including data from the Climatic Research Unit.... The graphic also included figures from six other research groups all showing the same overall trends.... The other six rising indicators were sea surface temperatures, collected by six groups; ocean heat to 700m depth from seven groups; air temperatures over oceans (five data sets); the tropospheric temperature in the atmosphere up to 1km up (seven); humidity caused by warmer air absorbing more moisture (three); and sea level rise as hotter oceans expand and ice melts. Another four indicators showed declining figures over time, again consistent with global warming: northern hemisphere snow cover (two data sets), Arctic sea ice extent (three); glacier mass loss (four); and the temperature of the stratosphere."

The strength of the study is that it analyzes data from multiple groups of scientists, including our own NASA. More signs are available from less technical sources, and they would have to be included to make a truly convincing argument, not to mention one that is comprehensible to an average audience. We'd add some examples, like declines in polar bear populations, to add a dimension of pathos about the effects.

Yet even this argument makes the key point: **Reasoning has to be made manifest for the arguments to be sound.** We've seen enough about how information can be manipulated not to trust authority on its own merits.

INDUCTION VS. DEDUCTION

The two broadest categories of reason are induction and deduction. They are commonly misunderstood terms. The usual definition is that induction is reasoning from the specific to the general, while deduction is reasoning from the general to the specific, which is fine as far as it goes, but there are other distinctions to be noted.

Deduction proceeds from a certain premise or accepted principle. Such reasoning moves from the general premise or principle to show how it supports a specific case. The result is a necessary or "valid" conclusion. A classic syllogism illustrates that point:

> All men are mortal.
>
> Socrates is a man.
>
> Thus, Socrates is mortal.

Deduction does not introduce new knowledge. It proceeds from what we already know. It simply notes an established truth about a class of knowledge, in this case "men," places an individual case in that class of knowledge, in this case "Socrates," and concludes that, since the individual case belongs in that class of knowledge, what's true of the class must be true of the individual. Of course, if you begin with an incorrect premise or principle, you can arrive at a false conclusion. In discussions of philosophy, for instance, we may hear "given that this is true, then this also follows," yet the givens are often a source of debate. Sometimes we use speculative premises about broader, more abstract matters of conjecture to explore deductions. You may practice this, for instance, in discussion of value propositions.

Inductive reasoning makes observations about specific cases in large numbers and tries to establish an acceptable premise or principle. It uses what is newly observed in research, collates discovered characteristics of the specific cases, and generates new understanding. Let's use a simple example of taste in wine we've sampled from a particular vineyard:

> I tried the vineyard's cabernet sauvignon, and it was very good.
>
> I tried the vineyard's chardonnay, and it was very good.
>
> I tried their sauvignon blanc, syrah, and merlot, and they were all very good.
>
> Thus, I conclude that the wines of this vineyard are generally very good.

Note that the result is not certainty, or formal validity, which deduction can, but probability. The probability may be strong or weak, depending on the number of cases analyzed, the credibility of the sources consulted about the individual cases, and the soundness of the observations themselves. Since so much of what we do in argumentation is research based, you'll find yourself more usually involved in a process of induction, gathering a lot of individual cases, and reasoning from those grounds, through warrants, up to your claims or conclusions.

Deduction and induction work hand in hand, one might say in a nearly cyclic way, toward the advancement of human knowledge. We could not have deductive principles unless we first go through an inductive process to establish an accepted principle from which we can deduct. As we discover new facts, we learn to adjust the accepted principles according to new inductions, refining our most trusted principles.

Basically, though, if you can strengthen your argument or hypothesis by adding another piece of data, you are using inductive reasoning. If you cannot improve your argument by adding more evidence, you are employing deductive reasoning.

Here follow more specific patterns of reason. Of these, only "reasoning by definition" is deductive. The rest are inductive in nature.

THE MAGNIFICENT SEVEN

There are a finite number of **reasoning patterns** that we use in argument building. This is a bit of an oversimplification, but **inductive** patterns work from specific information and work toward a general understanding. *Deductive* patterns apply known or accepted generalizations as a standard for analyzing particular cases. Inductive reasoning, by practical necessity, tends to precede deduction, though we can assume certain things to be true for the sake of argument. We'll call these patterns of reason, for the sake of memory (and fans of great western film) "*The Magnificent Seven*" (4):

Parallel Reasoning

Generalization

Reasoning by Definition

Reasoning from Sign

Reasoning from Cause to Effect

Reasoning from Dilemma

Reasoning by Authority

As our opening quotation mentioned, we may reason but we're not that reasonable. We make errors in reason called **logical fallacies**. Argument texts like this often separate discussion of reasoning from logical fallacies. This text will relate the two. We'll look at each kind of reason and ways it can go wrong. In fact, you'd be best served by reading one section and considering it for a bit before moving on to the others. It's a fairly long and very important chapter, so chew it in digestible bites. Please, do not get down on yourself if you don't understand this all at once. You have the whole semester, and you'll get a practical sense of these concepts through class discussion and doing the speeches themselves.

1) PARALLEL REASONING

Let's start with what is arguably the simplest pattern of reason after author-ity, parallel reason. **The primary mental action is a comparison:**

$$A = B$$

We know what each thing, being, and phenomenon is by **recognizing similarities and differences.** Otherwise, everything would be the same thing. We couldn't identify anything. We couldn't distinguish actions, causes, or effects, because there would be no separate agents for those dynamics. Parallel reason is that fundamental.

How can we think our way through anything if we can't **make distinctions** between these things and those? "These are fish. These are rocks. I won't eat the rocks. I'll also refrain from building a fence made of fish."

One of the first things we do as infants, besides following our instinctive impulses to eat and sleep, is to distinguish one thing from another. That's a face, and this is the fist I stick in my mouth. In early school, we play a game called "**compare and contrast**." We ask our children "**which of these does not belong**, a fish, a dog, a horse, or a ball?"

Also, since A equals B, we can expect similar things of each. We can then **make predictions** about the future from those expectations. "This storm looks like one that broke windows last year. I'd best close the shutters."

We may know this by **the more common term "analogy."** Parallel reasoning and analogy are like fraternal twins. It's the same process of comparison, but **the difference is how literal the comparisons are.**

Analogy is a poetic comparison. The literary concepts of metaphor and symbol evolve from analogy. These comparisons may be expressive aspects of style in speech or writing. We use them to make pithy and amusing social comments. One feminist graffiti is an example:

"A woman without a man is like a fish without a bicycle."

A woman is not like a fish in any literal sense, and a man is not much like a bicycle. The point of the comparison is to make a claim in a more colorful yet indirect way: "Women don't really need men."

While analogies are expressive, they are not without rhetorical impact. In a recent quip by a pundit, an analogy was used to make this succinct message: "The elephant and the donkey are outdated symbols for our political parties. They should be replaced with pit bulls and rabbits."

Another political writer made this more searing comparison: "A Star of David painted on a Palestinian home is like swastikas on a temple back in the U.S." That is, it's the same kind of disrespect for the religious differences of others. On the anniversary of 9/11, *The New York Times* reflected on events since 9/11. When considering if we'd improved our position in the global war on terrorism, one analyst said, "We've been hitting a glob of mercury with a hammer."

Parallel reasoning uses literal comparisons. Consider his quotation from a student on the veto of a gay rights bill by a California governor:

> "There was no reason to veto the bill. It does not interfere with any existing law, it does not mute the voice of the people, and it would have become law without the governor's interference. Governor Schwarzenegger has joined the opponents of equality who were on the losing end of segregation, anti-Semitism, and women's suffrage. History shows they will eventually lose this apartheid, too."

"Roe v. Wade is the Dred Scott decision of our age," said Edward Whelan, president of the Ethics and Public Policy Center, a Washington think tank, referring back to the Supreme Court decision that upheld slavery and was later discredited. "Like few other Supreme Court cases in our nation's history, Roe is not only patently wrong but also fundamentally hostile to core precepts of the American government (**5**)."

In an analysis of Tea Party positions, *Mother Jones* magazine made the point that, while it seems like a brand new revolutionary force, its simply another very typical response to Democrats taking power in the White House. They compare the Tea Party to The American Liberty League, which plagued FDR, and the John Birch Society that nipped at the heels of JFK (**6**).

There are **word clues** that can help us recognize patterns of reason in everyday writing and speaking. We will use such clues throughout the chapter. ***The language by which we identifyparallel reason includes:***

A word or phrase making the comparison clear: ***"like, as, is similar to, resembles, compared to, by contrast,"*** are all words or phrases that might signal the use of parallel reason. And, of course, there will be ***two nouns that are being compared.***

In a court of law, use of the word ***"precedent"*** indicates that the lawyer will refer to another earlier case like the present one to draw conclusions about how thejudge should rule now.

For instance, a *Los Angeles Times* photographer was first allowed to take pictures of a defendant by a judge, but she then changed her mind and forbade him to publish the pictures. A court concluded that she had violated the photographer's First Amendment rights calling it a **"classic**

prior restraint of speech." Prior restraints have commonly been ruled invalid, most famously in the case of *The New York Times* publishing the Pentagon Papers, a military analysis of Vietnam, which the Nixon administration tried to stop but which the Supreme Court allowed.

In policy discussion, the word *"model"* may indicate taking what someone has done effectively in a similar situation and applying it as a solution to the present circumstance. For instance, our national standards for welfare limitations are based on a model first tested in San Bernadino, California. Models are very important in developing policy solutions.

FALLACY: FALSE ANALOGY

There is *a wrong way to use parallel reasoning.* It's a fallacy, an error in reasoning, called "false analogy." This is making comparisons among things that are not really alike:

President Obama, who had made comments about Wall Street "fat cats" in several speeches, proposed that private equity fund managers should have their "carried interest programs," an aspect of their personal compensation, taxed as private income (%35) instead of as capital gains (%15). He thought it unfair for wealthy investors to be taxed at a lower rate than common working people. In response, Stephen Schwartzman, a co-founder of the Blackstone Group with personal assets of $8 billion dollars said, "It's a war. It's like when Hitler invaded Poland in 1939," shocking even his own stockholders (**7**).

The Washington Times used the term *"blood libel"* when referring to people questioning Sarah Palin's political qualifications. This is an historically inapt comparison. The term usually refers to the centuries-old accusation that Jews use the blood of gentile children in making matzos for Passover. The appearance of the blood libel label is often the prelude to massacres or other forms of anti-Semitic persecution and is alive and well in some parts of the world, especially the Middle East (**8**). The expression is also the appeal fallacy "emotive language."

When someone makes an analogy, his adversary should look for lack of commonality or significant exceptions. We'll discuss that further in the debate chapter.

2) GENERALIZATION

When we play "compare and contrast" and make analogies, we're actually beginning to create categories of living things, ideas, and people. Although it is not as simple as analogy, generalization has a natural relationship with it. ***Generalization, it might even be said, is an extended case of analogy.*** It seeks descriptive classifications of larger groups of comparable things, though, so it requires either many examples or figures and statistics.

The essential mental action is: A1+A2+A3, etc. = Class A.

The process involves ***description and classification.*** We gather sufficient information about enough individually described cases to classify like items into a group. We then attach generalized descriptions to that class based on our observations. "Mammals have fur and warm blood, breathe oxygen, and reproduce by live birth."

How did we come to know these things about mammals? First, we ***carefully observed many cases*** among apparently similar creatures. Then we noticed sufficient similarities to consider them a definable group or category. That's the process of ***classification.*** Finally, we made a list of generalizations about what is common among members of that class (Figure 5.1):

Circles are sometimes used to illustrate classification in logic. (9) You may be familiar with their use from a math class. Everything inside the

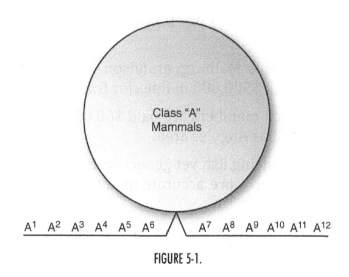

FIGURE 5-1.

circle is a member of the class, while everything outside isn't. This diagram intends to show many individual cases at the bottom, moving by way of our analysis into a general sense of what is contained in the circle: fur, oxygen, warm blood, and live birth.

When we generalize, we reason that **what is true of one member of a group will also be true of other members of that group**, to one degree or another.

Generalization is commonly revealed as **a list of examples**. In fact, it is often called "**reasoning by example**." In a recent scandal in the Los Angeles area, officials of the Bell city government were revealed to have taken extremely high salaries. While the city of Bell, California, has received a lot of attention for fattened salaries, Vernon next door is as bad. According *The Los Angeles Times*, over 99% of city managers make well below these kinds of salaries (**10**):

- Eric T. Fresch was paid $1.65 million in salary and hourly billings in 2008 when he held jobs both as city administrator and deputy city attorney.

- Daniel O'Callaghan was paid nearly $785,000 as a city administrator and director of light and power.

- Former City Attorney Jeffrey A. Harrison earned $800,000.

- Finance Director Roirdan Burnett made $570,000.

- Former City Administrator Bruce Malkenhorst made as much as $911,563.

- One ex-city administrator's pay topped $1 million in each of the last four years.

- Former Mayor Leonis Malburg, grandson of the city's founder, was ordered to pay back $500,000 in fines for fraud and conspiracy.

- Vernon City Council members are paid $68,052 a year, far more than other cities in the Los Angeles area.

This is a long and convincing list, yet generalization is often illustrated by **figures and statistics** for more accurate quantification, as is the case in this illustration:

> For women aged 55 and older who were followed for eight to eleven years, routinely being screened for tumors reduced the

risk of death from breast cancer by 55%, according to a new analysis reported in this week's edition of the international medical journal *The Lancet*. For women who were aged 45 to 54 at the beginning of the study, screening led to a 30% reduction in deaths, the researchers said (**11**).

Notice that generalizations may often appear as graphs, pie graphs in particular, like this one entitled "The Impacts of Mammograms" (Figure 5.2):

A 2010 article in *The New York Times Magazine* about new home size uses both statistics and examples to support their generalization that the new architectural trend is "less is more." An American Institute of Architects survey says that 57% of architecture firms reported a decrease in the square footage of home plans. The average size of homes, according to the National Association of Homebuilders, is now 2483 square feet, 100 square feet less than 2007.

- In Hermosa Beach, California, where ultra-small lots pose challenges, Dean Nota makes a house of 1600 to 1800 square feet.

- A 1300 square foot renovation on a corner lot in San Francisco by Dewey Dickinson is only 13.5 feet wide. Kitchen and dining room serve as hallway space.

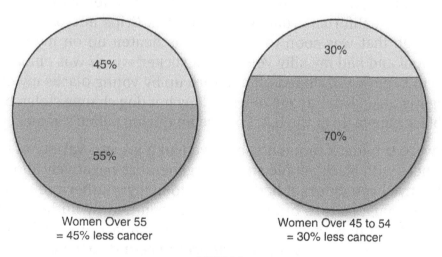

Women Over 55
= 45% less cancer

Women Over 45 to 54
= 30% less cancer

FIGURE 5-2.

- Rick and Cindy Black built a 1100 square foot home near the University of Texas, a series of cubes.

- The firm of Koch & Taalman sell ten models of prefabricated homes with average living spaces of about 1000 square feet, using recycled materials and solar panels.

- Path Architecture's prototype for "The Roho," is 200 square feet than the average garage with a glass wall and double height ceilings to create a sense of space (**12**).

The uniformity of things within a class may vary by degrees, but if exceptions begin to outnumber similarities, the class or category dissolves, and the generalization wouldbe considered unsound.

FALLACY: HASTY GENERALIZATION

Hasty generalization is probably the most commonly committed and most easily recognized logical fallacy. It is simply a matter of **too few cases counted to justify the generalization made**. We may have a particular personal experience of something, a type of person, say, that is so emotional to us that we "**jump to conclusions**" about that type of person.

I was in kindergarten when I had my first encounter with black gangs in Inglewood, California. That was before The Crips encroached on that area, though that was soon to follow. I was beaten up on my way home from school and had my silly yellow rain slicker, which was embarrassing enough to begin with, ripped off and torn up by young blacks my own age and slightly older. Later at age ten, I had my hot dog change stolen by some older black gangsters at the L.A. Colosseum during a Ram's game.

These were traumatic moments, but I've had a greater variety of positive experiences with black people and don't generalize negatively about them. It might have been different had I lived among my southern relatives, who had come from a culture of prejudice and been told by authority figures, "Well, that's just how they are." That's a major impact of this fallacy. **Hasty generalization is the very taproot of prejudice and racism.**

Here are a couple of examples, the first suggested by items from *The Los Angeles Times*, October 13, 2005. "I'm very curious how protesters arrived at the conclusion that a majority of Iraqis want the U.S. out of their country. I served two tours in Iraq and Afghanistan. I can state unequivocally that ***90% to 95% of all Iraqis and Afghanis*** were and are extremely appreciative of what the U.S. has done for them."

The speaker is certainly justified in using his expertise to say what his impressions are, but when he generalizes to all Iraqis and makes up a fake statistic to support his view, he's crossed the line into fallacy. Also, he generalizes about the Afghan population, though he never served there, and he concludes that the attitudes at the time of the quotation were the same as when he served. An emotional connection to the issue interfers with reason. The actual statistics near the time of his statement were that 71% of Iraq had negative opinions about the U.S. occupation (**13**).

A practical example of the fallacy's impact was seen in a Kansas appeals court in the matter of ***State vs. Smith***. Smith wanted to present evidence at trial that he was physically unable to commit a robbery and that he did not have a financial motive for the crime. His lawyer refused to present that evidence for his client and filed to withdraw from the case because he believed that his client was the person seen in a surveillance video of the robbery. He also refused to let a police witness offer his interpretation of whether the person in the video was Smith. The lawyer's filing was rejected by the judge and would not appoint a new attorney because "any lawyer would be precluded from presenting false evidence." However, the appeals court held that:

> Based on the lone assertion of Smith's attorney who refused to present potentially relevant defense evidence on Smith'[s] behalf because he believed that a suspect shown in a crime surveillance video was Smith, the trial court developed a general rule covering all attorneys who could have represented Smith, thus committing the logical fallacy known as a hasty generalization. Just because Smith's attorney believed that the suspect shown in a crime video was the defendant, it does not follow that all attorneys would have viewed that video in the same way as Smith's attorney, especially when the assertion is based on the

sense of sight. More important, this generalization theorizes that all attorneys would have refused to present potentially relevant evidence in Smith's defense (**14**).

3) REASONING BY DEFINITION

The natural counterpart to the inductive process of generalization is this deductive process of identification. Once we've generalized about a group, we've also defined it. "Birds are that group of animals which has feathers rather than fur, breathe air, are warm-blooded, but reproduce by eggs."

The essential mental action is using the generalized checklist of that class's qualities to see if an individual case fits into the class. We can than use that general definition to identify individual cases of living things as *that thing by definition.*

I have a home in the Santa Catalina Mountains above Tucson, Arizona. There's an active river wash behind my property. Birds come to drink and nest in the mesquite forest that grows along the bank. *Watching birds* has become a hobby. As I read more about the birds, I'm able to make more subtle distinctions between individual species. The local bird books are organized by predominant color, one form of classification. Birds are also distinguished by gender and age differences, by size, beak type, and habit. The cardinal is distinguished by its scarlet color and crest. The summer tanager has two shades of red—the wings being a purple-red—and it has no crest. My favorite, the cactus wren, doesn't live in nests like other birds; it hollows out a hole in a cactus, which is a wonderful defense system against its natural enemy, the thrasher, or a cowbird, a nest marauder.

In other words, *the major classification "birds" breaks down into sub-classes:* wrens, thrashers, hawks, hummingbirds, etc., each with unique characteristics. Sub-classes are illustrated as smaller circles within the larger one of a class. We typically adjust the size of the circle to representthe size of the sub-class relative to the base class. It is only by a significant observation of individual examples that we can induce reasonable generalizations, and I'm thrilled that scientists and more experienced birdwatchers have put together these generalizations because it allows me to identify birds. Others more experienced than I can even discover subtle differences in these generalizations and generalize about a new species.

This process of inductive generalization and deductive reasoning by definition, therefore, form a kind of cycle of ongoing refinement of knowledge.

Here is a legal example to illustrate reasoning by definition. Our classifications of **murder** are broken down into three basic sets:

First degree murder: In order for someone to be found guilty of first degree murder the government must prove that the person killed another person; the person killed the other person with malice aforethought; and the killing was premeditated. **Premeditation** means with planning or deliberation. It must be long enough, after forming the intent to kill, for the killer to have been fully conscious of the intent and to have considered the killing. Typical of such cases are lying in wait for the victim. Cases also include killing during certain felonies, such as armed robbery, rape, or arson.

Second degree murder: This is a non-premeditated killing, resulting from an assault in which death of the victim was a distinct possibility. These are often called **crimes of passion**. For instance, a jealous spouse comes home, find their mate in bed with another, and without forethought kills them. There is malice, but the killer does not have time to fully appreciate what he's doing.

Manslaughter: This is the unlawful killing of a human being without any deliberation, which may be involuntary, in the commission of a lawful act without due caution and circumspection. **Cases of negligence and of irresponsibility**, for instance, drunk driving that leads to death, are typical of this charge. Manslaughter is not as serious a crime as murder. On the other hand, it is not a justifiable or excusable killing for which little or no punishment is imposed. There are varying degrees of manslaughter with various degrees of punishment, just as there are many sub-classes of birds in the general class of birds **(15)**.

If you were on **a jury** for any of these charges, you would have to determine if the defendant was responsible for the general characteristics for the offense in question. You would be practicing **reasoning by definition.**

The language clues for definition includes words and phrases like: "it naturally follows that," "thus," "therefore," "it is necessarily so," "by definition," "if it's so that X then it follows that Y," "it derives from its classification that," etc. Traditional use of syllogistic logic employs this kind of language as well. For instance, the classic, "All men are mortal, Socrates is a man, therefore, Socrates is a mortal."

Think of your key areas of knowledge, the subjects you know about, then consider *the seemingly intuitive leaps you make*. If you know about horses, then you can glance up without really thinking and say, "Oh, yes, that's an appaloosa." You learned a long time ago that an appaloosa is neither an Arabian, nor a quarter horse. Perhaps you spot the larger head as a key element, along with the spots, typical characteristics of an appaloosa. You would have made a deduction based on your knowledge of various classes of horses.

It's important to recognize that there are often distinctions within a generalized class—like the varying degrees of manslaughter or the various kinds of birds—and that some characteristics about that class are true only to a certain degree. In other words, there are exceptions to what is generally true. Go back to mammals. If we see something that has all the necessary characteristics of a mammal, we would say that *"by definition" it is a mammal.*

Ah, but here's an interesting exception. Let's see, this new creature has fur. It is warm-blooded. But wait! It lays eggs! That's on other checklists, the one for fowl, for fish, and reptiles, too. How do we define and what do we call this remarkable thing? You may already know that this is an actual creature. It's called a platypus, and it's a partial exception to the rule of mammals. We would classify it as a mammal, because most of its features are mammalian. We would note the exception visually in a diagram, in which "M" stands for mammals, and "P" stands for platypus. It has features both inside and outside of the class of mammals (Figure 5.3):

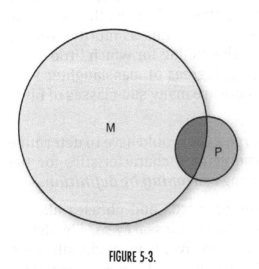

FIGURE 5-3.

This diagram also *reminds us to watch our qualifiers* carefully in our claims. It would not be technically correct to say "all mammals give live birth," since we've found at least one exception. We might modify this claim to "with small exception, mammals give live birth." We'd have to make similar distinctions with such biological anomalies as flying fish or flying squirrels, neither of which are birds.

FIGURE 5-4.

Here's another diagram to illustrate the essential mental action of reason by definition. If the creature observed has the characteristics of the class, it fits into that class as a matter of basic definition.

Further, it is possible to over-generalize about individual examples of a class of human beings leading what we've identified as stereotyping in the second chapter, but we can more formally recognize as a logical fallacy.

FALLACY: SWEEPING GENERALIZATION

This is the deductive counterpart to hasty generalization. "Hasty G"means you haven't gathered enough examples or sufficient statistics to make a generalization. On the other hand, *sweeping generalization too rigidly applies general principles to individual cases with exceptional features.*

Think about the earliest men and how they might have reasoned:*"Og"* is a typical Neanderthal man. He comes out of his cave, sees his neighbor "Ooga," and waves to him. Suddenly, Ooga hollers in pain. Og runs over to check on his friend and finds Ooga quivering and grimacing in death. Og sees a long squiggly creature, what we would know as a snake, baring its fangs. A man of action, Og hoists a rock and flattens the snake into a belt. He later crushes every snake that he sees, creating great fear in the land with his tales of deadly, squiggly beasts.

Are all snakes poisonous? Of course not, and even snakes that are poisonous break down into two distinct subgroups, "krates" including cobras, and "vipers" including rattlesnakes. As we know, some snakes are not poisonous and, in fact, contain rodent populations. Yet Og is out decimating king snakes and other helpful species, reasoning that all snakes are the same.

Og, an overenthusiastic naturalist, *lacked a reasonable sample* from the group examined. He committed a hasty generalization that all snakes are deadly based on a single emotional event. Adhering strictly to this hasty generalization, Og commits a sweeping generalization that leads him to murder all snakes.

As mentioned earlier, the process of inductive generalization and deductive reasoning by definition, therefore, form a kind of cycle of ongoing refinement of knowledge. Incorrect induction also leads to incorrect deduction and a cycle of growing incidents.

The essential mental action of sweeping generalization is the error of not recognizing individual differences in a group, arguing that all who share some characteristics shareall characteristics. For instance, we might believe that Asian-Americans are generally good math students, and statistics would support that, but would we then assume that every Asian-America is good in school?

You might believe that people from Hawaii are generally peaceful, and you may have evidence in the fact that Hawaii posts the highest rate of longevity of any state. Would you then be astonished to meet a bad-tempered guy from Hawaii, or one who died young?

If you discovered that most snakebite victims were young, white, beer drinking men with tattoos, the profile here in Arizona, would you consider that every beer drinking man with a tattoo has been or will be snake-bit?

You might think that blacks are good runners, and we could find support in the history of successful Kenyan runners who dominate world marathon competitions. Yet would we then encounter a single black man and say justifiably, "Oh, you're black, so you must be a good marathon runner?" Hardly.

As for **the key language**, the words **"always" and "never"** are good companions to this fallacy and should be watched carefully. "In every case," "categorically," "necessarily," or "certainly," are words that might accompany the overstatements that are typical of this fallacy.

4) REASONING BY SIGN

This is also called **reasoning by correlation**, and it sometimes resembles reasoning by cause, though a careful distinction between the two must be made. This is slightly more complex than parallel reasoning since we have to observe the relationship of at least two things over a period of time. ***The key mental action*** is "A tends to go along with B" (Figure 5.5):

A ➡ B

FIGURE 5-5.

Signs are a matter of recognizing how objects or traces of action are associated with related events. I sometimes call it "***almanac reasoning,***" as an almanac is full of such natural indicators, for instance, how certain phases of the moon may relate to luck with planting crops.

Think of "***Groundhog Day.***" In snowy areas, people wait for the ground hog to stick its head out of its hole. The myth goes, according to a February 4, 1841, diary entry in James Morris' Morgantown, Pennsylvania diary, "Last Tuesday, the 2nd, was Candlemas day, the day on which, according to the Germans, the Groundhog peeps out of his winter quarters and if he sees his shadow he pops back for another six weeks nap, but if the day be cloudy he remains out, as the weather is to be moderate."

This seems a little hokey, yet farmers have raised successful crops for many years based on careful observation of natural phenomenon by sign, well before there were weather channels and weather men named "Johnny Sunshine," or the like. In fact, scientific study suggests that groundhogs have an 80% rate of accuracy (**16**). However, since there are always six weeks of winter after Groundhogs day, the wily creature is much less accurate at predicting early spring

The language of sign may be quite literal in everyday discourse. "A sign of," "signifies," "indicates," "marks," "is an omen of," "a portent," are words that frequently suggest reasoning by sign. Another word for "signs" would be "***clues,***" as in signs of the crime. This victim suffered multiple knife wounds, possibly signifying a crime of passion. Also, "***symptoms***" in a medical sense may be the initial signs of illness. In the realm of economics, "***economic indicators***" are important signs for investors.

For instance, "To a surprising degree, economic misfortune has correlated with low top marginal tax rates. The marginal tax rate at the time of the 1929 crash was 24%. After his election, FDR promptly raised it to 63% (**17**)." The top marginal tax rate is the rate at which income over a certain amount is taxed. In other words, the point being made in this quotation is that there is a correlation between poor economic trends and lower tax rates among our top earners. Other examples of economic indicators would be debt, unemployment, housing starts, interest rates, etc. Unemployment rates and increased home repossessions have been worrisome signs of our economy.

A sign in the literal sense of *a tattoo* can have quite serious social consequences. A man, nagged by his son for a tattoo like dad's, finally relented and had the outline of a dog's paw print tattooed on the boy's hip. The mother saw it later and called the police. What could have been called a case of poor parental judgment turned into a criminal prosecution. The father and the tattoo artist wound up in jail, and the boy's tattoo was removed. It turned out that the paw print was the symbol for "The Bulldogs," a serious Latino gang that caused many problems for police. The father and tattoo artists had each been members (**18**).

A bombing killed 200 people and injured thousands during ethnic violence in the Xinjiang province of China. There have been struggles between Muslim Uighurs and the Chinese government. "Some observers... said the attack was *an ominous sign* of a renewed campaign of violence by separatists (**19**)."

We call this *a correlation, which is different from a cause.* For instance, while rain goes along with my aching knees, my aching knees don't cause the rain. Nor does the smoke on your backpacking trip cause the fire. There are a few of indicators for *the odds of getting bitten by poisonous snake.* The typical snakebite victim is an under 30 tattooed male. Does that mean that if you get a tattoo it will cause snakes to hunt you down and bite you? Of course not. *Signs indicate correlation between events, not their primary motive force*.

FALLACY: FALSE SIGN

Superstition is one form of this fallacy. People come to believe that breaking mirrors is unlucky, as is a black cat crossing your path. Some baseball players will refuse to change socks, or to shave during a playoff series. They fixate on what seems lucky as a way of coping with stress. All cultures have deep folklore that transcends reason.

Such errors are common in early American history. During the **Salem Witch Trials**, a physical anomaly like a third nipple was sometimes seen as a sign that one was a witch, and one might wind up in a life or death trial because of it. Suspected witches were tied to dunking chairs, chairs at the end of a pole on a fulcrum, by which they were dunked into the river. If one drowned, it would be accepted as a sign of guilt.

Simply misreading signs is a potential danger of this fallacy, which is a failure to prove a sound correlation among events based on sound observations. Clues in a crime are signs, for instance, but clues can be misread. A middle-aged man was roller-blading near the Upper Newport Bay on a road used by joggers, bikers, and skaters. He was found on the road knocked nearly lifeless with severe injuries to his eye and head. Splattered about him was paint from a paintball gun. People thought he'd been hit in the eye with paint balls, fallen and cracked his head. It was even implied in letters to the editor that paintball shooters were lurking in the bushes firing at unsuspecting skaters for a giggle. Police cited witnesses who reported that three "youthful males" were seen in the area with paintball guns. This was initially taken as proof paintball shooters had hit the man in the face, a serious matter since the man later died. However, an autopsy found that the eye injury was the result of the fall itself, not being struck with paintballs. The impact of falling backwards on his head caused his eye to leave its socket. Local papers retracted the incendiary headlines (**20**).

Consider the practical impact of this. Innocent youths might have been arrested and held responsible for wrongful death, had the scientific evidence of the autopsy not corrected a superficial reading of signs. A general distaste for paintball as a sport might ensue. Legal restraints may have increased unnecessarily.

5) REASONING FROM CAUSE TO EFFECT

Reasoning from cause to effect is perhaps the most **challenging** kind of reasoning, in part because there are several ways that it can go wrong. It's very important since we couldn't stop the sources of bad effects, or support sources of good effects, without this understanding. In other words, we couldn't solve social problems.

The essential mental act ion is A leads to B (Figure 5.6):

A ⟹ B

FIGURE 5-6.

A specific source of challenge is that our **burden of proof requires a "causal link."** That is, we have to find the specific agent of cause. For instance, consider the genius of van Leeuwenhoek, the father of microscopic science. His improvement of lenses eventually brought us the knowledge of microbes, which allowed us to locate specific illness origins and invent vaccines to kill them. Louis Pasteur, for instance, could not have developed his cures for anthrax, cholera, or rabies without knowing the causal. Here's an environmental example of a causal link:

> At Lake Mead, nature has done what humans had tried but failed to accomplish years ago—stimulate the food chain and rev up fishing with a record spawn of baitfish. Snowmelt and runoff from winter storms flushed tons of nutrients into the Virgin and Muddy rivers, which empty into the nation's biggest reservoir 30 miles east of Las Vegas. They carried a torrent of minerals that produce plankton that led to a surge of threadfin shad, the main forage for game fish (**21**).

The causal link for the Lake Mead example is the snow runoff thatflushed tons of nutrients into the rivers, which produced plankton, then shad, andthat provided an environment for game fish.

The key language clues in everyday argument is easily observable: "causes," "leads to," "produces," "activates," "provokes," "generates," "brings about," "results in," are active verbs suggesting a relationship between cause and effect. A phrase like "is a result of" is a passive version of the language of cause. Also, of course, "linked to" is a possible phrase, though that may also be used with sign. Clue words are highlighted below.

Offering suggestions to help the U.S. economy *The Economist* projected a future effect: "One priority is to encourage more write-downs of mortgage debt. Almost one quarter of Americans with mortgages owe more than their houses are worth.... Cleaning up the housing market **would help cut** America's unemployment rate, by making it easier for people to move to where jobs are." The causal link is enhanced mobility for folks stuck with homes they can't sell in this market (**22**).

On China surpassing the Gross Domestic Product of Japan to become the world's second largest economy, *The Los Angeles Times* wrote that: "Japan **has been stunted by** weak consumer spending and lower corporate investment.... China's population is 10 times the size of Japan (**23**)."

A new strain of corn (Bt corn) that has been modified to be more pest-resistant apparently **provides a halo effect by protecting nearby corn** from pests, even though it's not a pest-resistant strain. This is beneficial because it saved Minnesota, Illinois, Wisconsin, Iowa, and Nebraska nearly $7 billion in reduced damage from corn boring bugs (**24**).

Sometimes sorting cause out is the source of great social conflict and uncertainty, especially since other concepts related to cause are "**responsibility**" and "**liability**":

> In a study by the National Cancer Institute, breast cancer death rates in Marin were among the highest 10% of counties in the nation.... Those figures are not necessarily a surprise. Breast cancer rates rise with age, and Marin County's residents are substantially older than average. Rates are also higher among women who never had children or who had their children late in life—characteristics often found in women living in this collection of affluent suburbs. But for many women, those statistical explanations for the disease do not suffice... "We've got to take a closer look at the environment.... For all those scientists who have written off the idea of a cancer cluster, I say, you tell that to a community where six women in a three block area have come down with the disease (**25**).

It's true that there is a correlation between age and women who have never had children. That is, being older and childless is **a sign, an indicator** of vulnerability to cancer. The women are arguing, with some justification given the concentrationof cases, that there's a **more direct cause**, something toxic in the environment.

In truth, the mental action in difficult social, medical, and technological issues is not only a simple A to B relationship (Figure 5.7):

$$A \Longrightarrow B$$

FIGURE 5-7.

More often, it's **multiple causation**, and we have to sort through the various causes to see which is most influential and what we can practically do about each (Figure 5.8):

$$A \, \& \, B \, \& \, C \Longrightarrow D$$

FIGURE 5-8.

Several unrelated events can contribute to a problem:

> The massive Hurricane Katrina rebuilding effort will be even more expensive, thanks to the national housing boom. The rebuilding **will create** new demands for building material and construction workers, already in short supply because of strong home-building activity. That **could result in** even higher costs for those goods and workers, which in turn **could further boost** prices for new homes. "The recovery will make it more difficult for anybody operating in construction elsewhere," said Greg Gieber, financial analyst with A.G. Edwards & Son in St. Louis. He foresees that shortages **will reduce the pace of home building** across the country. Total reconstruction costs could run as high as $100 billion, based on latest estimates, making the Katrina rebuilding effort the most costly in United States history (**26**).

Cause and effect may also involve **complex chains of interlinked events:**

> Los Angeles County lost six emergency rooms in a little over a year, yet is facing even more closures that could jeopardize emergency care for tens of thousands. The next round of cuts is likely to target large, heavily used emergency rooms at private hospitals. That would further reduce emergency room capacity by 10% to 15%. That's on top of the 75,000 patient spaces already lost in the last 14 months. Public officials and some health care economists warn that further closures of emergency rooms could set off a chain reaction, due to the added financial strain on remaining E.R.s, including that from a greater number of uninsured patients (**27**).

FALLACIES OF CAUSE

As mentioned earlier, **the burden of proof for cause is heavy** because we have to locate a causal link. If we can't, we can only claim correlation. It's also difficult because there are **four common ways that we err** in the manufacture of causal reasoning. Each fallacy has a specific mechanism that allows us to say more than "that's a fallacy of cause."

False Cause: This is traditionally known as "**post hoc ergo propter hoc**" fallacy. That literally means, "After this, therefore because of this." Just because something A happens before something B doesn't mean that A caused B. Go back to "Og," the caveman:

He comes out of his cave and accidentally stubs his toe on a big rock imbedded in the soil. Even as he is hopping about, by pure coincidence, there's a total eclipse of the sun. Og is horrified. His primitive mind is certain that he has disturbed a powerful rock spiritand is being punished for his offense by the loss of light. He falls on his knees and begs the rock to forgive him. Others see him and join in his lament. As the sun comes back into view, the people are greatly relieved. They build a little fence around the rock and offer it regular worship, perhaps even (gulp) human sacrifices.

Don't laugh. It may not be far from how some tribal religions were created.

Early Americans who lacked our body of scientific evidence and expert opinion had to rely on crude interpretations of sign as cause. In **The Salem Witch Trials**, a citizen might testify: "Goody Proctor walked by my house, scowled at me, and an hour later I miscarried." To them, such reasoning was just cause for conviction for witchcraft. Goody Proctor's scowl may have been a sign... a sign that Goody Proctor didn't much like her neighbor.

A hurricane devastated some parts of the eastern seaboard, though not the prayer compound of evangelist **Pat Robertson**, who claimed to have diverted the hurricane with prayer. When it was pointed out that folks just north in Maryland had taken a terrific pounding, he replied, "They should have prayed," a comment for which he later apologized. Other evangelists made a similar analysis of **9/11**, claiming that it was God's repayment for our various evils, much like the flood of Biblical lore. Closer examination would reveal deep historical and political causes for the attack on New York.

Oversimplification is simply a matter of overlooking multiple causes for something, focusing on one cause to the exclusion of others. Under the influence of this fallacy, we may make misguided judgments about complex social issues. Someone who thinks ill of immigrants, for instance, may blame them for the cost of social services, though there are several reasons Social Security, Medicare, or other systems are strained. Here is an example of intelligent reporting avoiding oversimplification:

> A news report on the death of a man stabbed outside a Riverside gay bar in an alleged hate crime reveals that the man may have bled to death because of a hospital error. A nurse accidentally

gave Owens 100,000 units of an anticoagulant drug, 100 times the recommended dose, according to a report issued this week by the Riverside coroner's office. With blood unable to clot, Owens bled to death. Prosecutors said Tuesday the hospital error does not lessen the culpability of five Riverside alleged gang members charged with Owen's murder (**28**).

A man is stabbed by a gang, but a nurse accidentally gives him a huge dose of an anti-coagulant, and he bleeds to death. Who is responsible? Who caused the death? In auto accidents, we have the concept of "***contributory negligence***," recognizing that each person in an accident, for all their pleading, may be part of the cause.

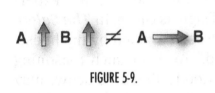

FIGURE 5-9.

Correlation vs. Causation is a confusion between reasoning by sign and reasoning from cause to effect. If you see a phenomenon in the vicinity of another phenomena often enough, you are likely to think of them as connected somehow. However, A going along with B is not the same as saying A is causing B (Figure 5.9):

While parallel reason and generalization are like fraternal twins, in which the action of one is multiplied many times by the other, ***correlation and causation are just distant cousins who happen to look alike.***

Go back to "Groundhog's Day." The groundhog coming out of its hole is a sign of early spring. Does the groundhog cause spring? No. We may say that housing starts, or the interest rates, or any individual feature of the economy is a sign of financial improvement or decline, but could interest rates cause an upswing in the economy by themselves? Probably not.

The key question to ask yourself when considering this fallacy is, what is the specific causal link? If you can't identify it, then you may be able to meet the burden of proof for correlation, but not cause. There may be a theoretical point at which many correlations begin to converge into the motive force of a cause, but you would have to locate and document it.

Slippery Slope proposes a landslide of bad effects from a single cause without establishing the causal links to each effect. The complex chain of causes that closed emergency rooms earlier was correctly reasoned. But the image of this fallacy is a landslide.

This error in reasoning has had considerable impact on U.S. history in the twentieth century. The cold war between the Soviet Union and the U.S. was largely defined, from the United States point of view, by the concept of "**the domino theory**." Ever set a series of dominos up on their ends, just to tip one and see the others automatically fall? In the domino theory, however, countries were supposed fall, one after another, to the communist threat. We neighbor kids used to wonder when the Red Chinese would show up on Catalina Island. This was a key justification for the war in Vietnam, but Red Chinese have yet to invade our beaches... except on vacation.

The language is frequently extreme, reactive, and fearful. During our debateson gay marriage, a typical argument has been that allowing it would lead to other terrible things. One of my students asked this question: "What's next, polygamy? Marriage with animals?" Whatever you believe about gay marriage, there is no evidence that a gaymarriage leads to polygamy, let alone bestiality. The statement is an emotional expression of the writer, not a logical argument.

Jay Leno made a joke aboutit on the "Tonight Show.""Boy, this Gay Marriage thing is really catching on. Just yesterday one man married sixteen guys in Utah."

On October 6, 2009, Representative Louis Gohmert of Texas argued that a hate crimes bill passed by Congress would lead to Nazism and legalization of necrophilia, pedophilia, and bestiality, "If you're oriented toward animals, bestiality, then, you know, that's not something that can be used, held against you or any bias be held against you for that. Which means you'd have to strike any laws against bestiality, if you're oriented toward corpses, toward children, you know, there are all kinds of perversions ... pedophiles or necrophiliacs or what most would say is perverse sexual orientations (**29**)."

Or consider candidate *Christine O'Donnell, during an appearance on Bill Maher's first show "Politically Incorrect."* "We took the Bible and prayer out of public schools, and now we're having weekly shootings practically. We had the '60s sexual revolution, and now people are dying of AIDS (**30**)."

6) REASONING FROM DILEMMA

Choices in public debate are not always clear-cut. There are advantages and disadvantages for both sides in most debates. Sometimes, though, we find ourselves in a *"dilemma,"* and that word **means something very particular**:

A)   A choice has to be made between two things.

B)   These things are "mutually exclusive," meaning you can't have both.

C)   There is no third alternative.

A real dilemma is **not just a problem** of some kind. It's also **not the same as a paradox**. A paradox unifies seemingly contradictory elements into a literary device or a complex philosophic insight. Things go together that somehow shouldn't fit. For instance, this Oliver Wendell Holmes quotation is aparadox: "The mode in which the inevitable comes to pass is through effort." For Christians, the idea of the Holy Trinity is a paradox. There are three separate yet unified entities. Yet adherents accept it. In quantum physics the same atomic particle can exist in two places at once. Also, dilemma is **not an enigma**, which is an unsolvable mystery, like what is the purpose of life?

As an example of dilemma, take the case of a Georgia woman, Carol Carr, 63, who is widowed by **Huntington's Disease**. Huntington's is a terrible disease with long suffering effects that she bore until her husband's death. She shot her two adult sons who were also suffering terribly from the disease. Her third son, 38, is in the early stages of the disease. Carr was charged with murder. Supporters say Carr could not stand to see her children endure more. She told one friend after the shooting that Andy was writhing, tearfully tugging at the sheets, and begging for release when she entered the room that day (**31**).

One's sense of logos may conflict with the pathos of the situation. On one hand, she's clearly broken the language in the law. Mercy killing is simply not legal. On the other, it is difficult not to feel sympathy for a woman who is aging and has already been through so much. Also, it's hard to forget the image of the son himself writhing and in pain. Put yourself on her jury. The dilemma is: Should we show mercy when to do so may set a precedent for future mercy killings? How would you vote? Perhaps more importantly for your study, how would you choose?

The language of dilemma would include phrases like: "either/or," "must choose between," "it's a question between," etc. You may hear dilemma discussed in terms of "advantages vs. disadvantages," or "costs vs. gains."

Costs vs. gains analysis is systematically listing the assets and deficits of the two positions in question then creating a value standard to decide between the two. This will be more important during discussions of value and policy. You'll learn how to make standards or criteria for decisions during your value assignment, and you'll need costs vs. gains analysis to determine which is best, side-effects of your proposed solution or the effects of the problem itself.

Environmental issues often create dilemmas: Which is more important, saving a forest or putting lumber companies out of business? Medical situations frequently put us in the situation of choosing whether the cure is worse than the disease itself. For example, the DEA is investigating pharmacists in five states for dispensing drugs to nursing homes without direct written orders from a doctor. Nurses at these homes typically send orders for pain meds like Percocet directly to the pharmacies because they don't have doctors on staff, and pain occurs over weekends. The agency says it's just trying to protect patients. If patients have enough pain to need such drugs, they should see a doctor. Yet patients affected by this scrutiny may wait two or three days to get orders filled or see a doctor. This particularly true in rural communities where doctors might need to travel long distances to see patients or reach their FAX machines (**32**).

FALLACY: FORCING THE DICHOTOMY

Not everything is a "for it or against it" proposition. There are ranges of opinion along a scale on many social problems. When you force a yes or no response toan issue with a variety of possible choices, you may be committing this fallacy.

The mechanism of this fallacy is omitting additional unrecognized options or arguing that two things are mutually exclusive when they're not.

For example, consider the phrase, "You're either part of the solution or part of the problem." It's a popular phrase, but it denies the possibility of being a neutral observer or undecided on an approach to solution.

This paraphrased argument also forces the dichotomy:

> So, there's a police brutality charge against an Inglewood police-man, and an Inglewood policeman tries to enforce the law against some kid who is resisting arrest, and he gets a fund raiser, while the officer gets a suspension. Representative Maxine Waters criticized the officers while seeking $10,000 in fundraising for the so-called victim. On the same day, 300 protesters staged a march to protest gang violence. Days later, in the same city, many FBI, police, and sheriffs hunted for the murderer of a child, a known sexual predator. Now, ask yourself, you who worry so much about the rights of a lone offender, which is the real threat to your peace? Gang violence and sexual predators, or a few overzealous, maybe even racist cops? Make a choice tonight after your prayers for your children.

First, there's a heck of *a hidden presumption* in the notion that the beaten kid is either a gang member or a sexual predator who deserves such treatment. The press reported that he was a mentally disabled teen who may not have understood what was going on and froze. The suspended officer said that the suspect had reached back to grabfor his privates ... while the officer was banging the boy's head on the hood of the car.

Second and more germane to the point, the writer provides us with **an unnecessary choice:** Choose either gangs and sexual predators as real social problems, or police brutality. Why do we have to choose? We can seek balanced solutions for all three issues. The further implication here, if we draw the argument out to its farthest logical extent, is that we have to allow police brutality for our streets to be safe. Isn't it possible for a good cop to fight crime effectively?

Another version of this fallacy is **the complex question**, when somebody tries to force you to a yes or no answer on a question that has a hidden presumption in it. For instance, take the question, "Have you stopped beating your wife? Yes or no!" The hidden presumption is that you beat your wife to begin with, also perhaps that you're married. These are three separate questions, parading as one. Answer with a direct statement: "I never beat my wife." Or, perhaps, "I've never married and have no wife."

7) ARGUING FROM AUTHORITY

We've saved this for last, because it's the easiest to manage. ***The key mental action*** is simply: It's so because the best and the brightest in a specific area of expertise say, as a matter of their own authority, that it's so. Their analysis of the evidence at hand is sufficiently superior to ours to be a cause acceptance of their conclusions.

This is an age of great specialization. It's this way, because we've experienced an enormous information explosion. It's impossible for everyone to be an authority on everything. (I myself have a separate doctor for each part of my body... and, boy, are they confused!)

A typical pattern for this kind of argument would take an authority's opinion, justify his authority by mentioning his credentials, then state his conclusion as the claim. The quoted opinion becomes the grounds. The warrant is that authority has sufficient expertise to be trusted for his conclusion.

Different authorities in the same field may conclude differently. ***Arguments from authority should be submitted to the common tests we use on source-based proof***: sufficiently specific expertise in the field, public recognitions of his authority, a lack of bias, first-hand observation, etc.

The key language would typically include phrases like: "in the words of," "as was established by," "according to," and other indications of authorship, along with source qualifications. You may also find "authorities conclude," "studies suggest," or "the consensus among experts is."

Students, when asked to identify the pattern of reason in warrants, sometimes answer "authority" simply because there's a source. Yet these phrases do not guarantee this pattern of reason, since they are also the words we use to document all evidence. By that reasoning, anything that comes from a source would be reasoning by authority. It's almost as tempting as trying to say that all warrants are implied to avoid grappling with the logic of it. You should ***be able to identify the pattern of reason used by the authority***, not just cite him.

FALLACY: APPEAL TO AUTHORITY

The fallacy associated with argument from authority is "appeal to authority." It's an odd label, as we know it's okay, in fact necessary, to mention authorities. It should really be called **appeal to fame**, since it consists of using celebrity rather than expertise to persuade.

The key mental action to remember is this: Not everyone famous is an expert. We hear from celebrities all the time in sales and politics. In sales, there's a parade of recognizable faces in commercials, none of which have any particular expertise in the issue at hand.

At the beginning of his term as governor, which he assumed after previously holding no political office whatsoever, Arnold Schwarzenegger made headlines asking for a part-time state legislature, because they make "strange bills" when they have too much time on their hands. It's not clear what an operational definition of "strange bills" would be, but, as a first-time office holder, he was too inexperienced to challenge the state Constitution. At the peak of his popularity, he also argued that foreign born citizens should have the right to be the president.

Any odds on that one, folks?

IN SUM

These are "**the magnificent seven**" of reasoning. You may not understand everything yet about **warrants**, which explain the connection between grounds and claims, but you can begin to examine your reasons for why you believe something to be true and spot simple errors. That's a good start.

More specifically, remember that there are **certain mental actions and word clues** for recognizing the patterns of reason in everyday text, and they generally can be found in the language of the grounds itself:

For **analogy**, identify the two things compared and look for words and phrases that include these words: "like," "as," "is similar," "are alike," "resembles," "compared to," "by contrast," "precedent," and "model."

For ***generalization***, look for many examples, sometimes in a bulleted list, and/or statistics. The language includes: "it is generally so," "usually so," "normally so," "customary," even "universally so."

For ***definition***, you may read or hear: "given that," "since we know that," "this case is typical of most," or simply "by definition this is so."

The language of ***sign*** may be quite literal: "is a sign of," "signifies," "indicates," "is an omen of," "a portent," "a symptom" or "a clue."

Causation language may also be quite literal and usually involves active verbs like: "causes," "leads to," "produces," "activates," "provokes," "generates," "brings about," or "results in."

Dilemma language would mostly be: "mutually exclusive," "either/or," "a choice between," as opposed to "a choice among," "it's a question of A or B," or "it's a dilemma."

Authority language is often: "in the opinion of experts," "as concluded by," "as established by," and "according to," along with citations of the particular qualifications of the authority involved. It's possible that you yourself may be an authority on a topic, but you must qualify yourself somewhere in the speech to gain that advantage.

VOCABULARY

Causal Link (not "casual" link)

Classification

Complex Question

Costs vs. Gains Analysis

Multiple Causation

Mutually Exclusive

Reason vs. Fallacy:

    Arguing from Authority vs. Appeal to Fame

    Arguing from Cause to Effect vs. Correlation/Causation

        False Cause

Oversimplification

Slippery Slope

Arguing from Definition vs. Sweeping Generalization

Arguing from Dilemma vs. Forcing the Dichotomy

Arguing from Generalization vs. Hasty Generalization

Arguing from Parallel Reasoning vs. False Analogy

Arguing from Sign vs. False Sign and Superstition

REFERENCES

1) Toulmin, S. (1964). The Uses of Argument. New York: Cambridge University Press.
Adapted from Nancy Woods' Perspectives on Argument.amath.colorado.edu/carnegie/humn/PDFdocs/
Toulmin.pdf.
http://changingminds.org/disciplines/argument/making_argument/ toulmin.htm.
http://www2.winthrop.edu/wcenter/handoutsandlinks/toulmin.htm.
http://www-rohan.sdsu.edu/~digger/305/toulmin_model.htm.
http://owlet.letu.edu/contenthtml/research/toulmin.html.

2) "Global warming pushes 2010 temperatures to record highs," The Guardian, July 28, 2010. http://www.
guardian.co.uk/environment/2010/jul/28/global-temperatures-2010-record

3) "Global Warming," Union of Concerned Scientists website, October 20, 2005. http://www.ucsusa.org/
global_warming/science_and_impacts/global_warming_contrarians/global-warming-skeptic.html

4) Ehninger, D.E. Influence, Belief and Argument. Glenview, 1974.
Golden, J.L., B., G.F., Coleman, W.E. The Rhetoric of Western Thought. Dubuque, IA: Kendall-Hunt (2001).
Toulmin, S., Rieke, R., Janik, A. An Introduction to Reasoning. New York: MacMillan.

5) The Los AngelesTimes, June 6, 2005.

6) "Recycled," Mother Jones, September/October, 2010.

7) "A Fat Cat Strikes Back," Newsweek, August 23 & 30, p. 10.

8) Right-Wing Media Rush To Defend Palin's Use Of "Blood Libel," Media Matters, January 12, 2011.
http://mediamatters.org/research/201101130013

9) There are several kinds of circles used to diagram reason. In somewhat progressive order, there are
Euler's circles, Venn diagrams, and Pierce's extension. For our purposes it's sufficient that you think of
each circle a class, or a set. This article is a good summary of each type of circular diagrams. "Stanford
Encyclopedia of Philosophy" at http://plato.stanford.edu/entries/diagrams/

10) "Hefty Paychecks for Vernon Officials Rival Those in Bell," Los Angeles Times, August 20, 2010.

11) "New Study Defends Mammograms," Los Angeles Times, February 1, 2002.

12) "Welcome to Smallville," New York Times Magazine, October 3, 2010.

13) http://thinkprogress.org/2006/09/27/iraqis-poll/

14) http://kansasdefenders.blogspot.com/2009/07/hasty-generalization-warrants-new-trial.html

15) http://www.lectlaw.com/def2/m053.htm
http://legal-dictionary.thefreedictionary.com/second+degree+murder
http://legal-dictionary.thefreedictionary.com/manslaughter

16) Randall, Mike. GROUND HOGS DO NOT AGREE! On 6 More Weeks Of Winter? WKBW-TV. February 2, 2009.

17) "Can't stop the greed," Los Angeles Times, August 22, 2010.

18) "Paw print leaves ugly, legal scar," Los Angeles Times, August 17, 2010.

19) "Blast Kills 7 in Tense China Region," Los Angeles Times, August 20, 2010.

20) "Paintball Assault Leaves Skater Critical," The Daily Pilot, April 19, 2002.
"Newport Paint-Ball Victim Declared Dead," Los Angeles Times, April 8, 2002.
"Sometimes Hasty Writing Requires Corrections," Daily Pilot, August 19, 2002.

21) "Feeding Frenzy," Los Angeles Times, September 6, 2005.

22) "Are we there yet?" The Economist, September 18-24, 2010.

23) "China leaps over Japan on GDP list," Los Angeles Times, August 17, 2010.

24) "Genetically altered corn helps protect cousin," Los Angeles Times, October 8, 2010.

25) "Breast Cancer Survivors on a Crusade," Los Angeles Times, March 18, 2002.

26) "Roadblock to Rebuilding," Los Angeles Times, September 4, 2005.

27) "Domino Effect Feared from Closure of Emergency Rooms," Los Angeles Times, August 24, 2004.

28) "Hospital Error Cited in Man's Death," Los Angeles Times, August 28, 2002.

29) http://soonerblue2.wordpress.com/2010/10/25/crazy-tea-party-quotes/

30) http://soonerblue2.wordpress.com/2010/10/25/crazy-tea-party-quotes/

31) "Georgia Woman Charged With Murder in Deaths of Two Sons, "New York Times, August 24, 2002.

32) "A Battle Against Prescription Drugs Causes Pain, " The New York Times, October 3, 2010.

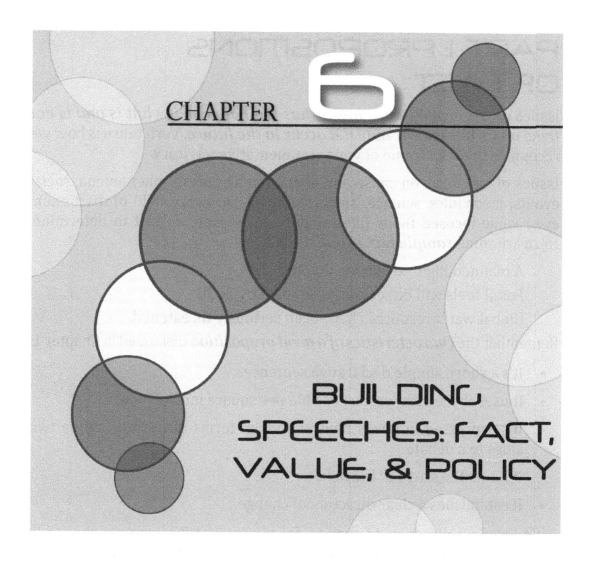

CHAPTER **6**

BUILDING SPEECHES: FACT, VALUE, & POLICY

"FROM NOW ON IT IS ONLY THROUGH CONSCIOUS CHOICE
AND DELIBERATE POLICY THAT HUMANITY WILL SURVIVE."

– POPE PAUL II –

The process of building complete speeches is discussed in this chapter. We will describe and exemplify each type of speech, including the stock issues relevant to each, and build fully integrated Toulmin arguments related to those issues. These speeches will defend the basic types of propositions, those of fact, of value, and of policy.

PART 1: PROPOSITIONS OF FACT

Issues of fact include **what has or has not happened; what is and is not true; and what may or may not occur in the future**. Verb tense is how we recognize the time frame of your argumentative territory.

Issues of fact focus on cause and effect among natural phenomena, social events, mechanics, science, and technology. Yet every field of discussion, even value-focused fields like religion, have issues of fact to determine. Here are some **sample fact propositions**:

> A manned flight to Mars is feasible.
>
> Fossil fuels will be seriously depleted by 2030.
>
> Global water resources have been seriously threatened.

Remember the **characteristics of a good proposition** discussed in Chapter 1:

- It's a short, simple declarative sentence.
- It uses the fewest words possible per square inch of idea.
- It's expressed in terms neutral enough terms that there can be two sides to a debate.
- It limits the scope of the debate.
- It establishes a clear direction of change.

Let's focus on direction of change, for a minute. What can we change in a proposition of fact speech? **Isn't a fact just a fact?** Why do we bother to argue facts at all? Yet facts aren't facts until we've agreed them to be so. We don't say, "Aha, this carpet is brown, so prove me wrong." **We only argue when there's confusion, controversy, or conflict about facts.** We have new knowledge that challenges old presumptions; questions of guilt, innocence, or liability in legal matters; or unanswered questions about the causes of significant phenomena that impact us.

When these factors are present, we have **rhetorical demand**, a reason to speak. We begin a search for the best possible approximation of what's factual, until the next challenge to our presumption comes along. We simply move forward with the advance of knowledge.

Here are other suggestions to help you firm up your fact propositions.

- Make a positive statement. Rather than saying what isn't so, say what is so.

- Define unclear words. That's especially important if you're talking about scientific, medical, or technical subjects with new specialized jargon.

- Don't artificially elevate your normal way of talking. Sometimes people think that they have to use a lot of big and unfamiliar words to sound educated. It's just the opposite with a speech. You're writing for the ear, not the eye. Even Aristotle said that we should speak in "the language that is common to the day."

- Avoid complex sentence propositions. It tends to increase and confuse the affirmative burden of proof. Often when students attempt a proposition like this, they really need two speeches, especially when they only have a brief time limit."

- Don't color the language with colorful adjectives and exaggerations.

A few of you may have seen old "Dragnet" episodes in re-run, one of the first great police detective shows. If so, you may remember Joe Friday. Whenever anybody tried to get emotional during an investigative interview, Joe would say, "Just the facts, ma'am, just the facts." Well, this is your Joe Friday speech. Stick to the relevant facts.

For those of you who have had a public speaking class and have done informative speeches, **this is not an informative speech; it's an argumentative one.** We don't use facts merely for the sake of their interest or amusement. The purpose of an argumentative speech is not primarily to inform. It's to use information to prove one side of a controversy, specifically to challenge a presently held presumption about what is true. If you find information too nifty to pass up, try to use it in an introduction or a conclusion, but don't build arguments that are not directly germane to these stock issues.

STOCK ISSUES OF FACT

How do we determine how many arguments to make and in what order? That's determined by the **stock issues, the basic required questions,** *relevant to each type of proposition.* There are also some unique, subject-specific issues that may come up as a matter of your topic choice. That is, any time we discuss capital punishment, we know we'll be talking about the issue of deterrence, whether it actually stops crime, but we fit that kind of question into the basic framework of these stock issues.

Stock issues are sometimes called *"inventional systems,"* because they help us to invent arguments. They do so by asking specific questions that have to be answered to make a complete prima facie case. In other words, they help us determine what our burden of proof is. There are *two stock issues of fact* sometimes broken down into a couple of sub-issues for the sake of clarity:

I: *What significant event* is happening, has happened, or will happen? In response, we need to prove two things.

A)   The phenomenon exists, has existed, or will exist.

B)   It has significant impact.

II: *What is the cause* of the phenomenon?

Using cause to effect reasoning is the key feature of this kind of proposition. We prove that something is the result of a natural phenomenon, or a result of human behavior, perhaps an aspect of present social systems, or sometimes how the present threshold of the law is insufficient to prevent the significant event.

These two issues are often reduced to the handy terms *"significance" and "inherency,"* another word for cause, though inherency is a term most directly relevant to issues of policy, which we'll explain below.

These stock issues *may be re-ordered*, depending on the particular topic and the way the evidence flows from point to point (**1**).

For instance, in some cases, just describing the way in which the present system or phenomenon operates may show it to be special, inefficient, or potentially damaging on the face of it. In that case, we may discuss cause first then move to the effects of the present system. This can create a kind of *"dramaturgic structure."* That is, we treat the speech like a play in which we build up to the most dramatic effects. Yet discussions of cause may be technical, involving explanations of political, scientific, or natural systems.

We may find it advantageous to capture the audience's attention with the dramatic effects of the problem or phenomenon, motivating them to have patience with the following explanation of cause.

Notice that the first issue is broken down into two sub-issues in this outline. That's because it's often taken for granted that a phenomenon exists. Novice speakers may go right to the significant effects of something and leave the existence of something as a ***hidden presumption***. Yet your burden of proof is to show that Hurricane Katrina occurred, even though we generally know it, before you tell us its environmental effects. This might seem obvious, even unnecessary. We can infer the presence of something through its effect. For instance, initially, we were only able to infer the existence of acid rain as a cause by reasoning back from the presence of its corrosive effects. Nobody even knew what to call it. We just saw that a significant phenomenon was happening and looked for a cause. Practically, though, it's best to start with a separate argument or a warrant within one that a phenomenon exists.

The key language used in propositions of fact are "is," "was," "will be," "did or will occur," "was or is responsible for," etc.

SAMPLE FACT ARGUMENTS

We discussed the process of ***building arguments from the "grounds" up***. We start with a hypothetical proposition, what we expect to be true then we adjust language to what the research actually says as we go. Go back to Chapter 1 and look at the BP oil spill argument, the first Toulmin argument shown and an example of a fact argument.

Let's say we want to argue—based on discouraging impressions of the Middle-East conflict and terrorism around the world—that ***"War is a more frequent common fatal event since WWII."*** Obviously, our burden of proof is going to require numbers to justify the term "more."

We research and we find three historical websites that can help determine if this is so. One is an anti-war website, subject to a charge of bias, but they collectively present raw data verifiable by government statistics. According to these sources the wars with the biggest casualties during the so-called "cold war" years were (**2**):

The Chinese Civil War (1946–49)	1.2 million dead
The Partition of India/Pakistan (1947)	1 million dead
The Korean War (1950–53)	4 million
Mao's "Great Leap Forward" (1958–61)	38 million
Mao's "Cultural Revolution" (1966–69)	11 million
Ethiopian Civil War (1974–91)	1 million
Mingitsu, Ethiopia (1975–78)	1.5 million
Khmer Rouge, Cambodia (1975–79)	1.7 million
Soviet Invasion of Afghanistan (1979–88)	1.3 million
Iraq/Iran War (1980–88)	1 million
Sudanese Civil War (1983–2002)	2 million

That's 64 million war casualties, more than the 55 million lost in WWII, compared to WWI which had 16 million deaths, and that's just selecting wars with roughly a million deaths. You'll learn quickly that you simply can't use all the research available on a given topic. You have to find a *criterion for grounds selection*. It's hard to deny that a million deaths constitutes a big conflict, but we can adjust how we define "war."

If we include wars of slightly less than a million deaths, Rwanda's 1994 Civil War for 900,000 deaths and Congo's Civil War from 1991–97 for 800,000, we're close to *66 million deaths* since WWII.

When you throw in other wars yielding more than *a half million deaths*— the Nigeria-Biafra Civil War, the Pakistani-Bangladesh Civil War, the Angolan Civil War, etc.—you can easily *add another five million*, and that won't include another three dozen wars adding from two to three hundred thousand deaths each between WWII and the early nineties. So far, there's pretty sound numerical support for our thesis, as we approach *72 million deaths.*

In the twenty-first century, add two million from a second Congo war, about a million deaths in Iraq, although estimates are continually disputed, a few thousand more from Afghanistan and terrorist incidents, and we can safely say that we're approaching *75 million deaths from war since WWII*. If we count all the wars mentioned and average them across the 65 years since the end of WWII, we can see that we get a war every three to four years, justifying the "more frequent" aspect of our proposition. **WWI and WWII combined had a total of 71 million deaths.** As impressive as the total deaths of the two world wars are, we've been even more deadly with each other since. Thus, we can build an argument based on these statistics for war being an increasingly frequent and fatal phenomenon.

As an argument for cause, we could name several reasons for this increase: the fatal potential of increasingly effective weapons, the challenges of tribalism and religious differences, and the fact that defenseless civilian populations are targeted more commonly, especially by terrorists. **Voila. You have the basis for a proposition of fact speech**, one argument showing significant increases in frequency and fatality, the second showing causes for more war, the stock issues necessary for a prima facie case.

At this point, a feeling human being may want to solve this problem. **You may not offer solution**. It may seem callous, but this cannot be done in a fact speech. You shouldn't even make any editorial comments about how awful the situation is, which students are tempted to do in conclusions on this assignment. We can make **no value-laden comments.** Don't comment that it's immoral or wrong. Let the audience have its own emotional reaction. Your job is to do an objective job of establishing a fact. Yes, you see it all the time on the news, but we're going to try to do better than that.

In Chapter 1, we discussed presumption. It is your role as an advocate to **challenge a presumption**. In the war example, we would simply be pointing out a fact about which people may be unaware, and that's fine. Yet the highest call of a speaker is to respond to a current controversy, **a subject with rhetorical demand**. We know that driving while using a cell phone is dangerous. We know that obesity is unhealthful. It's not an academic crime to reestablish these fact propositions, especially if there's brand new research that increases our awareness or modifies our previous conclusions. However, let's try to find something that is **a controversy of the moment**.

We could have determined, for instance, whether the Obama healthcare plan would really have hurt small businessmen, but the House has repealed the law, and we don't know enough about the Republican alternative to argue it's effects (**3**). There is some comment in the news that there is less an architecture of replacement than a simple repeal. A current question on everyone's mind, though, is whether or not the economy is or will be improving. Let's work with that:

Proposition: The economy is showing signs that it will slowly improve.

Claim 1: Currently the economy is moving slowly.

Warrant 1: Among positive indicators are that unemployment is improving slightly, improvement in the trade deficit, the housing market, increased consumer spending, and stable inflation.

Grounds 1A: Republican Mayor of New York and newsman Michael Bloomberg's website of August 8, 2010, invited several economic experts to speculate on the future of the economy. Treasury Secretary Robert Rubin, who served under President Clinton, said that the United States "is going to have a slow and bumpy growth." According to Treasury Secretary Paul O'Neill, who served under President Bush, "We are moving forward at a pretty gradual pace. But I don't think things are terrible (**4**)."

(**Note**: This is some of that conclusionary evidence that we warned about, and you cannot build a fact speech based primarily on evidence of opinion. However, it may be clarifying to use some such testimony to introduce or conclude an argument.)

Grounds 1B: "U.S. companies in July hired fewer workers than forecast, and economists in a Bloomberg News Survey project **unemployment will be slow to recede after reaching a 26-year high** of 10.1 percent in October 2009." Further, "Private payrolls that exclude government agencies rose by 71,000 in July after a June gain of 31,000 that was smaller than previously reported, according to Labor Department figures released in Washington August 6. Overall employment fell by 131,000, reflecting the dismissal of temporary census workers, and the jobless rate held at 9.5 percent (**5**)."

Grounds 1C: According to the U.S. Bureau of Labor Statistics website on January 7, 2011, "The unemployment rate fell by 0.4 percentage point to 9.4 percent in December, and nonfarm payroll employment increased by 103,000, the U.S. Bureau of Labor Statistics reported today. Employment rose in leisure and hospitality and in health care (**6**)."

Grounds 1D: Chief economist for Wells Fargo, Mark Vitner, who last year likened the economy to "a nosedive off a cliff," notes positive economic indicators in *The Daily Press* of January 21, 2011, "The good news is that *exports are stronger* than they have been in some time... Housing starts increased about 5 percent in 2010 and are projected to jump 15 percent in 2011, due mostly to apartments and senior housing... There's some *good news for commercial real estate*. Rents are up for apartments, and hotel occupancy and room rates have improved. *We don't see another recession on the horizon* (7)."

Grounds 1E: According to the Federal Reserve, as reported by Reuter's News Service on June 9, 2010, is improving in consumer spending and inflation. "Sales of spring and summer apparel were strong in Boston, New York, Philadelphia, St. Louis, Kansas City and Dallas districts. In the Boston district, retailers noted 'some potholes in the recovery path' but said *sales were generally positive*. Auto and parts production increased in the Cleveland, Richmond, and Chicago districts. Crop planting was generally ahead of the seasonal norm. On the *inflation* front, the Fed said wage pressures were limited... Prices of final goods and services were largely unchanged (8)."

(*Note:* All the signs promised in the warrant are delivered in the same order in the evidence, as the highlighted words demonstrate. This way, the links from ground to warrant are clear, and the warrant functions as a kind of preview for the audience of that for which they should look.)

Claim 2: There are helpful trends pushing the economy, even though there are inhibitions to more rapid growth.

Warrant 2A: Helpful trends include improved consumerism, the fact that slowly improving unemployment rates mean less inflation and that small businesses are gaining optimism, especially in light of the congressional extension of tax breaks.

Grounds 2A: According to a December 18, 2010, edition of *The Wall Street Journal*, growth of the GDP may be as high as 3.7% to 3.8%. They also project an unemployment rate of 8.6%, a drop of .8%. Here are some of the factors cited: "*Shopping is back.* Based on last week's Census Bureau release, November retail sales ran 7.7% higher than the same month a year ago, or about to 6.3% in real—that is, inflation-adjusted—terms.... **Slack labor markets reflected in *high rates of unemployment should mean tame price inflation.*** Slack labor markets mean wage hikes won't run much faster than productivity gains, curbing the rise in unit-labor costs.

The benefit through 2011 is that short-term interest rates will stay low.... High unemployment is precisely what should make it easy to keep short-term interest rates low... Probably because of the pickup in consumption, **the optimism index** of the National Federation of Independent Business continues to climb. Instead of applying drag to the economy, as it did in 2010, the huge small-business sector will apply a small boost—a swing that should make a difference **(9)**." Also cited was **the extension of tax cuts**, which could stimulate spending and, in turn, more employment.

Warrant 2B: Part of the reason that consumer spending is up, in spite of unemployment, is that people are working more hours. This could also help with unemployment, which may help boost the GDP.

Grounds 2B: According to *Fortune* of October 30, 2010, "The average workweek for all employees ... was 34.3 hours in November, a modest uptick from the 33.9 hours worked during the same time last year. An increase in worker hours is significant, since many employers dramatically cut hours during the recession that started in December 2007 and ended in June 2009. They'll usually use their existing workers for the maximum hours they can work before hiring new people. So a rise in the average workweek might suggest that sustained job growth is on the horizon **(10)**."

Warrant 2C: Having more money in the system helps stimulate activity in the private sector.

Grounds 2C-1: According to a November 4, 2010, article from the *RIS Media* website, "The Federal Reserve unveiled a controversial new plan to spur the faltering U.S. economy by pumping $600 billion into the financial system. The Fed's much-anticipated but unconventional strategy is aimed at driving down long-term interest rates in the hopes of spurring more home refinancing and other borrowing and spending by consumers and business **(11)**."

Grounds 2C-2: The previously cited *Forbes* article is hopeful about money flow into the economy, "Real money supply—the amount of money in circulation measured in traveler's checks, savings deposits, currency, money market accounts and the like—has increased, rising by 2% this year compared to the previous year. Nigel Gault, U.S. Chief Economist with HIS think tank, acknowledges that ... (this) indicates that activity in the private sector is picking up a bit. After all, the more transactions that happen, the more financing is needed and therefore the more money there is in circulation.

And real money supply last year was declining, so the fact that it has reversed is a positive sign (**12**)."

Warrant 2D: As a result of increased optimism and money supply corporations are beginning to spend money.

Grounds 2D -1: And, once more, from Nigel Gault, U.S. Chief Economist with HIS, "Just when it seemed like companies buying up computers, communications gear and the like would slow after seeing spikes during various periods throughout the year, business investment in capital equipment rebounded in November. Bookings climbed 2.6% after a 3.6% decline in October — a decline that was smaller than previously estimated, according to the US Commerce Department. If the trend continues into 2011, it could be a positive contributor to US growth (**13**)."

Grounds 2D-2: For a particular example, the farm industry is spending more money in ten Midwest and Plains states. According to the website of Michael Bloomberg, Republican New York Mayor and economic newsman, posted on January 20, 2011, "Profitable farmers have helped spur the economy in 10 Midwest and Plains states to 2007 levels, according to a new survey of bank CEOs released Thursday. 'From farm equipment to farmland to trucks, agricultural producers in the area are spending at a brisk pace,' said Creighton University economist Ernie Goss, who oversees the survey of rural bankers. The overall index for the Rural Mainstreet economic survey reached 59.3 percent in January, up from December's 55.4 and last January's 41.0. The index this month hit its highest level since June 2007. The index ranges between 0 and 100. A score above 50 suggests the economy will expand during the next six months (**14**)."

This sample proposition of fact speech was a good reminder to me of why we have to adjust our propositions and claims to what evidence actually says. I began with a much gloomier hypothesis of the economy but found moderately conservative business sources that had a cheerier point of view.

Notice the **Toulmin argument structure**. The first argument has but one warrant related to several pieces of evidence. The second is divided into several warrants, some with a couple of grounds apiece. Either type of argument is common. It's an organic process of building the argument from the grounds up, adapting structure to the specific facts. **Each of the basic types of evidence**—example, statistics, and testimony—were used in the grounds, and multiple sources were employed, making grounds stronger. Also, the speech demonstrates a lot of **reasoning by sign and by cause**, both within the warrants and between the two stock issues, the structure being basically one of cause and effect represented in two arguments.

There is no introduction or conclusion here, but they are customary. **Introductions** may consist of a description of the presumption that you're challenging, in this case, a gloomy financial forecast. **Conclusions** should not include persuasive appeals for change. That is the business of policy.

PART 2: PROPOSITION OF POLICY

There is good reason to move to propositions of value now. A critical thinking approach that examines the facts, then considers values, and takes both these issues into consideration for the construction of social policy makes sense. However, the stock issues of fact and policy overlap, so it also works to compare and contrast them here. Also, arguing values is a more subjective and challenging process with quite different stock issues.

Our most complex and important social discussions involve issues of policy. They include both questions of fact and value, as well as additional questions unique to the topic itself. Also, **they directly affect the daily conduct of your life**. Deliberation of policy impacts all of us, as it's a method practiced daily by lawyers, leaders, and legislative bodies at every level in America. You participate in making policy when you vote or support referendums. The very way that we function as a society and as a world is measured in terms of policymaking. What you can and cannot do in a car on the way to the market, or even in the privacy of our own home, are matters of public policy deliberation.

Policy speeches are **essentially problem and solution speeches**. It's easy to find problems. Being part of the solution is more difficult. **The main challenge is creativity with problem solving**, the essence of critical thinking.

If cause A—harm B, then solution C = −A

Or B harm—A cause = C solution

FIGURE 6-1.

Yet policy is also *an easy format*; it's very formulaic. The action of mind is an almost mathematical formula. If a problem has A cause, then a solution to the problem consists of eliminating "A" (Figure 6.1).

Thus, reasoning from cause is essential in policy, just as it was with fact. *Yet most don't reason to policy in that manner.* They see a problem and then suggest a solution that they've heard from respected authorities, or which reflects a subjective belief. In other words, they tend to come to policy from values and/or party loyalty more often than from careful analysis of cause. Unfortunately, in these partisan times, the cause is almost always said to be the other political party, but our problems are so much more complex than that.

The language of policy propositions almost always involves words like "should," "ought to," or "must" attached to an active verb, like "curtail," "increase," "improve," "implement," "modify," "eliminate," or "ban.

Sample policy propositions would include:

> We should increase tax breaks for the middle class.
>
> The Federal Government ought to increase matching funds to states for education.
>
> Californians must prevent forest damage from bark beetles.
>
> People over 65 should be more regularly tested for driving licenses.

The language of the proposition usually focuses on the solution, rather than the problem. *The solution is, in fact, the policy.* Yet we must justify change by establishing the existence of a significant problem.

STOCK ISSUES OF POLICY

There are four stock issues in policy (**15**):

1. *Is there significant harm from the problem?*

2. *What are the causes of the problem?*

3. *What workable solution could help with the problem?*

4. *Are there any side effects of the solution, either advantageous or disadvantageous?*

You'll notice that significant harm and inherency are essentially the same two stock issues as your fact speech. So you're somewhat familiar with the first half of this speech, though there are some slight differences.

Significant Harm: This issue often takes on more dramatic proportions than in discussions of fact. That's because ***harms are the motivating force for the policy change*** you seek. Ill-conceived policy in the present impacts people with whom we can identify. Telling their stories in the form of ***specific examples will build emotional appreciation for the issue.*** Pathos becomes a powerful persuasive force.

There are two terms to define for a fuller understanding, "harm" and "significant."

There are many ways that something can be harmful. The most dramatic would probably involve the ***death or physical damage*** of other human beings through violence, accident, or pestilence. People can also be ***psychologically damaged***. Consider, for instance, the mental effects of being raped, belittled over race or religion, or being made fearful of terrorists by ongoing violence.

There can also be ***environmental harms***: the disappearing ozone layer, over-fishing our waters to the point of species extinction, the polluting effects of industry, the obvious dangers of oil spills.

Economic harms can evolve from property damage, budget shortfalls, the Wall Street game of bulls and bears, and lately the loss of homes due to mortgage lending failures. Such harms can evolve from trade wars, the declining value of the dollar, rising interest rates, or inflation.

Harms to **human rights** are a pervasive and constant issue, such as controversies over racial profiling or ageism in hiring and firing practices. In sum, there are many ways in which we can be harmed.

The second term that needs definition is "significant." Harms can exist but be insignificant to a degree that there's no rhetorical demand. How do you determine whether damage is significant enough to change policy over it? The easiest and most obvious way is to **measure by quantity**. How many people were killed or made ill? How many illegal immigrants died of exposure? How much money was lost? We generally use figures and statistics to **"quantify"** an impact, in dollars or deaths. Significant harm arguments should not be generalities, but **be specific in impact.**

Some things just aren't measurable in terms of numbers. That fewer people may be affected by a problem does not mean that it isn't significant. Even in cases where harm is limited to a portion of the population, it may be **qualitatively damaging**. Should we not feel sympathy and offer medical support to people who have sickle cell anemia, merely because they're all black? We would make an appeal for them based on some basic sense of what is humane to all persons. Most Americans did not consider **AIDS** a big problem at first. The stereotype was that it was just a few gay men practicing unsafe sex in bath houses. The National Institutes of Health barely had funding to study the disease. Attention was paid only once it began to affect the heterosexual public. By then, it was an epidemic that put all at risk. Had we looked at the effects of the disease, in and of itself, perhaps we could have minimized this epidemic.

I'm reminded of **a saying** written from the viewpoint of Germans during WWII: "When they took the Jews I did not care, because I was not a Jew; when they took the gays I did not care, because I was not gay; when they took the intellectuals I did not care, because I was not an intellectual; when they came for me, I looked around for help...but there was nobody left to help me."

It's perfectly reasonable and typical for an audience to ask, **how does this affect those of us not directly impacted?** How does the impact of the initial harm to others ripple out to damage us collectively? So, a wise speaker will **show specific ways in which the audience is injured** by problems, though perhaps not obviously so. Take, for instance, motorcycle helmet laws. On the surface of things, you might think, "Well, it's their head, and it doesn't affect me if they crack their cranium on the concrete." Yet a closer look at the medical expense of accidents among those without helmets might change your mind. You might come to believe that we pay for the freedom of others with increased insurance costs. Since our rights can also be violated in harmful ways, we argue that even damage to the rights of a few is unacceptable as a principle.

Whether you are arguing quantitative or qualitative harms, **significant harm arguments should be dramatic** enough to motivate an audience to consider the present system's presumption. Storytelling is a critical aspect of persuasion, since we are by nature a storytelling species. So, the use of specific examples or personal testimony in a narrative voice can be very persuasive (**16**).

Yet it's also important not to pass over **the line between pathos to bathos**, a melodramatic use of pathos, or what we've described as the fallacy of **appeal to pity and fear**. A story can be dramatic, but the speaker has to decide whether it's so repellent that an audience may be alienated or tune out. They may insulate their feelings from your persuasion if they find the information or images too much to take. Students doing anti-abortion speeches have sometimes dwelled upon the details of surgery to the point that even those who agreed with them detached from the presentational effects. Graphic photographs from this and other subjects have caused some students to look away, register audible disgust, or even leave the room.

In April of 2004, four American civilians working in Iraq to rebuild the infrastructure were not only killed but burned and mutilated in Fallouja. Their hacked torsos were hung from a bridge while the wild crowd responsible danced beneath the corpses in celebration. Photos of that event inflamed the world, as did graphic footage of the slow beheadings of westerners like Jack Hensley and his colleagues by terrorists. The gruesome video is still online today for those with sufficiently ghoulish interest. Would oral description of this story be an appropriate use of pathos? Probably, but sensitivity to gory detail is a matter of reading natural audience reaction. On one hand, audience reaction to graphic detail varies from group to group. On the other, it may be wise to error on the side of caution and good taste.

Here is an example of a significant harm argument on bullying:

Claim: Bullying among the young is a significant problem.

Warrant 1: There have been recent dramatic incidents of young suicides in response to bullying from other youth, including cyberbullying.

Grounds 1A: According to ABC-TV News on September 30, 2010, a Rutgers student committed suicide after jumping from the George Washington Bridge after gay sexual acts were broadcast over the Internet by troommates. 18 years old, Tyler Clement became the victim of his roommate Dharun Ravi, a freshman at Rutgers, who has been accused of invasion of privacy by the police. He and fellow freshman Molly Wei left a spy camera in the room of Clementi. The two face five years in prison each. Both are 18 years of age. Clementi was a virtuoso violinist who had the talent to "blow away the public" with his music **(17)**.

Grounds 1B: The Boston Globe of January 24, 2010, reported a similar incident with Phoebe Prince, a high school transfer who made the mistake of briefly dating a popular football player. For this, she became the target of nine girls. "Kids can be mean, but the Mean Girls took it to another level, according to students and parents. They followed Phoebe around, calling her a slut. When they wanted to be more specific, they called her an Irish slut. The name-calling, the stalking, the intimidation was relentless. Ten days ago, Phoebe was walking home from school when one of the Mean Girls drove by in a car. An insult and an energy drink can came flying out the car window in Phoebe's direction. Phoebe kept walking, past the abuse, past the can, past the white picket fence, into her house. Then she walked into a closet and hanged herself. Her 12-year-old sister found her **(18)**.

Grounds 1C: The October 3, 2010 *New York Times* reported, "Seth Walsh, 13, also hung himself in Tehachapi, California, after cyberbullying. In 2008, Jessica Logan, 18, hung herself after a boyfriend circulated nude pictures of her that she had 'sexted' to him." The article continues, "A survey of over 5000 college students, staff, and faculty with alternative sexual orientation indicates that one in four have reported some kind of harassment. Another at Iowa State University with a smaller sample of 350 revealed that nearly half had been cyberbullied within a month of the survey. More than a quarter had suicidal thoughts **(19)**."

Warrant 2: It's harsh enough when youth bully youth, but there have also been incidents of adults joining in.

Grounds 2A: An Arkansas school board member was forced to resign and recant anti-gay comments that seemed to support the bullying incidents, reported CNN News on October 2, 2010. "McCance wrote on his personal Facebook page that he wanted gay people to commit suicide, according to The Advocate, a newspaper focusing on gay news. McCance used the terms "queer" and "fag" repeatedly, promised to disown his own children if they are gay and stated that he enjoys "the fact that [gay people] give each other AIDS and die (**20**)."

Grounds 2B: The previously cited *New York Times* article mentions, "An assistant attorney general in Michigan repeatedly attacked an openly gay student body president, Chris Armstrong, calling him a "radical homosexual activist." He posted a doctored photograph of the student with a rainbow flag and a swastika.

Notice that this argument uses examples to excite empathy for those at the effect of being bullied, and it quantifies to some degree the frequency of this problem with a survey. It also begins to suggest where we should place the blame, bringing up the issue of inherency.

INHERENCY/CAUSE

This is the most crucial yet neglected issue of policy discussion. People tend to argue from problem to solution based on their belief system rather than actual understanding of causation. Yet it's absurd to propose a solution without knowing how the problem comes about.

Loosely, inherency is *an analysis of what causes the significant harm.* We used this limited sense of inherency in the fact speeches, and the fundamental type of reason here is the same, though we'll be presenting a little more sophisticated version of the concept.

What does "inherency" mean? A problem is inherent when it is so woven into the present system that you can't manage positive change without removing that aspect of the system.

There are three dimensions of inherency: trend, structure, and attitude.

The minimum level of inherency is to ***discover a trend.*** You see signs of an emerging problem getting worse over time. When you find an increasing series of negative effects that you can quantify with statistical proof, you would normally reason that there is some cause for the trend to exist. If it is persistent and it's growing, then it's reasonable to assume that it's not going to go away on its own.

When we first saw ***acid rain***, like AIDS, we had no idea what it was. Yet, also like AIDS, there were definite signs that something was happening. Lakes in which bass had thrived for years were suddenly barren. Their ph level was equivalent to lemon juice or battery acid. Roads that were normally repaved every five to seven years required service every three to four. Even faces on national monuments like the Lincoln Memorial had begun to erode from what we now know as acid fog. With research, we discovered that acid rain is caused by a combination of sulfur and nitrogen in the atmosphere, especially when factories, power plants, and other "smoke stack" facilities burn coal or oil (**21**).

When we find a trend suggesting a new problem and the cause is unknown, our ***solution will usually be a research and development proposal***, i.e., research funds to systematically discover cause. Consider trend as distinct from general significance under harm. In harm, we may use figures and statistics to show that something is generally "big," but trend must involve showing a baseline number from which a present trend increases.

Structural inherency has to do with human process, system, and habit, a technological or natural process, and other aspects of the status quo. Among the physical causes of acid rain were some very tall smokestacks that were instituted by manufacturers, ironically, to help the local pollution. Yet they were so tall that they belched toxic materials into the cloud layer, contributing to acid rain. Other complex factors were influential.

Structural inherency may be a legal barrier, the presence or the absence of a law that blocks a solution. Inherency analysis should always ***determine the present threshold of the law.*** What is the present legal situation? What does the law do or not do that it shouldn't or should? Then we either eliminate bad laws or institute more helpful ones in our solution. In the case of acid rain, the 1975 Clean Air Act and its 1990 amendment forced certain industrial changes to curb acid rain (**22**).

There may be **an institutional barrier**, an agency or organization that inhibits solution. For instance, the NRA, the National Rifle Association, could be considered a barrier to gun laws. You could certainly argue that FEMA's lack of organization contributed directly to the extent of the damage and suffering from Hurricane Katrina. The lack of safety regulation by BP directly contributed to the Gulf oil spill in 2010. Also, there may be a need for such an agency or organization to regulate the problem. The existence of an unregulated nuclear energy industry would naturally call to the creation of the Atomic Energy Commission, just as pollution would demand the creation of the Environmental Protection Agency.

Here's an example of structural inherency. "Beaches from San Diego to the Bay Area are being tested less often and in fewer locations; some are going untested for months at a time. Statewide the number of tests for bacteria has dropped by nearly half since 2005." Baby Beach in Dana Point traps contaminated runoff and is often used by adults with kids, due to its sheltered calm, but no testing was conducted for five months. Cabrillo Beach has 80% less tests. Even wealthy Santa Monica had reduced tests by 65%. San Onofre had the worst test reductions at 94.1%. In Long Beach, home to the most polluted water in the state due to the presence of ships in the harbor, 40% of beaches aren't tested at all. This is due to state budget cuts **(23)**. So, the structural inherency is that state budget cuts have led to seriously reduced water testing, making beaches less safe.

This brings us to **attitudinal inherency**. Sometimes there are structural solutions in place to solve social problems, yet the attitude of the people against the system is so strong that it inhibits the system from functioning.

Consider the 1930s prohibition era. Not only did people respond by drinking all they wanted, there were people ready to provide illegal liquor, and gangsters were given a profit motive. Resistance to unpopular laws runs deep among American traditions.

Ever hear the phrase, "You can't legislate morality?" This point came home for me in dramatic fashion during high school. I was involved in Key Club, a youth service organization founded by Kiwanis, and I went to a convention. While traveling on a bus through the South in 1966, not long after **the Civil Rights Act** had passed, we visited the capital of Tennessee. When we entered the rotunda of the legislature, I saw that the raised metal lettering declaring "white" men's or women's bathrooms had been removed. Yet I was shocked to discover that the gaping rivet holes had been left and the marble left unpolished, so that the word "white" remained in stark relief. The letter of the law was enforced, but in a partial and sarcastic way, while the real attitude of the local people remained on the walls for all to see. That's attitudinal inherency.

We often hear some very heartfelt speeches about ***driving under the influence of alcohol and drugs.*** They usually end with the idea that we need "tougher laws against drunk driving." Is that really so? If you examine the present threshold of the law, you might be surprised to find that much more can happen to DUI offenders, even on a first offense, than normally does. In other words, the inherency is not systemic but attitudinal. It may be the propensity of courts to give warnings but to be lax about multiple offenses that keeps dangerous drivers on the street. Also, offenders evade enforcement, driving though they've been forbidden the privilege.

The lack of cooperation of British Petroleum in the 2010 Gulf oil spill is an attitudinal inherency issue. One might argue that the lack of a more aggressive response by the Obama administration was also an attitudinal barrier to solution.

Syndicated analyst Neal Gabler argues that financial reform fails because it ignores human nature, in particular, ***greed***. He explains that our economic policies have encouraged the worst in human nature. When President Reagan drastically cut the top marginal tax rate, the rates the highest earners pay, from 70% to 50% then 28%, reduced capital gains, and provided investment incentives, "that's when the trouble began—from the S & L crisis right through to the fall of Lehman Brothers. It wasn't enough for the rich to be rich... they had to be super rich.... Tax cuts, including the Bush tax cuts, fed some of the worst aspects of human nature and led to some of the worst excesses. It was just a matter of time before Wall Street went wild **(24)**."

When we have attitude as the key inherency factor, ***our workable solution will require either some enforcement mechanism or positive incentive*** to counter human resistance. We'll have to give people a reason to support the social system we advocate.

We may discuss only one level of inherency, or we may use all three. However, whenever we discuss solutions, we need to be aware of the various dimensions of inherency, as that analysis is key to making workable policy, something effective, not merely symbolic. It's important to note that the inherency section is not for general information about often complex causes for social problems. *Whatever you find to be the key causes are the specific ones that must be addressed by your solution.* Again, this is an argumentative, not informative, speech. Don't bring it up if you don't intend to solve for it.

WORKABLE SOLUTION

This section of your speech should *begin with a description of the policy,* the solution to the harms. Not everything we say in persuasive discourse is an argument. We use description and transition, too, between arguments. After describing details, you *make arguments* that the policy will work, applying the solution specifically to the harms. In this manner, you can achieve *"solvency."* Perhaps most important to solvency is making sure that you have discovered the right causes to the problem. *The most effective solutions are built from a thorough analysis of inherency* (Figure 6.2):

It makes no sense to pull solutions out of a hat like magic rabbits without knowing the causes of the harms and applying solutions directly to them. In the best of all possible worlds, *we'd like to eliminate problems*. Yet, as we've seen in the previous section, causes may be multiple and difficult. So, it is *acceptable to diminish the problem* by attacking some but not all causes, creating an improvement or a partial solution. You may be able to use statistics to suggest a percentage of a problem that comes from a particular cause. "We can diminish the problem by X%."

Remember that the issue is called *workable* solution. To determine if the policy you propose is practical and achievable, ask yourself about "*3M*," not the tape company, but the *manpower, machinery, and money* required to make things work. (I apologize for the sexist language "manpower."

A Harm   –   B Inherency   =   C Solution

FIGURE 6-2.

Chapter 6 | *Building Speeches: Fact, Value, & Policy*

I've sacrificed the more neutral phrasing "person power" to maintain the mneumonic device.) Roughly, 3M stands for who is going to do it, what they are going to do, and how we are going to pay for it.

Manpower means what is usually called *"agency."* Who is going to administer a solution? Is it an institution already established, but you're broadening or limiting its scope or authority? Are we going to use, for instance, the AEC for further development of nuclear energy, as they already have the necessary infrastructure? Is it a new agency that you're going to build? What personnel is required, and are they readily available? Does the agency require some special training? Are we going to have to hire and train a whole new profession, if the solution is something technical like an alternative fuel car?

The Bush administration restructured our national security agencies after 9/11, for instance, by creating the **Department of Homeland Security**. Independent agencies like the CIA and NSA were not functioning in a cooperative manner, preventing a larger picture of national threats. The new department's intent is to supervise interaction among these agencies.

One of the weaker approaches to solution is to appoint a committee to decide what to do. You often hear promises in elections to appoint *"a blue ribbon committee"* to solve some issue. Politicians either want to avoid being pinned down, or really aren't sure what to do. It's difficult to be convincing when you argue that we have a significant, indeed, imminent problem then defer the solution to secret "wise men." There are times it's appropriate to defer to committees. When we don't have a handle on causation, as with the AIDS and acid rain examples, the typical approach is an R&D solution. We fund R&D, research and development, searching for a solution.

Machinery means what are **the operations** of the solution to be? What are the steps of the plan to solve and how does it come about?

- Is it a research and development or **R&D solution**, as in the case of an inherency based solely on trends?

- Is it a **ban or a restriction**, making something entirely illegal or limiting it in some specific way?

- Is it a **law**, the repeal of a law, or a constitutional amendment?

- Is it an increased or decreased benefit of some kind to a particular cause?

Machinery may also be thought of as **details about the means**, or "the how" of stopping the problem. Is it enhanced border patrols to diminish the entry of illegal immigrants, or putting fingerprints on drivers' licenses to make it easier to trace criminals. I recently got a drivers license in Arizona. In a single day and place, they both deliver your license with photo and register you as a voter. They've eliminated bureaucracy and postal costs. They never mail out anything because they handle it on the spot. It's a good model. Other states could apply similar machinery to cut costs in the long run.

Machinery may be **literal machinery, in the sense of technology** required to solve something. We mentioned the acid rain problem. Part of the solution was to put "scrubbers" on the top of those tall smoke stacks to filter the effluents. You have catalytic converters on your cars to help with smog. When we first noticed water shortages, people were encouraged to use water-saving shower nozzles and toilets. Due to damage to the ozone layer, we changed the nature of home refrigeration to emit less effluent. Certainly, the current "**green industry**" movement will yield many new technological developments on a global basis.

INEOS Bio and joint venture partner, New Planet Energy, announced a conditional commitment for a $75 million loan guarantee from the U.S. Department of Agriculture's 2003 Biorefinery Assistance Program. A biorefinery is a facility that integrates processes and equipment to produce fuels, power, and chemicals from biomass like corn or distiller's grain. The Environmental Protection Agency and Chrysler announced a cooperative agreement to develop and adapt hydraulic hybrid technology for the light duty auto market. Walgreens announced the opening of the nation's first drugstore chain location to utilize geothermal energy for heating and cooling. India is beginning to use solar powered towers for communication. First Solar and China Guangdong Nuclear Solar Energy Development signed a memorandum of understanding to collaborate on the development of a solar photovoltaic plant in Inner Mongolia. Photovoltaics is a method of generating electrical power by converting solar radiation into direct current using semiconductors (25). This is an important area of research for a safer environment, and it could provide you with many topic ideas as well as solutions for policy.

Solutions often require money. How much financing is required? From where will you take it? Is there money in existing budgets that can be applied, or can you take it from some other less necessary program? Will you increase taxes? It may even be possible that the proposed program finances itself, like the several state lotteries, even providing extra monies. Will the cost actually be worth the benefit? You can't fiat money into existence, so you have to consider financing of the policy.

The cost of a solution becomes critical when we look at side effects. If you do something more cheaply, you can claim savings as an extra advantage of your program.

You may add *a fourth M for muscle*. People don't always like new systems. What do we do in a case when there is attitudinal inherency? We may have to think of *incentives and/or enforcements* to invite or compel compliance. Sometimes penalties, fines, and imprisonment must be provided. For instance, they're usually necessary when dealing with corporate resistance to environmental issues like illegal dumping of wastes. You can also consider incentives. Incentives are bonuses your plan can offer to win the public over, for instance, tax breaks to buy energy efficient cars or appliances. Cities have occasionally paid people in crime-ridden areas a fee to turn in handguns, which are then destroyed. Currently, you can get tax breaks for installing solar power cells, though the initial cost is high, and it takes some years to recoup your expenses in projected savings. In the long run, it can be quite cheap.

Enforcement may be particularly important if you have deadline for the solution's completion. *Timeline matters with many kinds of solutions*. Let's say we're concerned about wildfires that spread through the southwest damaging millions of dollars of acreage. If the solution is to clear dry brush and bark beetle-damaged trees, we wouldn't argue, "We should get around to it sometime." We'd probably set a timeline to help the problem before the next fire season. Some scientists have argued that fossil fuels will be used up by about 2030. If we propose a system of alternative energy, we'd have to reasonably demonstrate that it could manifest itself effectively by that time.

Where do solutions come from? Primarily, we look for *models* of solutions already applied elsewhere and achieving results and apply them to our problem. To the degree that the circumstances are analogous, we may expect similar results. Whether it be another country or a county here, we can at least see the idea in action and have some means of gauging solvency. Often, especially with newer harms, we may have to **rely on the best available expert advice**. In the case of relatively new problems, experts involved at the forefront of study may be the only ones with a clue about where to begin. Solutions can come from creative angles, including your own brainstorming. You can **reason backwards from inherency** that something is the direct cause of a harmful phenomena, and you can "cross-apply" some of the same, or similar evidence in your solutions.

Here's one example of integrating analysis of inherency with solution. A **Dole** food company project could be a model for increasing food safety for produce. A serious egg salmonella incident in 2010, during which half a billion eggs had to be recalled, involved someone who wasn't a real FDA inspector at all, just an egg grader. The weakness of the FDA is an obvious inherency point, and one solution could be to insist on stronger inspection standards. Yet that's expensive, as is the cost of such recalls to food companies.

Somewhat encouraging is new technology developed by Dole that could be applied across the food industry. They use massive servers in the Silicon Valley to trace particular batches of food from the fields, through harvester trucks, cold storage warehouses where the food is chilled, stored, then loaded onto refrigerator trucks. Within four days produce is delivered to customer warehouses and within a day to your market. The tracing ends at the checkout counter with bar code ID and purchase date recorded. That trail can be traced in seconds thanks to tiny high tech labels, allowing farmers to determine whether a leaky fertilizer bin, water pathogens, or unwashed hands on a factory floor caused contamination. This would reduce the time it takes to catch and repair public poisoning incidents, such as this egg salmonella incident.

Isn't the FDA supposed to insure our food's healthfulness? Yet estimates are that 56% of food is not inspected by the FDA. Many farming companies have not adopted this tracking technology, and food safety legislation that might encourage its use is stalled in Congress. Perhaps, besides just pressuring the FDA for more efficiency, we could convince food companies that it would be in their self-interest, both in terms of saving money from recall and attracting customers, to apply the technology. Perhaps tax incentives could be provided, along with more careful scrutiny by better qualified FDA inspectors (**26**). Businessmen are often critical of government solutions and want things handled by the private sector anyway, and it would limit their liability in future cases of food poisoning.

In summation, it isn't enough to propose something in principle. We have to show that it's possible and practical to manage it.

SIDE EFFECTS

After we offer a solution with solvency, we have to consider side effects that may result. Side effects may be either ***positive or negative***. It's possible that this issue will simply be a safety step in our critical thinking and that we won't present this issue in our speech. If there are positive effects, ***benefits beyond solving the significant harm***, they can be claimed as ***advantages.***

For instance, let's say you're going to offer new technology as a solution to a pollution problem. You may also argue the advantage of creating jobs for people manufacturing and installing the technology.

On the other hand, if we decided to boycott pre-washed lettuce in a bag to help solve water shortage problems, we might have the opposite problem. We could be challenged by opponents for a ***disadvantage***, since we're destroying an industry and creating unemployment. We put on the thinking cap of our imaginary opponent, attack our own plan, and fix any weak points. This would help to pre-empt potential side effect arguments, making this part of a speech unnecessary, and giving you more time with the other three stock issues.

Sometimes, though, a side effect may be commonly known and a matter of public debate. Rather than ignore challenges to your position, defend the notion that the harm you're solving is worse than the side effects of your proposal. This is sometimes called ***costs vs. gains analysis*** and is an argument similar to the type made in value speeches. We persuade the audience that, while some aspect of our solution may be a bitter pill, swallowing it eliminates much worse harms.

Here are examples of real world side effect of a policy. The U.S. Fish and Wildlife Service blamed the disappearance of Southern California kelp to marauding sea urchins in the *Los Angeles Times*, October 3, 2005. On October 6, three days later, they also mentioned their attempts to keep threatened sea otters out of Southern California waters to help fishermen. Sea otters, it turns out, eat sea urchins.

Much negative discussion of the Obama healthcare plan involves side effects. The Heritage Foundation, a conservative think thank, pointed out ten of them in a December 31, 2010, article in *The Foundry*, including higher insurance costs and taxes. They mention an item in the *Indianapolis Star*, "Driven by worries about the economy and possibly the effects of health-care reform, [health insurers] are raising rates this year for family coverage through employer-sponsored plans... from 8 percent to 21 percent, which is considerably higher than the 5 percent increase the Kaiser Family Foundation reported in 2009." Employers, they argue, will pass the price hikes on to their employees or switch to less expensive plans with higher deductibles, lesser coverage, or both. Tax levies on "Cadillac" health plans, on the other hand, raise concerns with unions. The problem with this tax is that it hits the very plans often enjoyed by their rank-and-file. Thus, besides helping people who are uninsured, it also may hurt people with good insurance now **(27)**.

Again, these kinds of side effects are not necessarily in every presentation. If we consider in advance what the side effects of our proposals may be, though, we can go back to our workable solution to add preemptive positions that may prevent the opposition's most likely attacks. So, this issue may have an advisory effect, rather than a presentational one.

The appendix of this text and the workbook have full samples of policy speeches, as well as those of fact and value.

PART 3: PROPOSITIONS OF VALUE

While policies are controversial, nothing brings more combative rhetoric than issues of value, **questions of what is right or wrong, ethical or unethical, even good or evil.** These are challenging issues because the words we use to express values are abstract and difficult to define **(28)**.

We're also deeply at the effect of our **cultural conditioning**, so examining our own values objectively is a challenge anyway.

A people's values may be **imbedded in their colloquial sayings.** Value statements are often proverbs. "A stitch in time saves nine," for instance, is an expression of handling problems before they get out of hand. "A rolling stone gathers no moss" advises us to keep active by way of preventing sloth. Your folks may have used a few on you, like "The early bird gets the worm" when you're sleeping in. If so, you probably wondered, "Who wants the worm anyway?"

Values may be about our personal conduct, not in the sense of social policy, but more in the way of personal policy, the **principles we use to govern our own behavior**. I recall my Boy Scout oath as a list of values suggesting how we should act. An oath is a promise to live up to these **goals**: trustworthy, loyal, helpful, friendly, courteous, kind, obedient, cheerful, thrifty (kids didn't have credit cards back then), brave, clean, and reverent. On the face of it, it's an easy pledge to make, but what do the words really mean in actual living? What constitutes courtesy? I could go on a bit about how we treat each other driving, defending the thesis that "Drivers should be more courteous to each other," but I still have to define what courtesy means in specific, behavioral terms. We have to **avoid the glittering generalities** discussed in Chapter 2.

When we talk about **human rights**, we're usually discussing values. When we compare the strengths and weaknesses of "**-isms**," as in arguing that capitalism is better than socialism, we're arguing value. When the Supreme Court looks at the Bill of Rights when its articles conflict in a particular case, they are also arguing values. Value arguments are concerned with **determining priorities** among important yet conflicting social goals.

It's hard to explain values in isolation, so they're **often expressed in competing pairs**. Socrates argued a value thesis when he said, "Mere survival is less important than a good life." Confucius said that, "It's better to be righteous than rich." This kind of comparison helps ground the conversation. Focusing more on **social priorities**, we might argue that:

Domestic spending is more important than foreign spending.

Environmentalism is more important than capitalism.

Private schools are better than public schools.

Notice that *the language of value* will usually contain variations of good, better, and best, as well as "right and wrong," "moral or immoral," even "virtuous and evil."

STOCK ISSUES OF VALUE

We need a larger framework within which to sort those values out, and they are different than fact or policy (**29**):

1. ***How shall we define the values in conflict?*** You have to explain what you mean by a value. You're for "love"? What do you mean? Platonic love? Brotherly love? Marital love? Sexual love? Love of country? What? Sometimes just determining what a value means can be the crux of a debate. Refer to the definitions section in Chapter 1 for more help.

2. ***By what standard shall we evaluate the values in conflict?*** This is the crux of a rational evaluation of values. We try to find some objective hierarchy by which to judge the issue. There should be a clear rationale for this choice. Hopefully, there would be some agreement about a standard by the two sides in a debate, a specific criterion for determining who wins.

3. ***Which value is superior when judged against the standard?*** Remember to consider the value in social action. Don't get lost in a cloud of abstract words. Bring values down to earth, concretizing them in real world experience. As I often say, ***the proof of the value is in the living***. Offer examples showing that the value is superior because it promotes a better life.

For our practical purposes, we're not looking for absolute philosophical truth. We're dealing with ***the relative world of practical social issues and probabilities*** rather than certainties. There is seldom an absolute right or wrong in most value debates, unless we're talking about something so odious that all but those with a pathological disorder reject the idea. The case of child molestation comes to mind.

STANDARDS

If we don't create standards, our debate will be reduced to silly utterances like, "My idea is just as good as yours." We need to understand and create some objective standards for evaluating the relative weight of values. We might think of this as *"ethical weight,"* being determined on an old fashioned scale (Figure 6.3):

In this illustration, we have value A against value B, but they are weighed against each other on a fulcrum, a point of balance, standard C.

A value standard is either a framework of priorities that you develop, with objective justification, or it's a framework already established and accepted by members of your community and your particular audience (**30**).

>   The Ten Commandments
>   The Constitution of the United States
>   Maslow's Hierarchy of Needs

FIGURE 6-3.

Value hierarchies are often sets of interactive and mutually influential ideas. For instance, **Maslow** said that we value our survival above all things (**31**). It's only when survival is guaranteed that we can value love. It's only when we have love that we are primarily concerned with social respect. Then it's only when we have social respect that we're likely to value issues of higher self-development, what Maslow calls self-actualization. Only a fully realized self can consider altruism, like sacrifice for the common good. It's certainly a standard that can be, and has been, challenged, but it is a widely used value standard.

However, we also need **a specific criterion** by which we can determine if we've met that standard. By Maslow's analysis, we could make "survival" the criterion for a value struggle: **Whichever value best supports human survival is the better value**, because without survival all other values are moot. Without survival we cannot exercise or support any other value. That is certainly arguable, but it's a typical analysis.

How do we determine what "best supports human survival?" Do we mean long term or short term? What may save mankind in the long run could possibly kill hundreds of thousands in the short run. Consider the casualties in WWII incurred to stop fascism from taking over Europe and Asia, especially our use of the atomic bomb on Hiroshima and Nagasaki. A criterion from this perspective might be "that which helps the species as a whole survive," rather than the short-term survival of individuals, best meets the standard. Other examples of people sacrificing themselves for their children could then be used as grounds.

What's clear is that different standards and criteria can be applied to the same real world situation. Creating standards and criteria are the essence of value discussions and debates. In fact, the second stock issue of standards can become the main point of a debate.

A pacifist might argue that all taking of human life is not only wrong, but counter-productive. Killing simply leads to more hatred and more killing. Some have argued that our tactics in the Middle East have simply created the next generation of terrorists. Iraq was a moderately secular state before the war, but it's now plagued by enflamed fundamentalism. By that perspective, the criterion might become "that which involves persons and nations in the least possible killing is best." Examples like Gandhi or Martin Luther King could be grounds here.

Three of the news magazines we discussed in Chapter 4 regularly put up "top ten" or "best of" lists. *U.S. News and World Report* put out its annual best hospitals list. Its stated criterion for selection is, "Hard data largely determined rank in 12 of the 16 specialties; examples include death rate, procedure volume, and balance of nurses and patients. The other four specialties were 'ranked by reputation alone **(32)**.'" *Forbes* compiled its "best college for your money" list. Their stated criterion says, "In this report, we rank undergraduate institutions based on the quality of education they provide, the experience of their students, and how much their students achieve **(33)**." Yet adding the criteria of affordability makes for a different ranking than a similar list by *U.S. News and World Report*.

Newsweek took on a big challenge when they announced "**the best countries in the world**." If you were born today, which country would provide you the very best opportunity to live a healthy, safe, reasonably prosperous life **(34)**. *Newsweek* chose five categories of national well-being: education, health, quality of life, economic competitiveness, and political environment. A "**weighted formula**" yields a list in which **the United States is eleventh** behind countries like Finland, Australia, Canada, and Japan. The analysis, which can still be seen on the Newsweek website, is very thorough, but the criteria lean toward countries providing a high degree of social services. Some of the highest have very high tax percentages. It is a progressive analysis.

So you can see that **standards and criteria are debatable** precisely because they themselves are value ridden.

Standards are also important in legal matters, as this *Los Angeles Times* article of August 30, 2005, suggests:

> The Meskwaki Nation in Toma, Iowa, began requiring DNA testing this spring to screen out pretenders seeking to cash in on the tribe's casino profits. But the DNA tests have opened fresh wounds throughout Indian country, unmasking complicated family relations and turning the unspoken bonds of community into impersonal laboratory results. Inevitably, DNA raises a

delicate question: What does it mean to be Indian? For example, Marilyn Vann spent her childhood among Cherokees. Her father received 110 acres from the federal government in compensation for lands confiscated from the tribe when it was forcibly relocated to Oklahoma from Georgia on the Trail of Tears in the late 1830s. In 2001, she applied for tribal membership but got a letter back stating that her father was listed on the 1907 tribal roll as a Freedman—a descendent of freed slaves—not a true Cherokee. Under the rules of the Cherokee nation, she could become a tribe member only if an ancestor appeared on that 1907 roll. "My ancestors helped build this tribe," Vann said, "My father and grandfather enjoyed Cherokee citizenship. I've been kicked out with no say-so in the matter."

So is this right or wrong? The rules for tribal membership vary with each of the 562 federally recognized tribes. Does the federal government have the ultimate say on what tribes can truly be called Indian? Further, Van's cohorts contest the controversial methodology of the testing. Ancestry tests look both at genes, of which there are 30,000 per human genome, as well as 255 mutations called single nucleotide polymorphisms. These polymorphisms are thousands of years old and link to specific contents indicating ancestry.

Yet genetic and genealogical ancestry aren't exactly synchronized. Each person has had four grandparents, but their *DNA isn't passed down in equal portions*. As much as 35% of genes can be traced to a single grandparent, for example, while as few as 15% might come from another, according to Tony Frudakis, chief scientific officer of DNA Print Genomics Inc., a Florida genetic testing company. Yet there is a need for some standard, since claims to be Native American have risen steadily since casino profits have improved. Also, health care benefits and other services are at issue.

More recent evidence continues to show that Marilyn Vann has not won the battle to have her ancestry recognized.

Again, there are complete *sample speeches* of fact, policy, and value in the appendix and the workbook of this text (**35**).

There are, however, *a few more concepts* that might help you do your best when debating values.

VALUES ARE NOT FACTS

At the most basic personal level, you might explore your own values by asking yourself **what you think is important in life.** What are your top personal priorities? Is there something you're so committed to that you'd put your life on the line for it, like our volunteer soldiers in the Middle East? What do you think is the ultimate purpose of your life? What civic duties do you think you owe society? What do you have a right to expect in return?

Maybe you haven't considered values seriously. Maybe you've been guided to a very particular set of values and heard them repeated so often that you didn't feel any need to examine them. **Many values are so deeply believed that they simply seem obvious and true.** We've been taught values by people we respect, have lived with on an ongoing basis. We have maybe not always practiced these values, but we've seen evidence for their wisdom in our own experience. Indeed, some values seem ingrained into our very personalities. What do we say, however, when asked, **"how do you know that?"**

Often we fall back on **circular reasoning**: "It's so because it's so."

Maybe we throw in a **bandwagon argument**: "Everybody knows it's so."

The temptation to be **aggressive rather than argumentative** surfaces when deeply held values are challenged. In fact, the whole range of bad pre-critical thinking habits and fallacies of appeal are likely to show up during this kind of discussion.

Yet values are **not facts**. They are neither true nor false. They are simply **deeply felt and believed opinions**. They are informed by facts, or should be, may begin as natural reactions to facts, but they are not themselves facts. This is one of the most difficult points of critical thinking, especially when exercised in everyday social discussion. The idea that values are subjective may be easy for educated people, yet even they may get red-faced with anger when pressed to defend a value.

So, not only do we have to consciously choose what we think is valuable, what has priority in our lives, we must also take a hard, logical look at why we believe what we believe. One way to look at it is that **values are the eyeglasses through which we examine facts.**

Maybe we need a new pair of glasses.

VALUES RESIST CHANGE

Yet they do so to varying degrees. Some values are so deeply held that it is next to impossible to alter them, even in the face of facts. Others are less resistant. **Milton Rokeach,** a social psychologist, defines values as specific sets of beliefs and attitudes that act as long term goals (**36**). He discusses **two kinds of values:**

Terminal values are ultimate life goals, like "I want to be rich," "I want to help the environment," "I want to accomplish something significant," or "I just want to be happy." **Instrumental values** are more changeable and immediate values that help us to achieve our terminal values. "In order to be rich, I must be industrious," or "in order to be happy, I need leisure time."Rokeach argues that **values are interwoven and fall into a hierarchy, like the layers of an onion.** Some are at the core and some are closer to the surface. The closer we get to the core, the harder it is to change a value.

There are five layers of belief:

1. **Primitive Beliefs (unanimous consensus)** are core beliefs gathered from personal experience, backed up by consensus from our peers. These rarely change. The fundamental belief that "killing is wrong" might be representative.

2. **Primitive Beliefs (zero consensus)** are also gathered by social experience but not backed up by others. These are idiosyncratic and privately held. They may include perceptions about our own worth and capacity, or our value of self. "I'm not special," or "I'm popular." These are not likely to change, but may be influenced somewhat. You may have had an interpersonal communication class in which your beliefs about yourself were nudged into a somewhat different direction.

3. **Authority Beliefs** are often controversial and depend upon our interaction with authority figures, parents or teachers, for instance. "You should show respect for your elders," or "Don't talk out of turn," might be examples. These are potentially changeable, but only through extended forms of persuasion and experience.

4. **Derived Beliefs** are taken from secondhand information from media figures like those discussed in Chapter 4, books and other reading

materials, or public speech. We derive personal beliefs from such information, without necessarily examining the ideas with any particular depth. By offering other credible evidence, it is possible to change such values.

5. **Inconsequential Beliefs** are usually individual preferences and tastes and are quite changeable.

It's also true, though, that **even widely supported values do change.** We may receive **new information** that forces reassessment. When Columbus showed Europeans that they wouldn't sail off the end of the planet by heading west, interest in the "New World" emerged. It made a value of exploration itself, and that became the motive principle for European economics and politics. That value contributed to the creation of our country and Eurocentric imperialism.

There is also erosion of values through time. People take them for granted. They pass away as people tire of them or they don't seem relevant, then they come back into vogue, like a pendulum swinging back and forth across the face of history. So, there are times when rhetorical demand is very high for intelligent discussion of values.

CORE AMERICAN VALUES

What lies at the very core of our principles as Americans? What are the values that are most enduring for us and, therefore, a basis for appealing to an audience's sense of value. Steele and Redding mention several, among them these:

The value of the individual: We rank the rights and welfare of the single citizen above those of government.

The value of achievement and success: We believe that citizens should be able to accumulate money, power, and status. We are an upwardly mobile population.

The value of change and progress: We believe in new actions leading to ever more positive change. Our very free market economy is based on the notion of growth.

The value of ethical equality: We believe that "all men were created equal" and should be treated accordingly.

The value of effort and optimism: We believe that even the most unattainable goals can be reached through hard work and positive attitudes.

The value of pragmatism: We believe in practicality, common sense, efficiency, and function. We like to say we have "Yankee Ingenuity" or "common sense" (**37**).

I would have to add, from my own experience as a forensic coach, as well as a sports fan and witness to several wars, that ***Americans believe in winning and winners***. "A winner never quits and a quitter never wins." It may be that you've heard this saying over and over from teachers and coaches. We hold winners up as media icons and invite them to our most prestigious talk shows. We also seem to enjoy tearing them down in fan magazines when we get tired of their celebrity, or they do something that makes them losers in the harsh eye of the media.

IN SUM

There are three distinct kind of speeches, each with its own set of stock issues, language style, and particular challenges. While your teacher will determine which order they should go in, I have found it useful to proceed in the order here described. I also make my value assignment a debate assignment, a more spontaneous exercise than the formulaic fact and policy speeches. The next chapter will discuss refutation and debate.

VOCABULARY

Costs vs. Gains Analysis

Criteria/Criterion

Hierarchy

Impact

Instrumental Values vs. Terminal Values

Inventional System

Qualitative vs. Quantitative

Stock Issues:

Fact—Significant Effect & Cause

Policy—Significant Harm

Inherency (trend, structural, attitudinal)

Workable Solution (money, manpower, machinery, muscle)

Value—Define the values to be debated

Establish a standard for decision

Apply the standard to the competing value

REFERENCES

1) Corsi, J.R. "The Continuing Evolution of Policy System Debate: An Assessment and a Look Ahead." Journal of the American Forensic Association 22 (1986): 158.
Ehninger, D., and W. Brockriede. Decision by Debate. New York: Harper & Row, 1978.
Freeley, A.J. (1993). Argumentation and Debate: Critical Thinking for Reasoned Decision Making. Belmont, CA: Wadworth, 1993.

2) http://www.antiwar.com/casualties
http://www.scaruffi.com/politics/dictat.html
http://www.antiwar.com/casualties/

3) "House passes health law repeal," Politico, January 19, 2011. http://www.politico.com/news/stories/0111/47831.html

4) "The economy is improving," Bloomberg, August 6, 2010. http://www.bloomberg.com/news/2010-08-07/u-s-economy-improving-more-stimulus-isn-t-the-answer-rubin-o-neill-say.html

5) Ibid.

6) "Employment Situation Summary," United States Department of Labor, January 7, 2011. http://www.bls.gov/news.release/empsit.nr0.htm

7) "Economy improving, job growth lagging," Daily Press, January 11, 2011. http://www.dailypress.com/business/real-estate/dp-nws-commercial-real-estate-20110120,0,7696461.story

8) "Economy improving modestly: Fed's beige book," Reuters News Service, June 9, 2010. http://www.reuters.com/article/idUSTRE6584V 720100609

9) Epstein, Gene. "Five reasons we'll get real in 2011," The Wall Street Journal, December 18, 2010. http://online.barrons.com/article/SB 50001424052970203319504576019543134370866.html

10) "Four reasons for optimism in the 2011 economy," Fortune, December 30, 2010. http://finance.fortune.cnn.com/2010/12/30/four-reasons-for-optimism-in-the-2011-economy/

11) "Fed Plans 600 Billion Dollar Bond Purchase to Spark Economy," RISmedia, November 4, 2010. http://rismedia.com/2010-11-04/fed-plans-600-billion-dollar-bond-purchase-to-spark-economy/

12) Fortune, December 30, 2010.

13) Ibid.

14) "Midwest bankers say economy improving," Bloomberg, January 20, 2011. http://www.bloomberg.com/news/2011-01-20/midwest-plains-bankers-say-economy-improving.html

15) Corsi, J.R., 1986.
    Ehninger, D., and W. Brockriede, 1978.
    Freeley, A.J., 1993.

16) Holihan, T.A., and K.T. Baske. Arguments and Arguing. New York: St. Martin's Press, 1994.

17) http://ustrendz.blogspot.com/2010/10/rutgers-university-student-tyler.html
    http://abcnews.go.com/US/suicide-rutgers-university-freshman-tyler-clementi-stuns-veteran/story?id=11763784&page=2

18) http://www.boston.com/news/local/massachusetts/articles/2010/01/24/the_untouchable_mean_girls/

19) "Bullying, Suicide, Punishment," New York Times, October 3, 2010.

20) "Arkansas school board member to resign over anti-gay post," CNN Wire Staff, October 29, 2010.

21) http://www.epa.gov/boston/eco/acidrain/causes.html

22) http://www.elmhurst.edu/~chm/vchembook/197acidrainsoln.html

23) "Beach Water Testing at Ebb," Los Angeles Times, August 30, 2010.

24) Gabler, Neal. "Tax cuts unleashed Wall Street greed," Los Angeles Times, September 3, 2010.

25) http://www.nrel.gov/biomass/biorefinery.html
    http://news.cnet.com/greentech/
    http://www.greenprogress.com/

26) "Could egg contamination have been prevented?" CBS News, August 25, 2010.
    "Farm to Table," Los Angeles Times, October 3, 2010.

27) http://blog.heritage.org/2010/03/30/side-effects-higher-health-insurance-taxes/

28) Christian, C.G., and M. Traber, Eds. Communication Ethics and Universal Values. Thousand Oaks, CA: Sage, 1997.
    Jensen, J.V. Ethical Issues in the Communication Process. Mahwah, NJ: Lawrence Earlbaum, 1997.

29) Perella, J. The Debate Method of Critical Thinking: An Introduction. Dubuque, IA: Kendall/Hunt, 1987.

30) Johanssen, R.L. Ethics in Human Communication. Prospect Heights, IL: Waveland Press 1996.

31) Maslow, A. Motivation and Personality. New York: Harper &Row, 1954.

32) "Best Hospitals," U.S. News & World Report, August, 2010.

33) "The Best College for Your Money," Forbes, August 30, 2010.

34) "The Best Countries in the World," Newsweek, August 23–30, 2010.

35) http://64.38.12.138/News/2007/001958.asp

36) Rokeach, M. The Nature of Human Values. New York: Free Press, 1973.

37) Steele, E.D., and W.C. Redding. "The American Value System: Premises for Persuasion." Western Speech 26(1962): 83–91.

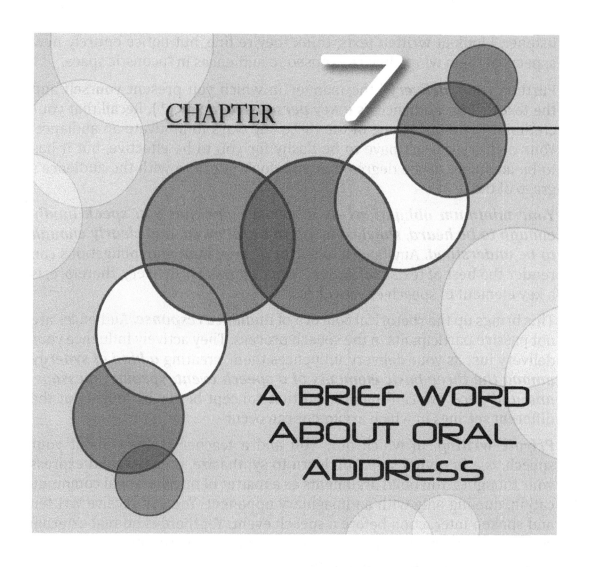

CHAPTER 7

A BRIEF WORD ABOUT ORAL ADDRESS

"GRASP THE SUBJECT, AND THE WORDS WILL FOLLOW."

– Cato –

It's important that critical thinking be spoken, not just written. You'll discover that the additional phase of discussion illuminates what we've written in surprising ways. *Speaking text out loud brings a different sense to arguments than perceiving them as merely written word.* Hidden presumptions and errors in language tend to show up to the ear in a way that the eyes don't perceive. Even as an experienced speaker and listener, I look at written texts, think they're fine, but notice entirely new aspects of them when they're exposed to audiences in "acoustic space."

Further, your "*delivery*," the manner in which you present yourself and the text to your audience, *is a key persuasive factor* (**1**). Recall that your credibility or ethos is one of the three key ways to motivate an audience. Your delivery doesn't have to be flashy for you to be effective, but it has to be adequate to the degree that you don't interfere with the audience's grasp of the text.

Your minimum obligations as a speaker are that you speak loudly enough to be heard, slowly enough to be followed, and clearly enough to be understood. Any failure to perform these minimum obligations can render the best of texts ineffective. Preparedness for delivery, therefore, is a key element of speech effectiveness.

This brings up the rhetorical concern of *audience response.* Audiences are not passive participants in the speech process. They actively influence your delivery just as your delivery influences them, creating *a kind of synergy among the three basic elements of a speech event: speaker, message, and audience.* We can understand that concept better by looking at the different settings in which argument can occur.

Private writing, in which only you and a teacher interact about your speech, is a first vital step. You learn to synthesize, organize, and express your thoughts. You build arguments as a matter of intrapersonal communication, dueling only with an imaginary opponent. You can receive written and spoken interaction before a speech event. Yet there is no real external challenge from the multiple viewpoints an audience presents.

Writing in a public medium, like journalism, draws the kind of vital interaction that promotes better testing of arguments. Multiple viewpoints from a variety of sources are the norm in that broader environment. The writer is also subject to criticism from the public at large, as well as other equally skilled professional writers.

Speaking before a live audience is a more dynamic, immediate process of interaction and is no less likely to draw contradiction from others (sometimes in overlapping and raucous chorus). This is the level at which you learn to defend your ideas, backed with the preparation you've achieved in private writing. Writing alone diminishes maximum opportunity for new information and perspectives. More considered and objective thought can emerge from the process of speaking, questioning, and answering (**2**).

Speaking in public promotes thinking on your feet. It's normal for audiences to ask questions after a speech and sometimes to disagree with you. When we disagree in public, we don't get to go away and write something down over hours and days. We stand and deliver our thoughts in the moment, hopefully disciplined by this training. After a little experience at this, you may find that your confidence to speak in a more extemporaneous manner may grow. It's not uncommon that some student speakers are actually better at answering questions spontaneously, given sufficient research, than they are reading canned text. That's not a bad thing, since extemporaneous delivery styles are more natural and useful in the working world.

This process benefits the audience as well. Not only does the speaker get a chance to hone his own thinking, the audience is forced to look at their presumptions and attitudes in the light of new knowledge and ideas. Sometimes student see things from a new angle, perhaps even more readily than one well versed in the subject. They may be less conditioned to certain assumptions about an issue, seeing it with fresh eyes. Therefore, no matter if it is a panel discussion, an open class discussion, or individual oral address, texts should be tested by open conversation and critique.

So, there are many reasons for speaking text, rather than merely writing it. However, that doesn't keep you from being a little nervous about the process. Whenever you stand or even sit to speak before an audience of peers, there's often a touch of stage fright, or ***"speaker apprehension."*** This feeling is natural, but it is ***always worsened by procrastination and insufficient rehearsal*** (**3**).

Don't worry so much! You're in good company. Most of us feel this apprehension. ***A little bit of well directed apprehension can even be a good thing, as it excites the energy of speech delivery.*** The key to handling this is a system of mental and physical discipline used in the rehearsal process (**4**).

BASICS

Let's go over a simple strategy for approaching delivery. First, attitude and mental process matter a great deal, both for you and your audience.

1) Do not put off the work. Do not procrastinate. Do it now. One of the worst enemies of good delivery is waiting until the last minute to write or rehearse. You may be afraid of delivery, so you put practice off, but that's a guarantee for a self-fulfilling prophesy that you won't do well. Adopt *a "do a little everyday" method* of writing and rehearsal. It's actually a better learning strategy to do a half hour of study per subject per day than to spend last minute time cramming on a given subject. That goes double for doing a speech.

This also means don't continue rewrites right up to the time of delivery. If you see something serious, fine. Adjust. Yet fussing with a text can be just another form of procrastination, like cleaning your desk before you write a paper.

2) It's actually good to rehearse what you're writing as you go. Novice speakers sometimes focus all their energy on writing the kind of paper they're used to doing for an English class then try to practice delivery at the last minute, if at all. They find themselves struggling with sentences that are too long, words that are too big, or unintentional tongue twisters that read well silently but trip up the living tongue.

Writing style impacts your delivery. There is a distinct difference between writing for the ear and writing for the eye. In other words, although it's good to expand our vocabulary and to experiment with it in written text, the ear is not the eye. Listeners may hear and recall as little as 25% of the average ten-minute talk (**5**).

When reading a text to yourself, like a book or a magazine, you can stop and muse about a thought or image, look up a word in the dictionary, then go on at your own pace. Not so when an audience listens. The language is coming at them in a linear manner, one word at a time. They can't skip back to the previous paragraph if they miss a few words. Therefore, we need a shorter, simpler writing style than we might use when writing other research papers.

Reading the text aloud helps. ***You'll realize that you're not only writing for their ears but for your own mouth.*** If a word, phrase, or sentence doesn't "fit in your mouth"—that is, it causes you to slip, to mumble, or to stop because you've run out of breath—then it's time to abbreviate your language.

Look in a thesaurus for simpler or more easily pronounced words. ***"Don't spend a dollar when a dime will do"*** when you're dealing with word choice. That is, don't try to impress anybody with big words. Keep your language clear and handily enunciated. Even Aristotle wrote that we should, "Speak in the language that is common for the day."

It will be necessary to speak the ***technical language*** of an expert's field. It can be embarrassing, as well as damaging to your credibility, when you mispronounce a word with which your audience is familiar. You should be looking up words you don't know, anyway. If you can't figure out how to pronounce a word with the dictionary, ask your instructor. Note any pronunciation problems when you turn in your rough draft, rather than just before speaking. Some common names are unusual. Just commit to a reasonable pronunciation rather than appear to be uncertain about it during speech.

Rehearsing while writing is a calming refinement that can boost your confidence. The very ritual of it can become a way of lessening apprehension: "I know this. I can do this. I say it every day." Rewriting, thus, should be part of the rehearsal process.

3) Make the manuscript your friend. The suggestion that you speak as you write does not mean that you'll be scribbling on your text just before you speak. I mention it because I've seen so many "final drafts" with last minute pen marks on them, and that's not college level work. There's a point, at least a day or two before you speak, at which you simply have to "play the ball where it lies." You do one last polished draft after which your time should be entirely devoted to practice.

You make the manuscript your friend when you ***make it easier to read.*** You're not merely reading, of course. You should be well enough rehearsed to glance at the text for content reminders yet interact with the audience. Small technicalities can help:

A) Double-space.

B) Boost your font size up to 14 from the usual 10 or 12.

C) Keep the script free of distracting marks or inserts.

D) Number your pages in case you lose your place.

E) Use a heavy enough grade of printing paper that you can hold the text without shaking it or letting it droop.

F) Don't wait until the last minute to print the script. You should rehearse with the actual pages you intend to speak with.

G) End your sentences at the bottom of the page rather than the top of the next. Otherwise, you may interrupt the flow of your delivery.

A clean draft both represents you and supports you. It represents you in the sense that an unsightly one has much the same effect as wearing dirty clothes. You should think of the impression your manuscript makes as the impression you make for yourself. It supports you in the sense that a more readable script becomes a kind of anchor for your memory and your nerves.

4) Focus on the content, not yourself. There are three basic parts of any speaking experience, according to Aristotle: audience, speaker, and speech; or, in today's communication parlance, a sender, receivers, and a message. Each is really equally important, yet beginners tend to focus on themselves in the process. Do I look all right? Am I making mistakes? Do I sound stupid? How's my hair?

Beyond a healthy discipline of self-preparation, you might *think of yourself as the least important of the three parts of a speech act.* The audience that represents your community is more important than your ego. A vital message is the main point of their gathering, not you. The speaker is the agent of the message and should submit himself to that role, rather than making the moment all about himself.

Speakers make themselves the focus in one of two ways. They may take such pride in their own delivery, "strutting their stuff," affecting their voice in overly dramatic ways, over-pausing as if each point were the most important, that the audience sees less of the message and more of their personality. This is a beneficial approach for someone with a weak message that won't bear much scrutiny.

The other way a speaker becomes the focus is by being so nervous that they require the sympathy of the audience to get through the process, further distracting from the message. Don't draw attention to yourself with comments like:

> I messed up. Can I start over?
>
> Oh, I'm so nervous.
>
> I'm sorry. I should have practiced more.
>
> What's wrong? Did I screw up?

You ask because you're projecting your own paranoia on an audience member who is probably doing nothing more than listening intently. You're nervous, so you think you're doing badly. Yet the truth is that the audience probably doesn't notice things about you that you do. Speakers may believe that the audience can see them shaking, for instance. We'll ask the audience if anyone's noticed, and generally they haven't. The speaker is simply struggling with themselves in their own mind. In the meantime, again, the message gets lost.

Think of it this way: **Your nervousness is not your audience's problem.** Their main problem should be to understand the arguments. So, get out of the way of the message and let it reach the community.

When you concentrate on message it leads the audience to similar focus. Minimize extraneous physical activity. Glance at the text. Make eye contact. Think the thoughts as you speak them. **Don't give way to self-critical inner monologues.** Save that for your own time. When you speak, you have a business appointment with your audience. Remember, they're not really looking at you with the critical eye you may think they are, anyway... at least until you make your nervousness obvious by emphasizing it with self-conscious fidgets and extraneous comments.

Notice, we do not recommend that you envision your audience in their underwear as some well-meaning teachers have suggested, only partially in jest. That's just another distraction you may never return from.

VOICE

We'll keep this very simple. ***Use your own voice***, not an impersonation of something you've heard in media. Don't try to sound like a radio announcer. Be yourself. Be conversational. ***Speaking is a conversation***, not unlike a conversation with a group of friends. It's a slightly larger group of friends, the subject matter may be more serious than party talk, and your attitude should be appropriate to the topic, but it is a conversation.

However, you do have ***some minimum obligations***: You must speak loudly enough to be heard, clearly enough to be understood, and slowly enough to be followed.

You must speak loudly enough to be heard in the last row of the audience. Don't yell at people. Use a technique called "***projection***." Our voices carry when we breathe the sentence out. It will be louder, but it will not sound harsh or angry. There's an old saying about this kind of delivery: "Breathe in the thought, hold the thought," that is, feel the sense of it, "then give the thought." We give the thought as an exhalation.

Rather than shout, just breathe it out. In other words, you look down at your text for your next line, "inhale it," look at your audience then exhale as you speak. It may feel mechanical initially, but with practice your voice will be heard.

There are several virtues of the method. Training yourself to look up at people in a regular manner ***improves eye contact***. Eye contact, discussed below, is important in engaging and persuading an audience. Also, lifting the head keeps your throat open, and that ***improves the quality of your voice***. Try tucking your chin down for a moment and speak. Notice that the voice feels flat and artificially lower in pitch. Now lift the head and speak. The voice becomes clearer, and you're easier to hear. Also, you ***reinforce content awareness and integrate it into your physical rehearsal***. That can help keep you from losing your place during delivery.

You don't, by the way, have to lower your whole head to read a line anyway. Just lower the eyes, making it easier to maintain audience contact. There's no need to look like a diving duck.

You must speak clearly enough to be understood. That is, your "***articulation***" needs to be more crisp and clear than in your usual conversations.

Students are sometimes surprised at how much physical effort is required to acquire clear speech. Articulating properly takes some vocal exercise for most students.

We tend to be a little lazy in our private speech, slurring words in the local vernacular. ("'Sup?") You may be used to speaking only by dropping the lower jaw. Most novice speakers barely use their upper lip in speaking, but we were given two for reasons other than eating soup.

It's simply harder to hear slurred language in public speaking situations. The problem is sound waves. You can slur at a table over coffee, and the person just across from you will understand. **Sound waves break up over distance**, though. Thus, slurring in even a small classroom is enough to limit the audience's ability to understand you.

Activate both lips in the articulation process to make sounds clearly. It takes some work to do it right. Your mouth itself can get tired with it. Don't be surprised by a cramp in your jaw, if you don't practice your diction.

Here are a few handy **tongue twisters**. You can use them to warm up for rehearsal and delivery, like stretching your legs before a race. Repeat each several times:

> Amos the amiable astronaut ascended into the astral plane.
>
> Isn't it horrid, Harold, when you're hot and in a hurry, and you have to hold your hat on with your hand.
>
> Marvin, a marvelous man with a muffler shop, makes muffins every Monday.
>
> Rugged rubber baby bumpers.
>
> She sells seashells by the seashore.
>
> Six thick thistles thrust through her thumb.
>
> How much wood could a woodchuck chuck if a woodchuck could chuck wood? He'd chuck all the wood that a woodchuck could if a woodchuck could chuck wood.

Sounds dumb? Try some phrases from more common text:

Israeli encroachment in Lebanon has leveraged the rhetoric of the Taliban.

Tommy G. Thompson, Secretary of Health and Human Services, spoke seriously at the Senate subcommittee about Katrina's shocks to the system.

Congressman Tom Tancredo seeks a symbolic one-issue run for the presidency. He'll likely be opposed by former Wisconsin Governor Tommy G. Thompson, governor of Massachusetts W. Mitt Romney, Secretary of State Condoleeza Rice, New York Governor George Pataki, Former Mayor of New York City Rudy Giulani, Former Speaker of the House Newt Gingrich, and Arizona Senator John McCain. Another gadfly candidate is Michael Jesus Archangel of Michigan, formerly known as Philip Jesse Silva, who calls himself "Saint Michael Jesus."

I mean it. Say these sentences out loud and you'll see. It's an articulation jungle out there!

You must speak slowly enough to be followed. If you go too fast, especially offering the kind of detailed data typical of an argument, you'll lose your audience. That's a common impulse among students who are nervous. They'll volunteer and say, "I want to get this over with," as if facing a spinal tap. Then they rush so quickly that they're done in half the time limit, leaving their audience entirely in the dark. Articulation almost always suffers as a result of this speed, so that even if the audience could keep up, they couldn't understand.

It doesn't help to go too slowly, though. It not only bores audiences, it fails to recognize the nature of human listening. The fact is that our minds can go a lot faster than the average human tongue. Professional speakers may speak much more quickly than the average human, and they do so with intention. They know that they can keep more energy and *dynamism* in their delivery with an increase in rate, but two things are key. You may recall that dynamism is one element of speaker credibility. *You can go quickly enough to keep audience interest as long as you articulate carefully and use the pause.*

Pauses matter for audience comprehension of the overall speech structure. It's typical that speakers will take *a pause of two to three seconds* between major junctions in the speech, say after a complete argument. That allows the audience to absorb what's just been said and realize that a new point is coming along. We represent paragraphing, in other words, with beats in our speech.

Some people have a tendency to speak more quickly or slowly than others. That relates somewhat to their locale and cultural background. You'll find your own best pace through rehearsal and when it's best to take a beat for breath. Just remember one thing: ***Never go anywhere faster than your lips can carry you.***

Our three minimums for vocal performance are that you project, articulate, and keep a reasonable pace, but ***vocal emphasis is also important.*** You are not very effective if you drone on in the same flat pitch, pace, and volume, making every word or idea of equal value. ***Some phrases are more important than others.***

If we only typically hear and remember 25% of a ten-minute talk, which on average we do, maybe we should make choices about what the most important 25% is and emphasize that language with our delivery. Find that language and highlight it on a rehearsal text. Your propositions are important, as are key words in the evidence that secure your claims, such as the causal link, or a figure you want to emphasize.

Then rehearse how to emphasize those key ideas. You may do so by ***bringing volume up or down*** at those points. Sometimes a well-projected whisper is as good as a shout when it's a contrast to the vocal quality preceeding and following it. You can use ***pace and pauses***, too. You could speak at a pace and then slow down the rate to emphasize a key point. You could also be talking at a slower pace and then accelerate for a new point to show a different level of excitement.

There are many possible ways to say a single thing. Experiment with it. You may find, once again, that the rehearsal process can affect the rewriting process.

PHYSICAL DELIVERY

Consider some practical physical techniques for delivery. A speaker's nonverbal communication can be even more important to persuasion than text content. When properly handled, ***the nonverbal frames the verbal*** in a way that makes the text accessible and easy to follow.

Nonverbal behavior communicates both outward and inward. The nonverbal creates an impression with an audience. Also, as you behave, so you become. If you behave nervously and uncomfortably, don't be surprised if you're nervous and uncomfortable.

There's a phrase that goes, *"Fake it until you make it."* For speaking, it's not bad advice. If you behave as though you have confidence, using the techniques discussed below, you may persuade yourself that you actually do.

Here are some of the **basic nonverbal elements** that you can consciously work with to improve your delivery.

STANCE: Just as you build good arguments "from the grounds up," *you build good speaking from your feet up.* The stance you begin with may affect both your comfort with yourself and the audience's attention.

Take a stable stance. Put your feet directly beneath you at about shoulder width apart, stagger one foot back about six inches, and turn that foot outward. A three pointed stance, heel and out-turned toe to the rear and the other foot with its toe forward, forms a kind of tripod. A tripod is the most stable plane of all. Such a stance is a bit like a military "at ease," a posture you take on the parade ground since it's easy to hold for a long time.

For the greatest part of your speech, you should **simply "stand and deliver."** Don't rock back and forth. Don't kick your feet. Don't pace about like some television evangelist trying to rouse the crowd. As you wander aimlessly, you may distract yourself as well as the audience. Using notes at a lectern can help you hold a place without too much wandering, as long as you don't drape yourself over it or kick it.

As you center yourself in your stance, take a pause to calm your mind and try to stand still for at least a paragraph or two while you speak.

EYE CONTACT: This is very important in audience communication, especially as the speech begins. **Looking at the audience is the gateway to communication.** Eye contact creates a bond with individual audience members. It's a positive persuasion factor. So, the next thing you do after setting your three-point stance is to look directly at the audience.

Let's define "look directly" more carefully using an exclusive/inclusive definition. It does not mean to look over the heads of the audience, nor at their foreheads. Well-meaning teachers sometimes offer such ideas, but there is no replacement for the interactive warmth of genuine eye contact. It creates an indescribable synergy.

Go ahead. Try looking over the heads of an audience, especially in a more intimate classroom setting. You'll look like you're doing a Stevie Wonder impersonation.

Lack of eye contact affects an audience negatively. You know when someone isn't looking at you. You can feel it, just as surely as you can feel someone staring at your back in a public place. The exchange of eye contact passes energy and support back and forth. It's a way that people recognize each other as important.

If you're not looking at the audience, why should they look at you? Just standing and reading into your text is like treating your audience to a radio show. Who looks at a radio? It's in the background, but we give attention to something else.

Since nonverbal communication communicates both outside and inside to you, *your eye contact has an effect on you*, as surely as it does the audience. At first, you may be very nervous looking, but you need the grounding that audience eye contact provides.

Try this "training wheels" approach: Look at one person, maybe someone you know and feel fairly comfortable with, then try another, then another from there. Don't look at "the crowd" in fuzzy outline. That's alienating, impersonal, and is likely to increase your apprehension. Pick individuals and talk to them, no differently than you would if waiting in the hall for class, passing the time. If you do this, you may be surprised how much support you feel from the others. You may feel energized by the synergy of your mutual focus on the topic.

FOOTWORK: Do you never walk then when speaking? Sure, you do. The longer the speech, the more points made, the more appropriate it is that you walk several times. Yet you will not wander aimlessly. Three points matter:

Choose when to walk. A good plan is to, literally, "move to the next point." Take just a single silent step, so that's there's a brief pause, no more than 1, 2, 3, seconds, between issues. This short walk will draw the audience eye to you if people have drifted during the last point. You attract their attention with the nonverbal and then deliver the verbal message once you've returned to your three point stance.

Audience attention will be drawn by the last thing that you do. As said before, the nonverbal works best when it frames, or sets up the verbal. If you speak the next point then walk, it will be an interruption of your own message. Done properly, walking becomes a sort of visual paragraphing. If you have three arguments, for example, walk four times, once for each point and once to move into your conclusion.

Lead with the toe that is already pointed forward. Don't cross your legs. Don't cross your right leg over your left to move left, nor your left leg over your right to move right. If your right toe is forward, simply swing that to the right and set it up as the back foot (heel set and toe turned out). Then bring the left toe forward to return to a three-point stance. If your left toe is forward, swing that to the left, set it up as the back foot (heel set and toe turned out). Then the right toe comes forward to complete your three-point stance. These are not big dramatic steps. You're moving no more than a foot or two.

Walk to the sides on a slight diagonal, which is easier to handle gracefully than moving straight up and back. Remember to start far enough away from the audience so that you don't run into them during your talk. That's generally thought of as unseemly. Make this walking reinforcement of your points a part of your rehearsal. It usually works best when you hold a manuscript in one hand and carry it with you.

GESTURE: The use of your hands to accent a point is worth only brief mention. You may complain that you don't know what to do with your hands in front of the room. Yet you do. ***You gesture naturally all the time***, some more than others, but normally in the flow of conversation. You just forget to do so when you're nervous, or have an unrehearsed manuscript in your hands.

Unless you stand around with your hands in your pocket all the time, you've learned how to gesture. ***Give your hands a chance to do what they know to do.*** Don't tie them up behind your back, or in front of you like a fig leaf on Adam. Don't clutch your elbows rigidly at your side. Let them come out from your body and reach toward the audience. Embrace the audience as the community with whom you intend to connect.

If you're thinking of your speech as a conversation with the audience, ***you should allow yourself to gesture*** as you would in other conversations, as we're called to do so by what we're saying. "He was about this tall." "It happened over there." "There are two ways to do this." You wouldn't even have to think about the proper illustrative gestures to go with these phrases.

You may also make some decisions about using some specific gestures to emphasize points, but don't rehearse gestures too much. That has a tendency to become wooden. Don't get trapped into rehearsing in front of a mirror either. A little is fine, to get a sense of what you look like when you take a step or two, but beware of locking into planned gestures in a mechanical way.

Manuscript familiarity is key to natural gesture. If you don't know what you're saying, you may be clutching the script with white knuckles. Be familiar with your text. Rehearse with the manuscript. Grasp it with the left hand, if you're right handed, or vice versa. Then use the opposite hand to gesture naturally, as the impulse or decision finds its way into your rehearsal process, then use the free hand to turn pages.

REHEARSAL

The only way to manage your delivery effectively is to *practice standing up and speaking at full volume.* Stand up, don't sit down, and speak the speech as if for an audience several times over a few days. Lying back on the bed or in the bath and mumbling the words may help your memory, but it doesn't replicate the physical act of delivery.

Part of your rehearsal responsibility is to time the message with a watch, so that you don't take more than your share of the audience's time. *You can't even time the speech accurately without a full volume reading.* Projection and good articulation each take longer than mumbling.

Lying back on your bed or in the tub while reciting the words is not a bad idea, nor is saying them when you're driving the car. Memorization is important. I have what I call *the 50/50 rule.* You need to know the material well enough to have at least 50% eye contact with an audience.

Yet memorization doesn't build the *stamina* taken by the physical activity of speaking. Speaking is more energy consuming than you might imagine. People who don't rehearse may run out of breath and wind up with choppy delivery.

Rehearsal, of course, relies on having a complete text in a timely manner. If you run up against a deadline, at least remember to integrate vocalization with the writing process. Then you can **employ the manuscript technique discussed with projection**. Glance down, inhale the thought as you look up at the audience, then breathe the thought out to them. This method can help even an only slightly rehearsed person to do better than someone who simply stares at the manuscript reading it word for word.

Rehearsing with a live person can help you prepare for possible distractions from disengaged audience members. It can also help you know if a joke doesn't work, or if something else that you hadn't expected is funny. Consider hooking up with one or two others in the class and practice for each other. Get some objective input about how you're coming across. Most folks don't notice their own fidgets and distracting idiosyncrasies, since they're a matter of habit. With objective input bad speaking habits can be broken.

PERFORMANCE

When you deliver the speech, try what may seem impossible: **Enjoy your interaction with the audience.** Look them in the eye, one individual at a time. Smile at the start, as you would when greeting a friend. Make contact. You'll be surprised at the support and energy that an audience can give back to you.

The whole dynamic of public speaking is interactive. There's a kind of community synergy that evolves when you and the audience focus attention together. It creates an atmosphere for a good speech.

So, don't take it all on. It's not all about you. It's about you, the important message that you bear, and the audience who came to hear it. You stand for a moment among the people you normally sit with. They will also be standing and speaking in a little while, and all of them will feel just as vulnerable as you do.

Many times **even a well-rehearsed person will hide** from the audience in the text as if afraid of the audience reaction. Don't hide in the text. Believe it or not, that will make you more nervous. You'll miss any appreciative nonverbal communication from your audience. It can be a confidence booster to notice that they're listening to you, even if they're not nodding in agreement.

Of course, there's a presumption here that the audience is listening.

The audience has a responsibility in the speeches of others, too. They should not be rehearsing their own speeches or paying attention to anything but the speaker. The speech of a fellow class member is a good time to remember the golden rule: Do unto others as you would have them do unto you. Even if you think it's boring or you urgently disagree, support your fellow speakers. Your good will toward them may pay you dividends when you speak.

IN SUM

Do not put off the work, but adopt a "do a little every day" method.

Rehearse as you write, both for their ears and your tongue.

Keep word choice simple.

Know how to pronounce the technical language and proper names you intend to say.

Make the manuscript your friend by making it more readable.

Clean copy represents who you are.

Focus on the content rather than yourself.

Your nervousness is not your audience's problem.

With regard to vocal performance, your minimum obligations are to project loudly enough to be heard; to speak slowly enough to be followed, though not so slowly that you bore your listeners; and articulate clearly enough to be understood. It's also useful to use your voice to emphasize some especially important words. Use your own natural voice but with a little rehearsed discipline.

With regard to your physical performance, the nonverbal should frame or set up the verbal. Move first, set your feet, then speak. It communicates both inwardly and outwardly, so be careful of certain nonverbal basics:

Take a stable stance.

Make solid eye contact with individual audience members.

Take a few small steps to emphasize changing subject matter.

Gesture naturally as in normal conversation.

Rehearse out loud, standing up, and holding the manuscript you intend to read. Be sure to time your speech so that you don't take more than your allotted time.

VOCABULARY

Articulation

Delivery

Eye Contact

Intrapersonal Communication

Nonverbal Communication

Projection

Rate and Pauses

Speaker Apprehension

Volume

REFERENCES

1) O'Keefe, D.J. Persuasion: Theory and Research. Sage Publications, Inc., 2002.
Gunderson, D.F. and R. Hopper. "Relationships Between Speech Delivery and Speech Effectiveness." Communication Monographs 43 (2003).

2) Kortner, A.N. "Debate and Communication Skills," ERIC Digest. Bloomington, IN: ERIC Clearing House on Reading and Communication Skills, 1990.

3) Brownell, W., and K. Richard. "The Communication Apprehension and Speech Anxiety Peak Experience." Paper delivered at the annual meeting of the Eastern Communication Association. Hartford, Conn: ERIC, 1985.
MacIntyre, P.D., and K. Thivierge, K. "The Effects of Speaker Personality on Anticipated Reactions to Public Speaking." Communication Research Reports. 12-2 (1995): 125–33.

4) Campbell, K.K. The Rhetorical Act. Belmont, CA: Wadsworth, 1996.

Rybacki, K.C., and D.J. Rybacki. Communication Criticism: Approaches and Genres. Boston, MA: Pearson, 2002.

Sonntag, L. Speeches for All Occasions. New Jersey: Mimosa Books, 1993.

5) Adler, R.B., R.F. Proctor, and N. Towne. Looking Out/Looking In. Belmont, CA: Thompson/Wadsworth, 2005.

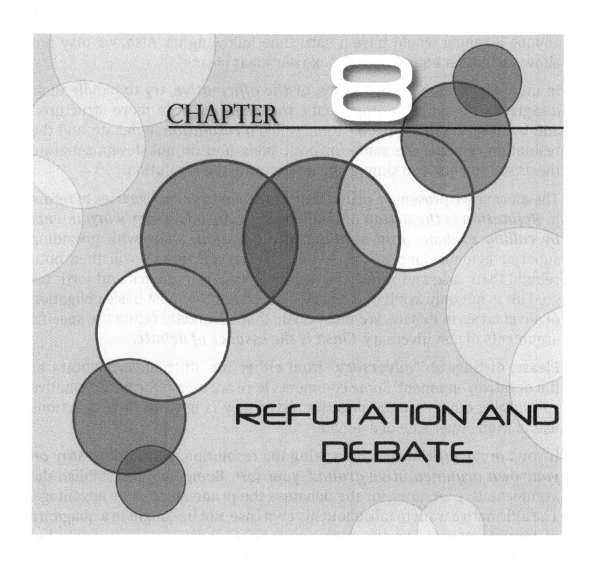

CHAPTER 8

REFUTATION AND DEBATE

"IT'S BETTER TO DEBATE A QUESTION WITHOUT SETTLING IT
THAN TO SETTLE A QUESTION WITHOUT DEBATING IT."

– JOSEPH JOUBERT –

By now, most people have some intuitive sense of how to respond to an argument. Give and take, agreement and disagreement, are as normal as conversation itself. That doesn't mean that we do it well. In the heat of a disagreement, we may revert to the merely reactionary responses we might have had before this study. We might also tend to be disorganized, so that anyone listening would have a hard time following us. Also, we may not allow each other equal time to make our ideas clear.

In more formal debate, advocates, or *the affirmative*, try to handle their disagreements with the opponents, *the negative*, in a more structured and fair way. There is a proposition, called *a resolution* in debate, and the resolution remains the same for both sides. You do not design separate thesis statements; you simply affirm or negate the resolution.

The affirmative presents a prima facie case then the negative tries to refute it. *Refutation is the action of challenging your adversary's arguments by calling evidence and analysis into question*, along with providing superior evidence and analysis yourself. The affirmative will then both rebuild their case and refute the negative attacks, and back and forth we go. This is not only askill that can be learned but the most basic obligation of adversaries in debate. We must clash, that is, directly refute the specific arguments of our adversary. *Clash is the essence of debate.*

Please, distinguish "*adversary*" from either the affirmative/advocate or the negative/opponent. Some comments here are meant for the affirmative specifically, others for the negative. Adversary is used to discuss actions useful from either side of a debate.

If you are the *affirmative* advocating the resolution, you want to *stay on your own argumentative ground*, your fort. Being able to establish the argumentative territory for the debate is the prime affirmative advantage. The affirmative want to talk about his own case, not be caught in a quagmire of negative attacks. The affirmative must be responsive to the negative, but it should do so in the context of the case that it presents.

The negative will try not to only tear down the walls of the affirmative fort, but *may draw the affirmative out into tangential territory*, distracting them from their case and forcing the negative advantage of presumption. If there is "*reasonable doubt*" about the efficacy of the affirmative case, doubt that they've met their burden of proof, *a tie goes to the negative's favor*. If we do a good enough job with refutation, our adversaries may wind up on the defensive, answering our attacks instead of being on the offensive with their own positions.

We'll learn the basic steps of refutation, debate formats that guarantee each side time to have its say, and a variety of strategies and tactics we can use to gain advantage in a debate.

LISTENING

There is no refutation tactic that is more important than careful listening. It's impossible to effectively refute an argument if you don't understand it. In fact, a good general principle for all criticism, rhetorical or otherwise, is this:

Understand and paraphrase the idea before you attack it.

It's been established through many studies that the average adult is a poor listener. We hear about half of the facts in a ten-minute talk then forget half of that within twenty-four to forty-eight hours. There is significant loss in retentionduring the first eight hours after a talk (1). In other words, **the average listening efficiency rate is 25%.** We absorb and retain about a quarter of what we hear. Often rates may be as low as 10%, while rates of 60% are so rare as to be phenomenal.

Therefore, it takes a lot of concentration to actually grasp the arguments that you're supposed to refute. This can be aided by the use of *a flow sheet*, a shorthand record of your adversary's arguments, which we'll discuss below. Just know for now that *you can't debate effectively without taking notes*. Indeed, you probably can't offer a very specific critique of a speech as an audience member without taking some kind of notes.

I've found, through practical experience in high school and collegiate debate, as well as many years of teaching speech, that listening is crucial, because *the seeds of an argument's defeat are sown within the language of the argument itself.* There is seldom an argument so perfect that it has no weak point. You can hear weaknesses in an argument only if you listen carefully. *Listen carefully to definitions*. They establish, not only the limits for discussion, but the burden of proof for the advocate. *Advocates must justify all the terms of the resolution*. Part of your job in refutation is to make sure the advocate meets his announced burden of proof.

Listening will provide the most important clues for which points may most invite attack. More importantly, *listening provides understanding*, a key aim of all debate education.

BASIC REFUTATION

Once you understand an argument, you can refute it using these steps (**2**):

1. ***Begin with an overview*** about the assembly of arguments, or the "case" of your adversary. Attack any key presumptions upon which the case depends, possibly revealing hidden presumptions not clearly defended. You should preview your own stance or philosophy for the debate as well.

2. ***Identify the argument*** you intend to refute. These will be numbered like our outlines. You should start with the first argument and work your way down the case, one argument at a time. Remember that the advocate has the right to determine the argumentative ground. It's both more courteous and easier for the audience to follow when you go in the order provided by the advocate. If you have additional arguments of your own, you may present them after you've satisfied your obligation to clash.

3. ***Paraphrase the argument.*** Put their position in your own words to secure understanding. It's possible that your opponent intends something different than you've understood, or that the audience has a view of its own. If the debate includes cross-examination, unclear intent can be clarified then.

4. ***Refute the argument*** in one or more of several ways described in more detail below, being sure to label your own counter-argument clearly and briefly. You may do one of the following:

A) ***Agree*** with the argument because it's relatively unimportant.

B) ***Diminish*** the argument's significance for the adversary's thesis.

C) ***Disagree*** with the argument by revealing its flaws.

- Point out any fallacies your adversary may have committed.
- Attack the grounds using the basic tests of evidence.

- Offer contradictory evidence from your own sources, arguing their superiority.
- Offer counter-argument that directly opposes your adversary's or opens other relevant but unmentioned areas of debate.

D) **Summarize** your position, especially emphasizing how your refutation affects the adversary's argument.

E) **Repeat** the above formula with each argument.

F) After you've refuted each argument, you may**offer an underview** summarizing the impact of your attacks on the adversary's case.

There's nothing fancy about the terms "overview" and "underview," by the way. It's pretty much the same as saying "introduction" or "conclusion." They're just customary terms from debate.

The opposition language of refutation usually has two grammatical parts:

"Their argument is..."

"Our response is...."

The affirmative language of refutation usually has three grammatical parts:

"Our argument is...."

"Their attack was...."

"Our response is...."

This language along with numbering the arguments as you go helps a listening audience to keep track of "the flow" of the debate from point to point.

DEBATE FORMATS

There are various formats for approaching a formal debate: Oxford, Oregon, and Lincoln-Douglas styles are among them.

Oxford and Oregon styles are generally **four person debates**, with two on the affirmative side and two on the negative. There is a **constructive** speech by each speaker—that is, a speech in which you build or construct your arguments—of lengths varying from 7 to 10 minutes. Constructive speeches are followed by a **rebuttal** for each speaker, usually of 3 to 5 minutes. The primary difference between the two styles is that **Oregon**

debate includes a cross-examination period by an adversary after each constructive speech, usually of 2 to 3 minutes.

Time limits are determined by various *forensic leagues*: the National Forensic League for high school, the American Forensic League, CEDA, NDT, and Phi Rho Pi, a community college league. There are also some international debate associations. Some have six person debate formats with three on each side. The word "forensics," by the way, relates to things judicial. In regard to debate, it means judicial reasoning. You may be familiar with the term "forensic medicine" from popular television shows like "CSI" or "Bones," meaning simply medicine or science related to law.

Lincoln-Douglas debate is named for a series of eloquent exchanges in 1858 between Abraham Lincoln and political opponent Senator Stephen Douglas. Basically, the difference from Oxford or Oregon styles is that it is a debate between *two people*.

We'll focus primarily on *parliamentary debate,* based loosely on British Parliament. They practice a rowdy form of interaction in which they frequently call for an opportunity to speak, peppered by *a spontaneous form of cross-examination*. They even hoorah and boo. This parent format can be seen on C-SPAN today. You may be surprised at how enthusiastic it is compared to our own Congress. NDT, or National Debate Topic style, uses a single topic all year requiring massive research for debaters. Students have to be prepared for both sides of a topic and lug massive amounts of proof. Parliamentary debate is *practiced in an extemporaneous manner*. Debaters are given a topic, have a limited time to prepare, and offer their arguments based on general knowledge of history and current events. Parliamentary debate differs also in that it only allows *one rebuttal per side.*

NDT and CEDA debate were waning in their ability to attract students. Parliamentary debate *renewed national interest* in debate at speech tournaments, and it's commonly practiced at many colleges today. It's also, in some respects, the easiest format to master, since it *involves less intense research*. It can be practiced as either two person or four person debates.

Also, since this is a more spontaneous activity than merely writing and giving speeches, it gives one *a chance to think on one's feet*, as we say. I allow my students a long preparation time on a resolution, unlike speech tournaments, so they research and have briefs on relevant issues. Yet the only speech that is entirely pre-written is the first affirmative speech. The rest is **responsive give and take** within given time limits.

PARLIAMENTARY DEBATE FORMAT

These debates may be practiced with policy propositions, as well, but we'll presume a value debate, which is what I use as the final assignment in my classes. The affirmative side is called **the government**, and the negative **the opposition**. These names are conventions of forensic competition. It's fine for class purposes to just call the two sides the affirmative and negative.

Constructive Speeches

A) **Prime Minister** (7 minutes)

1. Offer the exactly worded proposition.
2. Define the terms of the proposition, determining argumentative ground.
3. Establish an objective standard by which to measure the opposing values.
4. Prove that the value supported better meets the standard.

B) **Leader of the Opposition** (8 minutes)

1. Consider the definitions and either agree or disagree with them.
2. Either accept the standard offered by the government, or establish acounter-standard.
3. Offer direct refutation of the Prime Minister's case.
4. Present the opposition's case arguments, when applicable.

C) **Member of the Government** (8 minutes)

1. Defend definitions and standard, unless the opposition has accepted them.
2. Rebuild the government case and refute opposition attacks.
3. Attack the opposition's counter-arguments, when applicable.

D) **Member of the Opposition** (8 minutes)

   1. Defends the Leader of the Opposition's case.
   2. Attack the Member of the Government's responses.
   3. Extend and add arguments to the opposition's case.

Rebuttals

E) **Leader of the Opposition** (4 minutes)

   1. Extend upon and emphasize your key arguments.
   2. Offer some clear rationale why, given the standards applied, your counter-value is superior.

F) **Prime Minister** (5 minutes)

   1. Answer key opponent arguments.
   2. Rebuild the government case, ending on your own ground.
   3. Tell the audience why, given the standards, your value is superior.

Notice that the affirmative has one shorter constructive speech, but its rebuttal is longer, so both sides have equal time (**3**).

A timekeeper signals the countdown of minutes to help the speakers know how much of their allotted time is used up. This is usually done by holding up fingers for the number of minutes left at one-minute intervals. "Time" may be called out loud when the time is up, or they may make a "T" with two hands, the extended palm of one hand resting on the fingertips of the other. Nobody minds much if you take a few seconds to finish your sentence, but it's considered unfair, even rude to go overtime.

Notice that since there is only one rebuttal a side, the format requires that *the first speaker from each side also delivers the rebuttal*. If you're paired in a team, realize that the first affirmative speech from the Prime Minister is the most pre-prepared of all. Thus, it's not that great a burden for him to do a little extra time in rebuttal. Being the second speaker on either side is not a dishonor, though you have less floor time. That is where much of most important and extemporaneous refutation and counter-refutation occurs.

Note that there is *a curious shift in the order of speakers*. The negative gives the last constructive and the first rebuttal in a solid block of time.

That is another way that the negative advantage of presumption is balanced for the affirmative. They not only speak first, laying out the argumentative territory, they also speak last. Generally, beginning students find this confusing, and we're not required to use tournament rules, so I usually let them retain the normal alteration of order, allowing the negative to speak last. Also, a beginner in the Prime Minister position often finds it difficult to refute such a large block of opposition time.

It is usually easier **to have a clear debate**, one that focuses on the issues intended by the resolution, if the debaters **accept a common standard**. The same is true of accepting common definitions. The opposition should only presents **a counter-standard** or challenge definitions if the affirmative misrepresents the resolution somehow or unfairly limits the opposition's argumentative ground. In other words, affirmative definitions and standards should not violate **the neutrality rule** of propositions, which offers each side an equal opportunity to win. While the affirmative has the burden of proof, the opposition has to prove its arguments, too. Be careful about definitions and standards that may rob you of presumption. Neither side should allow itself to be cornered by standards that favor one side too much.

Time management is a critical aspect of debate success. If the government spends too much time refuting the opposition's arguments before rebuilding their own case with additional evidence and analysis, they'll almost certainly lose the arguments they've neglected. Both sides must also be careful to respond to all of the adversary's arguments during constructive speeches. Adversaries can argue that it's **unfair for you to wait until rebuttal to answer refutation**, as your adversary will have no additional speeches left to respond. If you don't leave time to refute your adversary's case, they can say that they must have won, since you have no response to their positions. You can offer **no new arguments in rebuttal**.

Observing the duties of each speaker as described above is another helpful method of time management. You don't want to waste time merely repeating your partner's arguments, unless it is to "extend" his analysis, offer additional proof, or respond to a new extension by the adversary with new analysis and evidence.

Time management in tournament debate is even more challenging due to three unusual conventions of this form of debate: *points of information, points of order,* and *points of personal privilege.*

While there is no formal cross-examination period, adversaries may ask questions during constructive speeches, as long as it isn't in the first or last minute of the time limit. You simply rise from your seat and ask if the speaker will yield to "*a point of information.*" Questions should take no more than about 10 to 15 seconds to ask and are not an opportunity for the questioner to make arguments. A speaker is expected to stop for a question or two, though it is **unethical for the adversary to continually badger** you during your speech. The speaker may refuse to take a question at a particular point by saying "**not at this time**" or "in **a moment,**" but to refuse all questions during your speech would be considered inappropriate.

Points of order are rarely used but are available in case there's a breach of the rules. For instance, **if someone offers a new argument or shifts ground in rebuttal**, you could stand and say "Point of Order." The speaker then stops and hasno opportunity to respond. You are addressing the judge or instructor, and he or she has the responsibility of making a ruling. They may make the ruling at that moment, or take it under consideration for the end of the debate. It may not bea significant enough matter to impact their immediate evaluation, or it may matter enough that it takes consideration.

Points of personal privilege occur even more rarely, but you may rise to point out that the adversary has **misquoted or insulted you** with an ad hominem argument. Noparticular judgment is required, though the speaker might apologize for his indiscretion.

In classroom debate, I usually suspend these conventions, except for my most spirited and confident students. Speaking extemporaneously is usually sufficient challenge for beginners.

It's also important to mention that **courtesy in listening** is a convention. While it's important to communicate with your partner over the positions you're hearing, do so by note, or wait until between speeches to confer. You'll be given some preparation time between speeches. Also, if you're too busy chatting, you might miss a key point for refutation. Your ability to ask just the right questions depends on paying courteous attention, too.

TOPICALITY: THE OTHER STOCK ISSUE

There is one stock issue not mentioned so far. It is relevant to all types of propositions, but topicality is particularly relevant in debate. It is considered **unethical when advocates exceed the generally assumed argumentative ground of the resolution**. If the advocate focuses on an extremely trivial portion of the resolution or uses definitions to twist its intended meaning, they've become non-topical or extra-topical. **This may be a strategic attempt** to confuse the opponent or render their preparation time useless. An advocate might focus on a minor topic aspect that nobody really knows much about simply to avoid refutation (4).

You might argue topicality from the negative side when there's an obvious attempt to avoid the main thrust of the proposition. When you do so, though, you put **all your eggs in one basket**, since it becomes the primary focus of your attack to argue that the affirmative is unfair. I don't object to someone arguing topicality then attacking the advocate's case anyway: "It's not topical, but even if it were they'd be wrong." Others, though, expect one to argue topicality exclusively. If it's not topical, they say, you don't debate it.

There are risks, though, in focusing on topicality arguments. At **Phi Rho Pi National Tournaments**, I judged parliamentary debate rounds. For the value, "The wall between church and state has grown too wide," the issue of topicality was key in a semi-final debate. The advocates took a European focus on the topic, using the conflict between Muslims and the French government's repression of their usual dress in public schools. Muslim women are not allowed by their religion to go bare headed but are not allowed to wear traditional head scarves to French schools.

During its fifteen-minute preparation time, the negative focused on the notion that this was about the separation of church and state in the United States. They issued a topicality argument that, since there is no formal separation of church and state in the constitution of France, the advocate's approach was outside the topic area. However, as the topic doesn't specify a constitutional sense of church and state, nor the United States, the judges found it appropriate to take a more global view.

Arguing topicality is not a tactic that I recommend for novices or classroom debate. You are topical as long as you stay inside the "fort" established by the terms of the proposition. For our purposes, it's just another way of saying something that you should already know: *Stick to the subject.*

QUESTIONS

Questions are one way *to understand and clarify positions*. If you don't clarify intent, you may target your argument strategy incorrectly **(5)**. *Once an advocate commits* to a point of view in cross-examination, his statements function as a sold basis for your refutation, and the person questioned *cannot easily shift ground*.

Questions should not be used merely to interrupt and rattle the speaker, though they sometimes are. There are other debate formats that have *separate question periods* aftereach constructive speech. In a class setting, questions may be much more informal, but they should come from the participating debaters rather than the audience.

What kind of questions should you ask in a debate? You may ask *open-ended questions*, those that invite some free elaboration:

> "What do you mean by X phrase?"
> "What is the significance of this argument?"
> "Can you give me another example?"
> "How did the source gather these statistics?"

It is sometimes necessary to *ask speakers to paraphrase their analysis* in words other than those used in their speech, to confirm your sense of their intention. The danger is that your adversary may ramble, wasting your time with evasive answers. The advantage is that speakers may inadvertently reveal a weakness that isn't apparent in a first hearing of the case. Sometimes the less said the better for the advocate.

You may ask *close-ended questions,* those that invite a yes or no response. The obvious advantage of close-ended questions is that you can more easily prevent abuse of your questioning time, and you can pin an opponent down, possibly even force him into a dilemma.

"Is it A or B?"

"Is it true or false that ....."

"Am I correct in paraphrasing your first point as...."

"Have you looked at the data from such-and-such a study?"

There is an ethic for close-ended questions, though. That last question would be to set up evidence for your side that you know of but which your adversary may not. It is not an opportunity to make an argument using that study as grounds. You should also **avoid the fallacy of forcing the dichotomy,** suggesting that there are only two alternatives whenothers exist. In courtrooms and debates, the fallacy appears in the form of **"the complex question"** in which a hidden presumption is assumed in a dilemma.

"Have you stopped using drugs? Yes or no? Yes or no?!"

The proper answer is to say, "I've never used drugs."

Some questions just can't be answered with a simple yes or no. It's the questioner's burden of proof to show that the person questioned used drugs. By presuming that inthe complex question, there's yet another potential fallacy, **ad hominem.** Thecomplex question is generally set up to diminish the credibility of the person questioned or to trick a person into an overly simple answer, not to clarify the truth. In many cases, a combination of closed and open questions is necessary to clarify and control debate time.

There are **strategic uses** of questions, though. You can use questions to attack the weakest point in the case, to pry it loose, and put the adversary on the defensive.

You can ask for additional evidence to press the burden of proof.
You can question the methodology by which the proof was gathered.
You can question warrants to set up a fallacy observation in your speech.

You may not make arguments in cross-x, but you can **use questions to set up your own arguments**. During your own speech, remind the audience of questions that you askedfor which the answers were unsatisfactory then launch your own position.

If you notice that two of your adversary's points seem in conflict, you might have an impulse to simply argue that it's a **contradiction** during your speech, but **a good fisherman knows how to set the hook.**

It would be clumsy to bluntly ask, "Doesn't A contradict B?" A clever person may simply answer, "No, and let me explain why." Instead, **lead him to repeat the contradiction**. Ask about point A with an open-ended question. If the adversary wanders, step in with a closed-ended question, "but didn't you also say B in your speech?" It may take some time, but you will have **attacked not just one but two arguments**. If two points contradict each other, the speaker doesn't get to choose one and continue to defend it; he loses both. Also, you may have created a sense of dramatic irony between you and your audience. Since the adversary made the contradiction, he or she will be unaware of it, even as you subtly dramatize the point.

Let's emphasize that word "subtly." **The tone of questioning should be respectful, even conversational.** Please, don't behave like some television lawyer. No drama. No histrionics. Questions aren't a time to fight, except in the time honored sense of a duel of wits. A person who comes across too aggressively may alienate audiences and cause sympathy for the adversary.

Consider **the Bush/Gore presidential debates** and the public reaction to Gore's audible sighing and condescendingly negative headshakes. Though Gore beat Bush soundly on issues in that first debate, public reaction forced himto back off into a defensive position and may have changed the tide in the election. Few noticed that President Bush spent much of the debate clenching and unclenching his fists, a nonverbal sign of suppressed anger.

REBUTTAL

Many debates are decided by rebuttals when the leader of each side says why their side has won and leaves a lasting impression with the audience.

You generally cannot cover very much material in a rebuttal, because they're shorter speeches. Also, audience attention span will erode at the end of the debate. Thus, the major purpose is to focus on the key points in controversy and to **"crystallize" issues**. That is, we must isolate and clarify those issues that we think are critical. Of course, some of those should be the ones that we think we're winning.

Do not merely summarize when there are outstanding questions from your adversary to be answered. Manage your time carefully so that you can emphasize all the points you think are key to your side in the debate.

1. *Answer any outstanding questions.*

2. *Extend upon and emphasize your key arguments.*

3. *Point out attacks to which the adversary hasn't responded.*

4. *Offer some clear rationale why, given the standard, your position is superior.*

It's up to the audience to decide which positions are most persuasive, but it's very important that you do more than rattle off individual points. Don't completely ignore anything. Even experienced judges may not consider arguments that go unmentioned in rebuttal, or may grant points for your adversary if you ignore them altogether. Just realize that ***not all points are equally important.***Go back to your standard, weigh key arguments against it, and explain clearly ***why you better satisfied the standard than your adversary.*** If you've each defended different standards, you argue why your standard is the superior choice.

This is also the time that the negative wants to ***make an issue of your affirmative burden of proof.*** Mention that they haven't proven what they've promised. Likewise, beable to mention ways in which you have met your promise of proof.

As much pressure as you may feel to cover arguments, just try to use good, clear word choice and ***don't panic or try to speak too quickly***. Try to save a little time to make a persuasive appeal at the end. The last argument you make may be the last thing they remember when they decide on the issue for themselves.

REFUTATION STRATEGY

There is one key question of strategy that most informs your use of debate tactics discussed below. Do you choose a straight refutation approach or make counter-arguments?

Since the negative has presumption, it is sometimes useful to use ***straight refutation.*** That is, you only attack the advocate's arguments without building any of yourown. You simply rely on the fact that the advocate has the burden of proof, force that burden of proof, andcreate no additional burden for yourself other than pure attack. ***If negatives defeat one stock*** *issue, they often win.* They simply put most of their time and effort on weak points of the case. Affirmatives sometimes put out a few **independent justifications**, just in case they lose one. Even with this simple offensive approach, negatives will generally open with some kind of opposing philosophy in their overview.

Straight refutation also makes sense because, just as the affirmative has the burden of proof, **the negative has the burden to clash**, to challenge the affirmative's arguments. A straight refutation strategy makes sure that the negative focuses on their primary obligation in the debate. It also helps with time management. If the negative does a good job of attacking arguments the affirmative builds, the affirmative may wind up either on the defensive or dropping their case in rebuttals.

However, when you don't offer yourself **the chance to be for something, rather than just against something**, you may surrender the opportunity to create identification or inspire your audience. Hence, some choose to create their own positions andapply them against the affirmative case, offering the audience a choice between two clearly expressed philosophies on the topic. That's called **counter-argument.** Just as the opposition has an obligation to clash with the advocate's arguments, **the advocate is also obligated to refute the arguments from the opposition** (6). It is possible that carefully constructed counter-arguments from the opponent may draw the advocate out of his fort and distract him from defense of his own case. Just remember that **if you offer a counter-argument, you must defend it** as well as attack, which can make your time management more difficult. There are at least **three ways** that you can manage a counter-argument strategy:

- You can build **an argument at the start** then apply it to the affirmative arguments as you go down the case. I said earlier that it's best to wait until after you clash with each argument before you make your own, but it is possible to build a kind of super-argument that defeats several points as you apply them specifically to the case.

- You can build individual counter-arguments that correlate directly to the advocate's on a point-by-point basis. They could constitute your refutation or be offered in addition to it.

- You can do arguments at the last or "the bottom" of the case, reflecting on how they impact earlier positions. The main advantage of this approach is that it's easier for audiences to follow. Also, you can achieve your primary obligation to clash with each argument directly first before you run out of time. As long as you introduce a simple version of the counter-argument in the first constructive, you can further develop it as you go.

No matter which approach you take, your refutation and counter-arguments must relate directly to the affirmative case. You can't just make points about the proposition in a general way.

REFUTATION TACTICS

There are three refutation tactics with which you already have some familiarity: applying fallacies, especially to warrants; attacking the grounds of the adversary'sargument; and countering the adversary's evidence with evidence of your own.

Applying Fallacies: You've had a chance to see fallacies in action. Let's review them by sub-groups, with nicknames, and in alphabetical order:

Fallacies of Appeal—Six Silly Slaps
Ad Hominem
Appeal to Ignorance—unfairly shifting the burden of proof
Appeal to the People (Bandwagon Argument)
Appeal to Pity and Fear
Appeal to Tradition or Novelty
Reductio ad Absurdum (Appeal to Humor)

Fallacies of Evasion—Four Horsemen of the Apocalypse
Avoiding the Issue
Red Herring
Seizing on a Trivial Point
Shifting Ground

Fallacies of Language—The Three Stooges

> Emotive Language
>
> Equivocal Language
>
> Jargonese

All of these can be called upon, **especially in a value debate where these kinds of fallacies are frequent** due to the common use of emotional appeals when we deal with deeply held values.

You've also seen logical fallacies that relate directly to the seven patterns of reason, but there are **other logical fallacies** that may happen as a matter of getting flustered while speaking "off the cuff."

Sometimes our reason runs in a circle, chasing its own tail, not unlike a dog at play. This is called, appropriately enough, circular reasoning. The mental action can be defined easily in terms of Toulmin. **Circular reasoning occurs when warrants merely repeat claims.**

> "All of us cannot be famous, because all of us cannot be well known."

So, what's wrong with that? "Well known" is just a synonym for "famous." The language consists of a repetition of the same thought with slightly altered word choice or grammar. The clue is that the argument, on the face of it, will likely seem redundant, with the speaker merely repeating the claim over and over as if to persuade by sheer force of repetition. Repetition may be persuasive, but it isn't necessarily logical. Other common names for this fallacy are "begging the question" or "tautology."

Here are a couple of contemporary examples:

Tom DeLay is a former House Majority Leader sentenced to prison for his involvement in a money laundering scheme discovered during a campaign finance scandal. *The National Review* criticized *The New York Times* for saying that, "Many of Mr. DeLay's actions remain legal only because lawmakers have chosen not to criminalize them." In other words, *The New York Times* asserted that DeLay is guilty by tautology (**7**).

MSNBC newsman Chris Matthews offered this circular reasoning, "I don't believe he had a responsibility to even answer that question—you have no responsibility to answer personal questions that people have no right to ask you (6)."

Non sequitur literally means "*does not follow*" in Latin. It occurs when an argument makes a huge inferential leap that doesn't make sense because steps in the thought process are missing. Sometimes ideas will pop out of us that aren't really connected, though they may seem to make sense to us at the time. A phone call from an animal lover to a talk radio show used this argument:

Grounds: Now that Saddam Hussein is gone, Iraq is a hotbed of looting, crime and rebellion. There's dog fighting and even camel fighting.

Claim: I say, "Bring back Saddam!"

Notice that there's no warrant. Warrants are commonly missing with non sequitur. There is no connective thinking to link the grounds to the conclusion drawn in the claim. It makes perfect sense to the speaker, in the midst of his disgust about dog fighting, but it's not a logical argument about Hussein... especially since he's been executed.

During the 2010 New York state elections, Tea Party backed candidate Carl Paladino had to explain why he sent emails including pictures of a woman having sex with a horse, President Obama and Michelle Obama dressed as a pimp and ho, and various other pornographic and racist chain letters. His answer was, "I'm in the construction industry." That's it. The missing warrant could have been an admission that such humor was common in his line of work and he didn't realize it was inappropriate as public discourse, but that's not what he said (8).

Other non sequiturs make even less sense, having no argumentative structure at all, such as this bumper sticker about illegal aliens that I saw in Arizona:

> "Men don't drop 'anchor babies,' illegal alien mothers do."

If you can explain that one to me, please, drop me a note.

Transfer fallacies are errors that extend reasoning beyond what is necessarily so. We'll focus on two, *composition and division.*

Composition fallacies conclude that because a part of something is a certain way, the whole of that something is the same. Simply recall the phrase, ***"What's true of the part is true of the whole."***

For instance, if you were buying cars and wound up being taken in by cool rims and a snappy leather interior—and it's red, too—you might tend to infer that the appearance of the car is reflected in the quality of the car as a whole, though it may not necessarily be so.

Let's say you've built a debate case on the proposition that unemployment is rising across the national economy, but you only used examples from two states to illustrate your point. While the claim may be generally true, you would have committed a composition fallacy by virtue of your limited evidence choice: "Because it's true in this state, it's true of the nation."

If you chose a college because they have a really good program for your major, you couldn't necessarily infer that it was a really good college overall.

Composition gets confused with hasty generalization. The difference between the two is the integrity of the whole. The example about a car part for the whole car is apt for composition, or a single department for a corporation. It isn't that there's too small a sample in a counting process, like hasty generalization. It's that a singular part of something is inaccurately perceived as necessarily representative of the whole.

One of the better examples of dual error, both hasty generalization and a fallacy of transfer/composition, came from an exercise in the third edition of Rybacki and Rybacki's *Advocacy & Opposition* (**9**).

Claim: Sports is a veritable hotbed of steroids use.

Grounds: Why, just last week, three more football players were suspended for steroids.

If we made the warrant manifest it would be:

Warrant: Three is a significant number, and football represents all sports.

There is hasty generalization, as three players are not a particularly large sample for football, let alone sports. Also, sports is a large class including several smaller sub-classes, football, baseball, basketball, soccer, etc. To characterize football is not to characterize all of sports, and that's the transfer fallacy of composition. So, another way to explain the fallacy is that a sub-class is not necessarily representative of the whole class (Figure 8.1).

Division is the reverse. It infers that what is true of the whole is necessarily true of the parts. Remember the phrase "What's true of the **whole is true of the part**." The transference here is from larger class to sub-class (Figure 8.2):

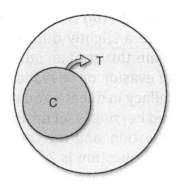

FIGURE 8-1.

I have mostly enjoyed being a Chrysler AWD Pacifica owner. For someone who camps, its roominess is convenient as is its roof rack, upon which I can carry a kayak. The mileage hasn't been all that bad for a crossover vehicle either. Yet it would be a transfer fallacy of division to say that, because I like the car overall, each part of it is good. For instance, there is a known defect that I've twice had to repair, a tendency for the engine mounts to shear off.

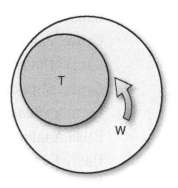

FIGURE 8-2.

Fallacy of division gets confused with sweeping generalization. Again, the difference is the integrity, the unity of the classes involved and whether the whole is representative of all its parts. If California as a whole votes for a Democratic candidate, does that mean that all the counties in the state voted Democratic? As strong a Democratic state as it is, you can usually count on Orange County to go its own way. The county itself is an excellent example for division because there are extremes along the political extreme among the various voting districts. Laguna Beach and Santa Ana are strong liberal strongholds while Newport Beach is among the most conservative in the state, indeed, the nation. If we reasoned from the overall tendency of the county to vote Republican and told an individual in Laguna Beach, "You're in Orange County, therefore, you're a Republican," that would be sweeping generalization. If we said, "Orange County went Republican, therefore, Santa Ana went Republican," that would be a transfer fallacy of division.

Red herring is often classified as a third kind of transfer fallacy, but it does have a slightly different dynamic and is an attempt to distract from the main thrust of an adversary's argument, so it's classified here as a fallacy of evasion or relevance. Regardless of where you classify it, it is a common fallacy in debate. You may notice in political debates how often and easily a red herring is set up. Panel members from the news corps will ask a pointed question, and the candidate will reply: "That's not the real question. The real question is X." Then the candidate goes his merry way arguing some tangential issue for which he is better prepared.

So, we can add these other logical fallacies to our list:

Fallacies of Logic - The Dirty Dozen
> Cause: Correlation vs. Causation
> Cause: False Cause
> Cause: Oversimplification
> Cause: Slippery Slope
> Circular Reasoning
> False Analogy
> Hasty Generalization
> Non Sequitur
> Red Herring
> Sweeping Generalization
> Transfer Fallacy of Composition
> Transfer Fallacy of Division

When applying fallacies as refutation be sure that you clearly identify the "giveaway"in your adversary's argument—the smoking gun, so to speak—the specific wording that reveals the fallacy. The process should look something like this.

1. *Establish the argument attacked.*

2. *Establish the part of the Toulmin format in which the fallacy exists.*

3. *Read the specific wording that reveals the fallacy.*

4. *Identify the fallacy.*

5. *Emphasize the impact on the adversary's case.*

Fallacies may occur at every level of a Toulmin argument. Fallacies of appeal and language may appear in **the wording of a claim** or a warrant. Fallacies of evasion are often seen in reworded claims, or in their sudden absence when an argument is dropped.

Logical fallacies will usually be imbedded in the **warrant**, especially above weak grounds. Isolating the warrant for scrutiny may determine that, no matter how good their evidence is, the reasoningthat fastens arguments together doesn't hold.

Overly dramatic examples in **grounds** could signal an appeal to pity or fear. Hasty generalization, perhaps the most common of logical errors,can occur due to sheer lack of evidence. The burden of proof for arguments of cause is especially difficult, so remember to look for the four causal fallacies when examining grounds beneath a claim for cause. The evidence may prove only a correlation (sign) rather than provide the necessary causal link to meet the burden of proof.

The use of "jargonese" or "equivocation" may be used in answers during **cross-examination**, a means of being intentionally evasive. Equivocation can be an intentional set-up in affirmative case building. An equivocation is presented to allow a shift in ground later in the debate, an act I sometimes call "**the amazing sliding rebuttal trick**."You spend a constructive speech attacking what you think your adversary means, but they come back and say, "Great argument, but it's a red herring because that's not what I meant at all." You'll then have wasted a constructive speech and lost the time management game to an unethical ploy. If you're already in rebuttal, you're stuck because you can't make new arguments more relevant to the "intent" of the case. It would be appropriate at that point to call for "a point of personal privilege."

You can do a more complete review of these fallacies in chapters 2 and 5.

Evidence Attacks

To the degree that grounds are **the foundation of an argument**, if you can undermine the evidence, the argument should fall. Tests of evidence should be appliedto grounds anyway, simply as a matter of course. **Here is a checklist for the "ten commandments" of evidence tests:**

Are the grounds **consistent** with other grounds offered in the case?

Was the evidence observed *first hand*, or is it hearsay evidence?

Is the *method* for gathering figures or statistics explicit and sound?

Are the sources *qualified*?

Are the sources *objective*?

Are the grounds *recent*?

Are the grounds *relevant* to the claim?

Are the grounds *representative* of the preponderance of evidence available? In the case of statistics, are the samples used representative?

Are the grounds *sufficient* to support the claim? This may be one the most common evidence errors. We may be more hopeful that the evidence supports our claim than correct.

Are the grounds *verifiable*? Can I find the same evidence elsewhere?

Think of these two catalogues, tests of evidence, as well as the fallacies, as checklists for refutation. Note that they're alphabetized to help you with memorization.

When you apply the tests of evidence, remember to take these basic steps:

1. *Identify the argument.*

2. *Identify the evidence to be tested.*

3. *Summarize the content attacked.*

4. *Apply the evidence test.*

5. *Describe the impact of the evidence attack on the argument and the case.*

There is one last evidence attack worth mentioning. Sometimes an adversary's evidence simply doesn't jibe with our everyday common experience. We call such evidence *counter-intuitive.* For instance, in anti-smoking speeches, I've heard second-hand smoke arguments for decades. That second-hand smoke is dangerous forthose near smokers is well-established. One argument that has never made intuitive sense to me, though, is the notion that second-hand smoke is even more dangerous for the non-smoker. Why? Because the smoker has a filter, the argument goes. Well, maybe he does, and maybe he doesn't, but I've never been convinced that being in the room with smoke could possibly be more dangerous than inhaling and holding it in one's lungs.

When arguing that something is counter-intuitive, it's more an appeal to audience logic than a formal attack. Yet, if the evidence seems to contradict their basic common sense or everyday experience, they may side with you.

Offering Counter Evidence

The above evidence refutation illustrates more than how to take evidence apart. It reminds us that it's easier to refute other people's evidence when you have better evidence of your own. Take, for instance, the evidence test of recency. If you have more recent evidence that takes new facts into account, you would simply note the date of your adversary's evidence, perhaps as a question during cross-examination, then offer more recent evidence in your next speech. Debate is sometimes decided by which side has the stronger grounds.

Offering counter-evidence proceeds much like other refutation tactics:

1. *Name the argument.*

2. *Identify and summarize the evidence to be challenged.*

3. *Offer superior evidence.*

4. *Establish why it's superior.*

5. *Describe the impact, the failure of your adversary's claim.*

Apply the tests of evidence to your own sources first to avoid counter-refutation. Attacks that are good for the goose are good for the gander, too.

Evidence can be superior in several different ways. It can be superior in terms of the tests of evidence, more easily verified multiple sources, for instance. It can use more recognized and qualified sources. It can also be superior in the sense that you have more evidence.

You probably know that in a capital case the standard for evidence is that it must be acceptable "beyond a reasonable doubt." However, in civil courts, the standard is "*the preponderance of evidence*," and that is probably closer to the standards used by the average listening audience when hearing arguments about social problems. An example would be the O.J. Simpson murder trial. By the first standard, there was sufficient reasonable doubt for Simpson to escape a murder charge. However, when the civil trials from the victims' families applied the second standard, the preponderance of evidence was against O.J.

It's time for a caution: The potential downside of using more evidence to beat an adversary is that you may be tempted to yield to a **shotgun, or spread refutation** strategy. This occurs when you attempt multiple levels of attack against every single point, trying to overwhelm an opponent with the sheer amount of evidence. Apart from being inaudible to an audience, speeding is often an attempt to cover up poor quality arguments. If you're going touse counter-evidence in refutation, use enough, but **prefer quality over quantity.**

As a debater, I would usually apply two pieces of my best evidence to each one of my opponent's. Yet I was always careful to edit my evidence carefully so that it was not too lengthy. Further, I would save at least one piece of good evidence, perhaps even my best, for the coup de grace in rebuttal.

You can do a more complete review of evidence tests in Chapter 3.

ADVANCED REFUTATION TACTICS

There are other tactics that you can try once you're confident about the morebasic techniques described above. You can argue alternative causation; point out contradictions, dilemmas, and double standards; observe that an argument isn't unique; use the adversary's own evidence against them; argue counter-productivity; and run an adversary's argument out to its farthest logical extent, sometimes approaching a point at which the adversary's point becomes absurd.

Alternative Causation

Whenever you perceive that the pattern of reason in an argument is cause, observe whether the adversary is committing **a fallacy of oversimplification**. Recall that there are usually multiple causes for difficult social problems. More than namingthe fallacy, though, you can **offer evidence of several other causes**.

For instance, if an advocate made the popular argument that violence in the media has increased the likelihood of assault and murder, you could point out a variety of other events linked to violent crime: childhood abuse, liquor and drug addiction, which are both linked to childhood abuse, poverty, and pathological disorder.

Janet Curry of Columbia University and Erdal Tekan of Georgia State University compiled research on abuse and crime in 2005. They included cases of famous killers who were beaten as children, including sniper John Mohammed. They also suggest links between violence and alcohol or drug abuse and poverty (**10**). In fact, the majority of people in jail for violent crimes have these links in common, so there's statistical support, too. There's a significant body of evidence for each of these counter-causes, while the links between media violence tend to be ***anecdotal.*** It's a perfect set up for arguing alternative causation. This tactic would put the adversary in the position of having to prove that his cause is more important than any of these others, a significant burden of proof. Also, it would make it harder for him to win the time management game, as he'd have to offer some responses to the alternative causes that you've provided.

By the way, recall that when we say that evidence is "anecdotal," we mean that there are some examples but no consistent statistical measure. When you drop that word, it's best that you have numbers supporting your side.

Here's a real life example of arguing alternative causation:

> Barry Marshall won the Nobel Prize in medicine for his discovery that peptic ulcers were caused by an infection—not stress, smoking, or alcohol.... (He) opened up a line of research that has utterly changed the way scientists think about infection and illness. Simply put: Many deadly, chronic ailments typically blamed on lifestyle—heart disease, cancer, diabetes and others—may actuallybe triggered by viruses and bacteria. If true, the repercussions are almost beyond imagining (**11**).

What does one do when confronted with an alternative causation argument? One responds by fortifying the causation you defend with figures and statistics, arguing that it is the main or a significant cause and that dealing with it will be useful, even if it doesn't account for all the potential causes. One can also press the person offering alternative causation to quantify the degree of influence his causes have on the issue at hand. In other words, it becomes a debate of percentages over which cause is the most important.

Contradiction and Dilemma

We've already noted that *contradictory arguments eliminate each other*.

In an article in *The New Republic*, reporter Amitai Etzioni made this point about contradictory positions among Afghanistan insurgents who complain about civilians being killed by the United States:

> Insurgents are violating the rules of war while demanding to be protected by them. The rules require that those engaging in warfare separate themselves from the civilian population with uniforms or insignia, on uniforms as well as vehicles. What is at issue here is not a small matter of a logo on one's hat or sleeves. It is a matter of enabling adversaries to separate the fighters from the civilians and to spare the latter **(12)**.

Pointing out contradictions is a strong debate tactic. However, another possibility is to *place an adversary in a dilemma,* forcing a choice between two critical aspects of a case, the loss of either of which is damaging. Also, one can simply show that what your adversary wishes to support creates an alternative damage of some kind.

A student group was discussing the value topic that "We should better honor soldiers defending us in the Middle East." The advocate's line was that the mission in Iraq and Afghanistan is noble, that we're helping to create freedom and democracy,and that protesting against the war undermines their mission. The opponent arguedthat the advocate is in a dilemma when he asks us to support the official line,since the official line itself dishonors soldiers. The official line has included sendingsoldiers to war without sufficient numbers or even adequate body armor to protect-them. The soldier's friends and families have had to gather money so that they can buy their own body armor. How is it honoring the soldiers to place them in danger without the means to do the job we supposedly honor? Further, the opposition asked, does it make sense to say, "We honor our slain soldiers," but then conceal their bodies from public scrutiny upon their return? Evidence cited included that the Bush administration enforced a ban on photographs of the caskets arriving at military bases. The same has been done with casualties. Between 9/11 and mid-2005, the Pentagon's Transportation Command transported 24,772 patients from battlefields. All the transport is done literally in the dark. In most cases, photos were banned. As one mother of a slain soldier said:

> Does it make sense for people to be outraged at parents who have lost children in the war but oppose it, because they lost children and find it a noble death? At the same time, those who support the war are loath to increase health benefits and pay for veterans and their family. Is "honor" only in the words (**13**)?

The dilemma is that we can blindly support the war as a means of honoring soldiers, but that means implicitly that we do things that dishonor them by putting them at risk without sufficient support. The best way to honor them, the opposition argued, is to support the soldiers by challenging policy that dishonors them. In other words, how can you both support a war that dishonors soldiers and ask that we honor them more?

Dilemmas could be common in debates over **_alternative fuels_** for the future, one of the hottest topics of the day. The justification for alternative fuels is that fossil fuels pollute, yet alternative fuels also yield environmental damage with significant side effects. Take **_ethanol_**, for instance. Brazil is the world's largest exporter of ethanol fuels made from sugar cane and has been held up as a model for flexi-fuel cars that can run on mixtures of gas and ethanol alcohol (**14**). However, there have been serious charges of air and water pollution, as well as deforestation. Burning sugar cane fields is used to drive out snakes and protect workers from sharp cane leaves, worsening air pollution. There's a law in Brazil that they have to stop... by 2017, but that's a lot of burning in the meantime. Massive amounts of fertilizer are used that run off into already limited clean water sources. Rain forests critical to global oxygen production have been cut back for huge acreage of sugar cane. Brazil and other developing countries convert land in undisturbed ecosystems, such as rainforests, savannas, or grasslands, to biofuel production, and they limit crop production when agricultural land is diverted to biofuel production. Thus, we may place ourselves in **_a dilemma between worsening world starvation and reducing global oil consumption_** (**15**).

Some have argued a "**biofuel carbon debt.**" Land use change releases more CO_2 than the annual greenhouse gas reductions that these biofuels would provide by displacing fossil fuels. Sugarcane ethanol and soybean biodiesel each contribute to nearly half of the projected indirect deforestation Another problem is that while gas consuming cars can be converted to flexi-fuel cars, they will get lower fuel mileage and have a shorter shelf life than gas, forcing more production and worsening the other side-effects mentioned above. Also, due to the corrosive nature of ethanol, engine life is shorter and so would require increased use of other resources, such as steel production that also pollutes **(16)**.

So, on one hand, you get a new fuel that reduces certain kinds of pollution and boosts the economy of formerly poor countries like Brazil; on the other, you create a whole new set of environmental problems that may be just as bad or worse, along with the threat of world starvation.

When confronted by a dilemma, one may argue that the adversary is "*forcing the dichotomy*" because there is a third alternative, a middle road between these two sides. For instance, we could engineer improvements in the fuel that would not threaten engine life, develop additives to preserve shelf life for ethanol, or phase in pure ethanol engines. We could take measures to balance land use between subsistence crops and the economic temptation of conversion. One can also update the evidence of the adversary showing that some aspects of the dilemma have already been solved.

Double Standards

There is a common psychological tendency for people to perceive things in their own favor, to apologize sometimes for themselves while accusing others who behave no differently than we do. Likewise, your adversaries may fall into the problem of "*the pot calling the kettleblack.*" In other words, they've applied a criticism to your position that may equally apply to theirs; or they've applied a standard to one thing though not to another of similarkind. We call these "double standards," and they can be reversed to your advantage. It's an especially useful technique in value debates, since standards are both critical and subjectively interpreted. Here is a potpourri of statements in the press arguing that someone else has practiced double standards **(17)**:

- "Is turnabout fair play? If members of the Christian right truly believe that it is only fair and reasonable to teach intelligent design as an alternative to evolution in public schools, would they not agree that it is equally fair to teach evolution in their churches as an alternative to intelligent design?"

- "I'm saddened that the senators feel it is appropriate to ask John G. Roberts if he will allow his Catholic beliefs to influence his decisions on the Supreme Court. Would that same question be asked if he were Jewish, Baptist, or any other religion? This country was founded on tolerance for all cultures and religions. Since when has Catholicism become a stigma for judicial service?"

Catholic belief was a huge issue in the election of President Kennedy. One wonders if the Mormonism of Mitt Romney, a likely candidate for President in 2012, will become an issue for his election.

As thrilled as many were to hear Pope Benedict XVI say in 2010 that condoms may be used in certain situations, the situations themselves seem to apply a curious double standard. The Pope says that a gay male prostitute, for instance, can use a condom to prevent the spread of AIDS. However, a normal couple trying to practice safe sex or avoid unwanted pregnancy may not. It's a step forward from the previous Pope, who said that condom use may actually worsen AIDS, but the new edict suggests that male prostitution can have advantages that faithfully married Catholics can't **(18)**.

In another amazing turn, the U.N., which has often been a bastion for human rights, recently removed "sexual orientation" from a resolution addressing extrajudicial, summary, or arbitrary executions. The vote was mostly driven by a majority of African, Middle East and Caribbean nations. These are nations that have the highest incidence of gay hate crimes. While the resolution aims to reduce extrajudicial, summary or arbitrary executions in general, the removal of a specific reference to sexual orientation could lead some to interpret that it is now okay to kill someone merely because they are gay. The new standard says, "Don't extradite, don't execute," but it excludes gays as those to be protected by the standard **(19)**.

Not Unique

You may be able to note that an attack from an adversary is not unique to your position. A bad effect that your adversary associates with your position or present circumstance may be just as likely with other positions and circumstances, perhaps even the adversary's.

Return to the "media causes violence" argument (one of my favorite whipping boys, I confess). We could easily observe that violence is not unique to the era of media.If media is a primary cause of violence then why was there so much violence throughout history? The Old Testament is one of the bloodiest books I've ever read. There's certainly an abundance of information suggesting that we didn't suddenly degenerate into savages as a result of playing video games. I would then argue that violent human behavior is non-unique to the media age.

Let's say that we're debating the resolution that "environmentalism is more important than capitalism," and we discuss clear cutting, the process of denuding whole areas of trees through logging and agriculture practices. As the affirmative, I argue that this is bad because it creates erosion; it exposes brush to direct sun, causing it to dry more easily and lead to fires; and it damages animal habitats increasing species reduction. The negative argues that we need clear cutting because it provides employment. I then argue that unemployment is not unique to stopping clear cutting. First, unemployment exists as a natural economic phenomenon and sometimes requires retraining for other jobs. Second, clear cutting itself creates unemployment for the logging industry. Once you've clear cut the area around your homes, what do you do for work? During the most intensive period of clear cutting in the American Northwest, when logging increased by 15%, employment for loggers and sawmill operators dropped by 12,000. A more managed and selective logging system not only keeps people employed in the present, it guarantees logging jobs for the future (**20**).

Reversal of Fortune

There is also the opportunity to *ju-jitsu evidence to your own advantage*. Warrantsare somewhat subjective. Different speakers may infer differently from the same evidence. If you look carefully at your adversary's grounds, you may find that they really don't support his points. In fact, you may be able to *steal their grounds for your own counter-claims by applying a different warrant.*

One example is a discussion of the three-strikes law in California. Someone with two prior convictions for serious crimes can be sentenced from twenty-five years to life for even minor offenses. Some argue that it's the most effective law ever, imprisoning more criminals and deterring future crime. Others say that it is ineffective, expensive, and constitutes cruel and unusual punishment.

An adversary argues that the three strikes law is effective because 26% of the prison population is there because of this law, not counting another 80,000 that are in prison for lengthier sentences on second strikes. He further argues that 44% of third strike prisoners committed serious and violent crimes against others. He has a chart from the California Legislative Analysts Office to prove his point. The obvious question for you is what did the other 56% do? If you look at the chart from which these statistics were derived, you'd find that only 14% of all convicts committed assault, and another 5% were convicted for weapons possession, though they had not in fact used the weapon. 30% were property crimes like burglary, and 24% were for drug offenses. Almost as many people are in jail for simple possession as a third strike (13%) as are there for assault, twice as many as for assault with a deadly weapon. Using the same evidence presented by your adversary, you then reason that the law is ineffective because less than half of third strike convicts did anything that serious for their third strike. Also, the same chart shows increased costs to the state of $3 billion a year (**21**).

Using either the same source or the particular piece of evidence as your adversary against him is ***an economical and damaging tactic***. All evidence may be subjectively read. Listen carefully, and you may find that you can interpret their grounds with a different warrant so that it supports your claim rather than theirs. It's an especially handy tactic when you don't have much research of your own, or get caught off guard by ideas you hadn't expected. There's ***a benefit to your ethos*** since you may look like you're giving the more honest and objective analysis of the same source. Further, since you're applying different reasoning, you may ***set up a fallacy charge*** for the adversary's warrant.

Counter-Productivity

Observing that someone is working against themselves, shooting themselves in the foot, as it were, is useful in both value and policy discussions.

When we support a value, we set up goals to live by. Yet our approach to the value may inadvertently damage those very goals.

Let's say we're debating corporal punishment as an effective parenting tool, and an adversary argues that a little judicious spanking creates more respect for parents and improves behavior. Yet spanking children to make them "be good" tends only to make them more aggressive and contributes to the well-known cycle of abuse, a 2009 study reveals (**22**).

There are several studies suggesting that DARE programs are not only ineffective at preventing drug use but may inspire young people to be more curious about drugs. The General Accounting Office declared the program a complete failure (**23**).

Some have argued that it's counter-productive to draft soldiers, since we need an army thatwants to be on the front lines.

Some have argued that Israel's tactics in suppressing Palestinians is counter-productive to the long-range goal of self-defense, let alone peace, since it inspires retaliation. After an Israeli assault on the Gaza alleyway, an Israeli soldier commented openly on his surprise at the civilian damage they had inflicted. He was shocked by some of the scenes inside Gaza, describing whole neighborhoods leveled.

Soldiers expressed their sincere regrets that any civilians died. After only a few weeks of combat, the battlefield looked like it had been active for years, the destruction was so extreme. Palestinian doctors say that more than 900 people have died, half of them civilians, since Israel began Operation Cast Lead in Gaza on December 27, 2009. Thirteen Israelis have died, three of them civilians (24).

The argument goes that using force against countries harboring terrorists, rather than targeting individuals and groups more carefully, is simply breeding the next generation of terrorists. Some have made the same argument about our involvement in Iraq, which was a relatively secular state compared to Iran but now has a solidified core of Muslim extremists.

Running Arguments to Their Furthest Logical Extent

One way of attacking an adversary's warrant is to apply their logic to circumstances that go beyond their intent but that remain logical. It may sometimes be combined with humor for maximum effect.

A gay student of mine was upset about an editorial, "Sex and Safety," published inthe *Los Angeles Times* of March 19, 2006. It advocated closing ***gay bath houses*** as a solution to HIV. The student argued:

> Unsafe and safe sex occurs everywhere and between both genders. Should the country also close motels? Shall bars be shut down because people go home together and have unsafe sex? Shall we go into people's homes and make sure that they're wearing condoms?

Now, there's a point at which you can run into a slippery slope fallacy.In this case, that point would be going into people's homes to make them wear condoms. That's not really analogous to shutting down public places. Yet comparing what an adversary criticizes to similar situations that we generally like can be effective. If the advocate argued that bath houses were different, you could point out that it's a double standard. One could have the advocate in a dilemma: Either you're going to apply the law to everyone, regardless of sexual orientation, with all the likely outcry and problems of enforcement, or you're practicing a double standard that discriminates.

There's a popular notion that we should phase out ***Social Security*** and allow younger people to invest in their own retirement plans rather than pay into a system that is allegedly going bankrupt. By that logic, when we can't make the family budget because of a low bank account, we should stop putting what we make into the account, making ourselves less able to pay for our household needs. The system is in danger of going bankrupt; let's make it a self-fulfilling prophecy by reducing payments to it. What then happens to those who have paid into it all their lives? And how well do you think the average citizen is going to do gambling on their futures with Wall Street?

There have been recent Tea Party arguments that ***taxation*** is basically a form of theft, that we should have more of our own money to spend as we like, and that the vast majority of government services could be administered by the private sector. While I'm about ready to throw the postal system up for grabs among privatized agents, and I'd like a more direct say as to whether my tax dollars are used for war, let's think this no taxation position through to its farthest logical extent.

A clever young woman who identifies herself only as "Anok" did an analysis on an anarchist website called "Identity Check." Would you agree with her, for instance, that even in an anarchistic society, we'd have to pool some resources together to maintain a minimum standard of living and basic public safety? We need water, we need sewage run-off, roads, garbage collection, and education, correct? If the government doesn't give us these things, we'd have to calculate out their costs per household and pay them by other means, right? What might those costs be?

Anok's research found that these are the average per household costs for various services over a year: Waste Disposal, including sewage and garbage pickup is about $102 per household per year. Public Schooling is $5,000 per year per student, unless you want private schools that often charge upwards of $8,000 per year in tuition. Fire Departments cost $778 per household per year, according to data from the largest cities, though smaller towns may be cheaper. Road Maintenance is a surprising $3592 for a little over half a mile. How many miles of road do you think you need in your new world without taxes? What if you do something wrong on those roads, hurt somebody, and get sued? The average legal assistance per household based on current public services is $3000 for 20 hours worth of work, assuming a $300 per hour attorney rate. If you're poor, you're out of luck because there would be no budget for public defenders.

What if someone attacks you in your home? We could dispense with police, cling to our right to bear arms, and forego any expense other than weapons maintenance. On the other hand, police protection is about $584 per household per year. Based on our bills from private security companies in the Middle East, we might suppose that they'd be a little higher. Unless you want to buy all your books or rely entirely on the internet, public libraries are about $41 per year per person. Maintenance of public parks and recreational areas is about $13,235 per acre per year. Even if you don't have large parks, there are many public spaces that need maintaining, and that adds up. So, the total cost per household per year for even these minimum services is $26,332 per household. This includes no military, no government medical care, and no Social Security.

Then Anok looks at taxes. The average household income in the United States is $40,000 per year. The average tax is 18% at the federal level and 5% at the state level. The average property tax is $2000. So the average income household pays about $11,200 in taxes. Take a wild guess at sales taxes, gas taxes, etc., and you're about $11,700 a year. In sum, she reasons, *the average*

household would be overpaying by $14, 632 a year for basic expenses in a world without taxes. Throw in the fact that 91 million Americans live near the poverty level of $17,000, and 80 million of them get medical care only due to Medicaid. Probably, these impoverished households could not fork out enough to cover education, medical treatment, or help from police and firemen. Maybe a little taxation isn't such a terrible thing, reasons this young woman considering anarchy as a political position (**25**).

It only requires a little imagination and some parallel reasoning to damage the logicof an adversary by revealing that logic at its extreme.

EXTEMPORANEOUS THINKING

We've been primarily concentrating on text building in a written sense. There are basically **four ways to deliver a speech**:

Entirely without specific preparation, or "impromptu";

Reading from a manuscript;

Memorizing a text, then delivering it without a manuscript;

Or extemporaneously with an outline, but not a fully worded speech. **Debate requires that we speak in a more extemporaneous manner**, using some language from prepared briefs but spontaneously forming the language of our refutation. This is a little scary for some at first. Yet the most useful, even necessary, skill for maximum function in employment, as well as social and civic interaction, may well be extemporaneous speaking.

In real life careers, we often have to pull our thoughts together in a brief time, organize them, and present them "**off the cuff**." That phrase, by the way, is a literal reference. In the old days, when men wore starched and detachable cuffs, they would literally jota few notes on their cuff to prompt them during presentations.

But what would you write on your cuff if you had one? Confronted with masses of thoughts and information, the mind reels at the prospect of responding so immediately. The common phenomenon of speaker apprehension can be increased beyond situations in which you have a fully worded manuscript to depend upon.

We've seen **certain checklists** and forms throughout this text: stock issues, tests of evidence, and fallacies. Of course, Toulmin's model is our standard form. We can call these checklists and forms "*cookie cutters*." They help us to look at a mass of information, the cookie dough and, by applying the form of a particular cookie cutter, we can distinguish distinct uses of this information mass.

After a certain amount of experience with these standardized forms, you can use them to respond to argument, almost instinctively, in a natural and organized way. So, extemporaneous speaking is not being unprepared. It's having a grasp of the above cookie cutters and applying them to open questions within a brief time of preparation. Even an impromptu speaker can use these typical patterns of speaking to shape his or her thoughts:

> What's the who, what, when, where, why, and how of this?
> What's the past, the present, and the future of this?
> What are the causes and effects of this?
> What is the problem, the cause, and the solution of this?
> Which is the least important and the most important of these things?
> Or ask the stock issues of the three types of propositions.

You get a topic. Your mind is blank. Your pulse starts to race. Your mouth getsdry. Your hands get wet. You start thinking about your sense of personal insecurity instead of the issue at hand. Stop. **Take a cookie cutter and apply it to the topic.** You can't know everything about the topic. Nobody can. Yet you may be surprised how much you do know, if you ask yourself systematically, "What are the effects and what are the causes?"

When I teach, and I suspect this is true for other teachers, what I do in front of the room is both spontaneous and the result of long planning. We have learned many bits of lessons and examples, just as a comedian has memorized many jokes, and we pull them out of memory based on the structural outline that best evokes them.

When you can manage extemporaneous speaking in real-world settings, you'll create a more authoritative and confident image for yourself. Even very successful businessmen join Toastmasters to practice this very skill. In a market in which most jobs will require at least some oral communication competence, it's important. For leadership, it's critical. And there's one other tool you can use to help, the flow sheet.

A student sample has been inserted to give you a sense of how one might look. Everyone's will be a little different, as some will want more notes than others.

Affirmative

Democrats 8trongr Platform for 2004 election

D. Civil Rights - Vehicle for Reform

1. D platform on economy will benefit Americans
   &1. Raising min. wage ($7/Hr.)
   &2. tax reform to create Jobs
   &3. Middle class is bombarded
      — will insure 98% will get tax cuts

2. Federal Responsibility for Education
   &1. Smaller classes, elem. Secondary
   &2. No Child left behind
   &3. Better teachers
   &4. Student aid & tax credits for all students

3. Clean up envir./future Pollution
   &1. Strengthen envior. act
   &2. Restore "Polluter Pays"
   &3. Restore leased land & respect nat'l Parks

Negative

Republican platform will deliver

1. Economy
   &1. Sweeping tax relief
      W - saved Americans $
   &1. reduces, trade agreements
      W - reinforces SS
   &1. SS won't be cut taxes not raised

2. education need to meet obligations
   &1. Children have access to free 1st rate education
   &2. No Child left behind
      W - Higher education
   &1. 73 billion increase in fin. aide
   &2. tax credit

3. Environment Improving? Yes
   &1. CleanSkys report
   &2. Bush cleaned up Browns fields as promised.

Affirmative

1. Economy
   1. Republicans want to keep min. wage @ $5.15/hr
      — 200,000 a year or more a year will have their tax cuts repealed.
      — 2003 & 2004 tax cuts will be permanent under Rep. platform. (7 trillion?)

2. Education
   — No child left behind born D & R disagree on.
   — R. Want to turn it over to the federal gov.
   ✱ — most places that need the funds won't get it because they can't pass.
      — Military: troops to teachers
      — D: after School Care, Shools open til 6 pm.

3. Environment
   — Clean Sky Initiative lets businesses to pollute
      《Browns fields (D & R's)》
      — Arctic Nat'l will put life & drilling
      ✱ huge Republicans want to drill here
      — Interfer w/ Research

Negative

1. Education
   — no child left behind
   — more qualified teachers
      (reduced restrictions on than

2. Economy
   — Dem. raise min. wage
   — Implies it will help economy
   — Reduced taxes 25 million
      Sm. business owners.
   — After 9/11 = Recession
      Unemployment 6.3%
      This year dropped to 5.1%
   — Strongest economy
      (140 million in workforce)

3. Education
   — 17 mill. new grant $ to improve quality (NCLB)
   — Troops to teacher, highly qualified people & funds
      Injured soldiers from Iraq war.

4. Environment
   — Reduced 70% of some emissions.
   — EPA: by 2020 emissions from power plants will be drastically reduced. — increased wetland

Negative Rebutal

Rep. better platform

1. Economy
- Alternative min. tax
- Economy is strong it's in "the numbers"
- 1.5 mil. New Jobs from last year.
- Unemployment down in 49 States.

2. Education
- Edu. is a state obligation
- must assume a majority of the Responsibility and Obligation.
* Scapegoat?

3. Environment
- Free 1st Rate education
- R. Policies geared towards results.

(lead for over 100 years / fresh platform) Contradictory

Affirmative Rebutal

1. Economy
- America is asking for a better economy.
- taxes not accounted for outsourcing
- Worst since the depression

2. Education
- 27 billion less than promised
- Promised affordable education and she being Middle Class doesn't see that as foreseeable

3. Environment
- 20,000 facilities to spew more smog
- Promised 5 Billion to Nat'l parks
- only delivered a fraction of this.

FLOW SHEETS

A flow sheet is *a note taking system for debate* that will help listeners and speakers keep track of the "flow" of arguments from speech to speech. Take a sheet of 8×10 or legal-sized paper, hold it long side up, then fold the paper in half. Fold that half by half again, and you're left with *four creased columns.*

You write notes in the first column on the left for the Prime Minister, being sure to leave some blank space at the bottom of the column for opposition arguments yet to come. This is important, as you want to be able to *follow each argument and theresponses to it from left to right*, all the way across four constructive speeches. You can then flip the paper over and use the columns on the back for rebuttals.

The language has to be abbreviated. Unless you have shorthand skills, you'll getlost trying to write every word down. Lean back, listen carefully, and when you have a sense of the whole argument, jot some quick notes down. Try to include some notation of sources on grounds and be sure to jot down key statistics.

IN SUM

We've seen that there are various refutation strategies and tactics. Yet I'd like to offer a word about *being a team*, if your instructor chooses to stage team debates. If debating alone in a Lincoln-Douglas format, you don't have to worry about satisfying a partner's goals. In a team, however, you have to coordinate your attack, both to avoid contradicting each other and to leave each other a reasonable amount of argumentative ground. If you listen to your adversaries and each other, each may pick up things that the other has missed. You will each do better if you respect your partner as you would yourself, and your experience will be more enjoyable and satisfying. Even if you don't have a lot of time to meet, sharing ideas by email can help prepare you for a mutually supportive and enjoyable debate. Relax. You can do it!

VOCABULARY

Adversary
Alternative Causation
Closed-Ended Questions
Constructive Speech
Contradiction
Costs vs. Gains Analysis
Counter-Argument

Counter-Productive

Cross-Examination

Dilemma

Double Standard

Extemporaneous Speaking

Extension

Flow Sheets

Forcing the Burden of Proof

Furthest Logical Extent

Government: Prime Minister and Member of the Government

Lincoln-Douglas Debate

Logical Fallacies

    Circular Reasoning

    Non Sequitur

    Transfer Fallacy of Composition

    Transfer Fallacy of Division

Non-Unique

Open-Ended Questions

Opposition: Leader of the Opposition and Member of the Opposition

Oregon Debate

Oxford Debate

Parliamentary Debate

Rebuttal

Refutation

REFERENCES

1)   Adler, R.B., R.F.Proctor II, and N. Towne. Looking Out, Looking In. Belmont, CA: Thomson, 2005.

2)   Freeley, A.J. Argumentation and Debate: Critical Thinking for Reasoned Decision Making, 8th edition. Belmont, CA: Wadsworth, 1993.

Hill, B., and R.W. Leeman, (1997). The Art & Practice of Argumentation & Debate. Mountain View, CA: Mayfield.

3) Coco, F., Instructor at Orange Coast College and Debate Coach.
    Handouts Describing Parliamentary Debate Formats, 2003.
    Crossman, M.R. Burden of Proof: An Introduction to Argument.
    Mason, Ohio: Thompson, 2003.
    Zarefsky, D. "Criteria for Evaluating Non-Policy Argument."
    CEDA Yearbook 1 (1980): 9-16.
    http://www.csun.edu/~dgw61315/debformats.html
    http://42explore.com/debate.htm
    http://www.idebate.org/teaching/debate_formats.php

4) Perella, J. The Debate Method of Critical Thinking: An Introduction to Argumentation. Dubuque, IA: Kendall/Hunt, 1987.

5) Larson, S. "Cross-examination in CEDA Debate: A Survey of Coaches." CEDA Yearbook 8 (1987): 33-41.

    Miller, T.H., and Caminker, E.H. "The Art of Cross-Examination." CEDA Yearbook 3 (1982): 4–15.

6) The National Review, September 20, 2010.

7) http://www.brainyquote.com/quotes/authors/c/ chris _matthews.html

8) wordpress.com/2010/10/25/crazy-tea-party-quotes/

9) Rybacki, K.C., and D.J. Rybacki. Advocacy and Opposition: An Introduction to Argumentation (3rd edition). Boston, MA: Allyn & Bacon, 2004.

10) http://64.233.161.104/search?q=cache:t2oeHOK7aq8J:urban. hunter.cun

    http://www.ojp.usdoj.gov/aac/

11) "An Infectious Discovery," Los Angeles Times, October 8, 2005.

12) Etzioni, Amitai. "Unshackle the Troops," The New Republic, August 12, 2010.

13) Los Angeles Times, September 13, 2003.

14) "2010 Ethanol Industry Outlook" Renewable Fuels Association, 2010. http://www.ethanolrfa.org/ industry/ outlook/RFAoutlook2010_fin.pdf.
    "Brazil's road to energy independence," The Washington Post, August 20, 2006.

15) "Brazil SP cane growers to ban burning by 2017,"Greenpeace UK , May 9, 2007. http://www.greenpeace. org.uk/blog/climate/biofuels-green-dream-or-climate-change-nightmare-20070509.
    "Brazil SP cane growers to ban burning by 2017,"Reuters & UK Yahoo News, September 4, 2009. http:// uk.news.yahoo.com/rtrs/20080904 /ntwl-environment-cane-brazil-suppliers-dc-1202b49.html.
    Grunwald, Michael."The Clean Energy Scam". Time, March 27, 2008. http://www.time.com/time/ magazine/article/0,9171,1725975,00.html

16) Davis, Jeff. "The Effects of E85 on Gasoline Engines," December 27, 2010. http://www.ehow.com/ list_7691892_effects-e85-gasoline-engines.html

17) Los Angeles Times, September 15& 28, 2005.

18) "What the Pope Really Said About Condoms," Time, November 20, 2010. http://www.time.com/time/ world/article/0,8599,2032433,00.html

19) Hoffman, Regan, "The Pope Allows Condoms for Male Prostitute; The U.N. Allows Executions for Gays," POZ Blogs, November 22, 2010. http://blogs.poz.com/ regan /archives/2010/11/the_pope_allows_cond.html

20) "Deforestation," National Geographic Website, 2011. http://environment.nationalgeographic.com/environment/global-warming/deforestation-overview.html
Berg, Linda. Introductory Botany: Plants, People, and the Environment. Belmont, CA: Thompson, 2008.

21) "A Primer: Three Strikes – The Impact After," Legislative Analyst's Office Website, October, 2005. http://www.lao.ca.gov/2005/3_strikes/3_strikes_102005.htm

22) "Spanking detrimental to children, study says," CNN News, September 16, 2009.

23) "Youth Illicit Drug Use Prevention: DARE Long-Term Evaluations and Federal Efforts to Identify Effective Programs, " Report for GAO-03-172R, January 16, 2003. http://www.csdp.org/news/ news/ darere-vised.htm

24) "Gaza: Israeli troops reveal ruthless tactics against Hamas," The Times, January 14, 2009.http://www.timesonline.co.uk/tol/news/world/middle_east/article5512123.ece

25) Anok. "Is Taxation Actually Theft?" Identity Check: A Blog for the Anti-State of Mind. January 14, 2011. http://identitycheck-anok.blog spot.com/2010/01/is-taxation-actually-theft.html

Chapter 8 | *Refutation and Debate*

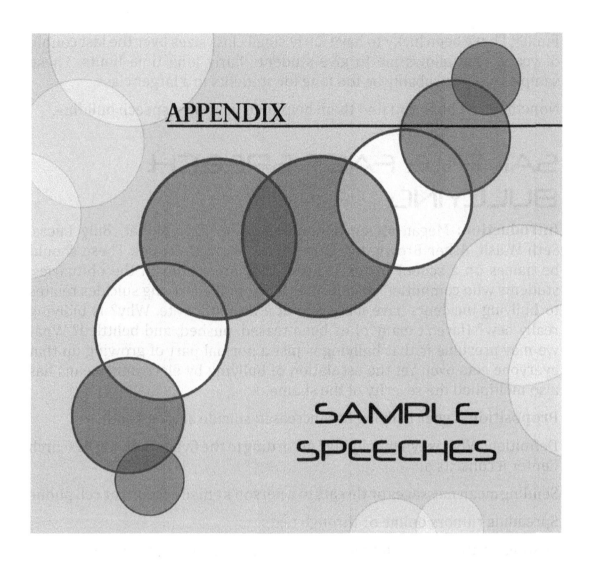

APPENDIX

SAMPLE SPEECHES

The following are examples of speeches, one each of the three types of proposition. They are student samples with some corrections by me. They're not perfect. In fact, I invite a criticism of them to be a part of your class discussion, but they're pretty good examples of top student work among freshmen and sophomores.

I have recommended that students use actual quotations in classroom assignments. I think of sharing the real evidence as simply fair to adversaries, a little like the discovery phase of a trial. However, academics and copyright law don't always get along, so most of the evidence in these speeches has been digested and paraphrased to avoid legal conflict.

Finally, I have been lucky to have fairly small class sizes over the last couple of years. That allows me to give students fairly long time limits. These samples would probably be too long for students in a larger class.

Nonetheless, I hope you find them helpful to your own speech building.

SAMPLE FACT SPEECH: BULLYING

Introduction: Megan Meier, Jeremiah Lassiter, Eric Mohat, Billy Lucas, Seth Walsh, Asher Brown, Jon Carmichael, Michael Cooper. These should be names on a school roster. Instead, they are names in the obituaries, students who committed suicide after being bullied. Young suicides relates to bullying incidents have increased at a dramatic rate. Why? Is bullying really new? Haven't many of us been teased, pushed, and belittled? What we may presume is that bullying is just a normal part of growing up that everyone gets over. Yet the escalation of bullying by electronic means has also multiplied the severity of the shame.

Proposition: Cyber bullying has increased suicide among youth.

Definition: What is cyber bullying? According to the Cyber Bullying Research Center it consists of:

Sending mean messages or threats to a person's email account or cell phone

Spreading rumors online or through texts

Posting hurtful or threatening messages on social networking sites

Spreading unflattering pictures through cell phones or the internet

Sexting, or circulating suggestive pictures of a person

Stock Issue A: Significance

Claim 1: There is an increasing public profile of bullying suicides involving electronic medium.

Warrant 1A: There are several recent highly publicized cases.

Grounds 1A-1: There is the case of Phoebe Prince. According to *The New York Daily News*, March 29, 2010, nine teens were indicted for driving a

15 year old girl, new in the school from Ireland, to suicide. The even involved traditional physical abuse. "Her books were routinely knocked out of her hands, items were flung at her, her face was scribbled out of photographs on the school walls," and, ultimately, on the day she hung herself at home, a large can of Red Bull was thrown from a car and hit her in the head. But there was also a series of threatening text messages to her cell phone, and she was called "Irish slut" and "whore" one Twitter, Craigslist, and Facebook. Even after her death, her tormentors posted vicious comments on her memorial page.

Grounds 1A-2: Tyler Clementi's suicide at Rutger's University is an even clearer example of the impact of electronic bullying. An accomplished violinist, Clementi was secretly filmed by his roommate having a homosexual encounter. The roommate and another girl live streamed the encounter for all to see. Dahrun Ravi tweeted this comment about the event, "Roommate asked for the room till midnight. I went into Molly's room and turned on my webcam. I saw him making out with a dude. Yay." Tyler then jumped off the nearby Washington Bridge after posting an apology on Facebook announcing his intentions. The event was documented by ABC News on September 29, 2010.

Grounds 1A-3: Hope Whitsell was just thirteen when a single impulsive act ruined her reputation and cost her life. The Florida teen tried to interest a boy she had a crush on by texting him a topless photo of herself. The boy "sexted" the photo all over the school bringing about constant ridicule and bullying, until Hope hung herself in her bedroom. According to *MSNBC* of December 2, 2009, there was an earlier incident in the same year. "In March, 18-year-old Jesse Logan killed herself in the face of a barrage of taunts when an ex-boyfriend forwarded explicit photos of her following their split."

Warrant 1B: Statistics reveal that these are less isolated incidents than we may believe. The following is a summary of research from 2004 to 2010 accumulated by the Cyber Bullying Research Center:

Grounds 1B-1: According to the I-SAFE Foundation, a non-profit organization concerned with youth problems, over half of adolescents have been bullied online, and about the same number have engaged in cyber bullying. More than 1 in 3 youths have been physically threatened online. Over 25% of teens report being bullied repeatedly on the internet.

Grounds 1B-2: The Cyberbullying Research Center did another series of surveys and also found that about half of young people have been cyber bullied. They also found that girls are just as likely as boys to use this form of bullying. Cyber bullying transcends race. Perhaps most significantly, cyber bullying victims are more likely to suffer low self-esteem and consider suicide.

Grounds 1B-3: *The Hartford County Examiner* also supported the statistic that half of teens have been cyber bullied. They also found that 1 in 10 teens have had damaging or embarrassing photos taken of them without their permission and broadcast by cell phones. They, however, found that girls are slightly more likely to use cyber bullying than males.

Stock Issue B: Cause

Why is this phenomenon occurring with such frequency and damage?

Claim 2: Young people are increasingly less empathetic with peers.

Warrant 2A: While empathy, the ability to relate to the emotional circumstances of others, is a cornerstone of society, recent studies show that the young have become more narcissistic, a characteristic that can be measured objectively by a test called the Interpersonal Reactivity Index.

Grounds 2A: According to *Scientific American*, January 19, 2011, refers to a study indicating a serious dip in empathy over the last thirty years. "The research, led by Sara H. Konrath of the University of Michigan at Ann Arbor and published online in August in *Personality and Social Psychology Review*, found that college students' self-reported empathy has declined since 1980, with an especially steep drop in the past 10 years. To make matters worse, during this same period students' self-reported narcissism has reached new heights, according to research by Jean M. Twenge, a psychologist at San Diego State University." The research was supported by a systematic look at 14,000 of students who took the Interpersonal Reactivity Index.

Warrant 2B: Other research indicates a lack of appropriate socialization and a lack of parental involvement.

Grounds2B-1: A 2007 Yale Study suggests that empathy is a genetic trait, yet social context can have a profound effect on trait enhancement or decline. "In the past 30 years Americans have become more likely to live alone and less likely to join groups—ranging from PTAs to political parties to casual sports teams. Several studies hint that this type of isolation can take a toll on people's attitudes toward others. Steve Duck of the University of Iowa has found that socially isolated, as compared with integrated, individuals evaluate others less generously after interacting with them, and Kenneth J. Rotenberg of Keele University in England has shown that lonely people are more likely to take advantage of others' trust to cheat them in laboratory games."

Grounds 2B-2: Research collected by the Cyber Bullying Institute also says that half of the victims never say a word to parents about the incidents. Thus, the parents are not involved in any attempt to counsel or help the victim.

Warrant 2C: However, it is also true that even in cases when the parents are involved, states and schools are inadequate in their anti-bullying programs.

Grounds 2C-1: In the case of Phoebe Prince, school officials were continually notified of parental complaints and did virtually nothing. They simply declared that they had an anti-bullying policy. Yet the bullies who attacked Phoebe Prince.

Grounds 2C-2: A state by state look at what cyber bullying laws say reveal that thirty states have laws that mention this relatively new phenomenon. However, those that do generally simply say that school districts must have an anti-bullying policy, though few mandate any specific programs to promote student empathy or a requirement to punish.

REFERENCES

"The Current State of Cyberbullying Laws," Cyberbullying Research Center Blog, August 3, 2010. http://cyberbullying.us/blog/the-current-state-of-cyberbullying-laws.html

"NJ Gov. Wonders How Rutgers 'Spies' Can Sleep at Night After Tyler Clementi's Suicide." ABC News, September 29, 2010. **Error! Hyperlink reference not valid.**om/US/suicide-rutgers-university-freshman-tyler-clementi-stuns-veteran/story?id=11763784&page=3

"Phoebe Prince, South Hadley High School's 'new girl,' driven to suicide by teenage cyber bullies," NY Daily News, March 29, 2010. **Error! Hyperlink reference not valid.**.com/news/national/2010/03/29/2010-03 29_phoebe_ prince_ south_hadley_high_schools_new_girl_driven_to_suicide_by_teenage_cy.html?print=1&page=all

"'Sexting' bullying cited in teen's death," MSNBC News, December 2, 2009. http://today.msnbc.msn.com/id/34236377/ns/today-today_people/#

"State Cyberbullying Laws Range from Guidance to Mandate," Education Week, February 4, 2011. http://www.edweek.org/dd/articles/2011/02/09/02cyberbullying-laws.h04.html

"What, Me Care? Young Are Less Empathetic," Scientific American, January 19,2011. http://www.scientifi-camerican.com/article. cfm? id=what-me-care

SAMPLE POLICY SPEECH: PRESCRIPTION DRUG ABUSE

Introduction: In December of 2009, Joey Rivoro and friends from ASU went on a road trip to Rowland Heights, California. They weren't coming for the beaches or to visit girls. They were going to visit Dr. Lisa Tseng, one of dangerous breed of doctors who hand out prescription pills like candy at Halloween. The young men left with several prescriptions, including a large amount of Oxycodone, an opiate analgesic, as well as Percocet. Nine days later, Rivoro was dead of an overdose at 21. He was one of at least six men in their early 20s who have died of similar overdoses from drugs like Vicodin, Soma, and Xanax prescribed in large amounts, sometimes with overlapping prescriptions.

Young people in high school and college face a lot of pressure, and we're all familiar with the fact that drug use if fairly common in school, but there's been a shift from street drugs to prescription drugs because they are far too easy to get, and the effects are fatal. That is why I believe...

Proposition: Steps should be taken to make prescription drugs less easily accessible to the young.

Definitions: The particular drugs that are being abused are class 3 narcotics like pain killers, muscle relaxants, anti-anxiety medictions, and anti-depressants.

Stock Issue: Significant Harm.

Claim 1: There are significant damages from prescription drug use among the young.

Warrant 1: Joey Rivoro is just one of many examples of death from prescription abuse, not just from overdosing, but from suicide as well.

Grounds 1-A: Matt Stavron of San Clemente had a compound leg fracture at the age of 13 due to a motorbike. He was given morphine for the pain. Over the next ten years, he was in and out of rehab for drug addiction. His father later noted that Stavron kept crashing his bike on purpose to get drugs. After a problem with a girlfriend, Matt's mother found him curled up in fetal position on the bathroom floor from a mixture of OxyContin, Soma, and Xanax. His OxyContin dosage was 80 milligrams, the maximum strength. All of these prescriptions came from one doctor.

Grounds 1-B: Ryan Latham was born with a minor case of spina bifida and had broken a jaw in a fight, neither of which was causing him any particular pain, according to his parents. He was a sensitive young man, however, and was depressed about a breakup with a girlfriend. Yet he joked with friends that a doctor had told him that he could any drugs he wanted with an old x-ray. He overdosed from the combined effects of Hydrocodone, Soma, and Xanax.

Grounds 1-C: After getting seven prescriptions totaling 325 pills—Adderall, an amphetamine commonly prescribed for attention deficit disorder, Xanax, Soma, hydromorphone, and OxyContin—Jeffrey Neal West of UCLA shot himself to death. The Soma including overlapping prescriptions of 90 pills each given within a week of each other by the same doctor.

Grounds 1-D: Ryan Winter was given ibuprofen and recommendation for physical therapy for a knee injury. Wanting more, he drove to Dr. Tseng, previously mentioned, and got Opana, a morphine like narcotic, Xanax, and Alprazolam. Five days later, he was found dead outside a Santa Ana supermarket.

These examples are taken from the *Los Angeles Times* of August 29, 2010, and the *Orange County Register* of August 31, 2010.

Warrant 1B: These are not isolated examples. There is a demonstrable statistical trend.

Grounds 1 B-1: A *Christian Science Monitor* study showed a 400% jump in prescription drug abuse between 1998 and 2008. The number for prescriptions of pain killers in emergency rooms rose from 40,000 in 1994 to over 300,000 in 2008.

Grounds 1 B-2: In a 2005 survey by the Partnership for a Drug-Free America, 19% of U.S. teenagers—roughly 4.5 million youths—reported having taken prescription painkillers such as Vicodin or OxyContin or stimulants such as Ritalin or Adderall to get high. They actually have what are called "Pharm Parties" in which bowls of undistinguished drugs are taken by the handful. The euphemism for such bowls is "trail mix." After one such party, Eddie Capello died with 134 milligrams of Xanax, roughly 67 pills, and other opioid derivatives in his system.

Grounds 1 B-3: A 2009 survey from the Centers for Disease Control and Prevention shows that prescription drug abuse is on the rise, with 20% of teens saying they have taken a prescription drug without a doctor's prescription.

Grounds 1 B-4: According to the a survey from the National Center on Addiction and Substance Abuse, August 20, 2010, more than a quarter of school students say that such drugs are freely available on their campuses.

Transition: Can there be any doubt that this is a growing problem that cannot be ignored? Why? Why this shift from the street drugs we've so long feared to over the counter prescriptions?

Stock Issue: Inherency

There are both structural and attitudinal barriers to the solution of this problem.

Claim 2: Unscrupulous doctors have a profit motive.

Warrant 2: Giving a minimal exam with charges attached in exchange for drugs allows, not only rapid and loyal addicted patient turnover, doctors can charge government medical programs.

Grounds 2-A: An influential senator some doctors have written thousands of prescriptions for painkillers and anti-psychotics. Among these doctors are Columbia psychiatrist who wrote nearly four thousand prescriptions in a year and billing $1.3 million to Medicaid. A Summerville doctor billed $640,000 for 2400 prescriptions. An Atlanta, Georgia, doctor wrote 1300 prescriptions for $720,000. A Sumter family doctor billed more than half a million dollars for 860 prescriptions.

Claim 2: Drug companies are partially to blame.

Warrant 2A: Drug companies have a serious profit motive. It leads them to market a drug for one purpose, get it past the DEA, then turn that drug into a miracle cure for everything. Unfortunately, this happens quite frequently with anti-psychotics and relaxants.

Grounds 2A: According to the Justice Department in a *New York Times* article, October 2, 2010, drug companies trained their salesman to rebut valid medical objections, like suicide among the young, to their drugs.... Last year, both Eli Lilly and Pfizer settled the largest criminal investigations. Lilly had to pay $515 million as part of $1.4 billion settlement with the government for deceptive sales practice, the side effect of which is teenage suicide.

Warrant 2B: The profit motive is increasing for this kind of unethical practice. Drug companies operate like street drug salesmen. They distribute samples that doctors give to patients who then like the effects and increase demand, which in turn allows pharmaceutical companies to raise costs.

Grounds 2B: According to the *Kaiser Family Foundation* website, spending in the US for prescription drugs was$216.7 billion in 2006, more than 5 times the $40.3 billion spent in 1990. Growth in drug spending is at least partially due to increased use of drugs, lower rebates from drug companies, and increased prices, with increases as high 12.6% per annum in recent years.

Claim 3: There are porous elements of the present prescription system that are easy for the young to evade.

Warrant 3A: Local pharmacies are relatively careful about tracking drug orders and sometimes refuse to fill even doctor signed prescriptions. Dr. Tseug who killed at least six was only tracked by DEA after a pharmacy started to refuse her prescriptions.

Grounds 3A: Studies have revealed that driving long distances to get drugs are a signal of the kinds of deaths we've seen above. Doctors apparently do not correlate home addresses and pharmacies with someone driving hundreds of miles to get drugs. The cross borders—Arizona and Florida are notably easy states for giving drugs to contiguous states.

Warrant 3B: It's also too easy to get drugs online, including from other countries.

Grounds 3B: According to a 2008 *Online Free Library* article quoting Blue Cross, Aetna, and other domestic insurance companies, nearly 20 million packages of prescription drugs are estimated to be shipped into the United

States each year—a supply worth more than $3 billion. The importation of contaminated drugs from Mexico by mail order have hospitalized some Americans.

Transition: Pharmacies can keep track of addresses and amounts of drugs. Why can't doctors and their regulatory agencies?

Claim 4: Our own national attitude about drugs is partially to blame.

Warrant 4: We tend to have a sort of automatic tendency to reach for pills and not tolerate any kind of psychological pain. Doctors are supporting this tendency.

Grounds 4: The 2010 *Christian Science Monitor* article cited earlier notes this tendency. They note that doctors have been pushing along with pharmaceutical companies for more aggressive approaches that have increased the use of opiates. The abuse of these strong drugs is an indication of a much more widespread cultural problem, says addiction specialist Clare Kavin of The Waismann Method, a treatment center for opiate dependency, which has treated many celebrity addicts."We are in a culture of immediate gratification and nobody will put up with even the slightest discomfort anymore," she says. This underlying attitude leads many patients to push for stronger painkillers when lower strength—but non-addictive—drugs would have sufficed in the past."

Stock Issue: Workable Solution

There are several things that must be done. First of all, we need to refocus our anti-drug enforcement policy to acknowledge the fact that pharmaceuticals are now the second leading drug abuse problem in the country. We're spending billions to stop marijuana from coming across the border when far more potent drugs are easily accessible from our medicine cabinets.

Second, there needs to be a national interactive prescription monitoring system to prevent people from traveling long distances to get around local pharmacies. If you get a traffic ticket in California, for instance, other states will know that by computer and vica versa. Yet we allow people to hop counties and states to avoid wary pharmacies. What if we had a national system that would reveal prescriptions filled anywhere alerting pharmacies and, even more importantly, doctors of young people, any people, trying to fill multiple prescriptions. According to Dr Scott Glaser, president of Pain Specialists of Greater Chicago, 37 states have some monitoring, and federal monitoring laws were signed by Congress in 2005 but they are unfunded. Dr. Glaser and The American Society of Interventional Pain Physicians have been lobbying Congress for $55 million to implement and nationalize this monitoring. Let us add our voices to theirs in the name of our own safety and that of our children to come.

Third, the FDA needs to be much stricter in authorizing drugs that have dangerous potentially fatal effects that are then heavily marketed by pharmaceutical companies for multiple uses. I didn't have time to get into suicides caused by anti-depressants among the young, or 478 sudden cardiac deaths from FDA approved anti-psychotics noted in a *New York Times* article of January of 2009. In that case, the FDA approved drug had a 3 in 1000 rate of death from side-effects. We're simply not watching these companies carefully enough.

Fourth, lets shut down internet drug sales. According to a 2011 report by the National Association of Boards of Pharmacy, about 96% of drugs purchased online are fake or contaminated drugs. 75% of them are opiates like hydrocodone purchased from, not only Mexico, but India and China. Lets support this group in their efforts to create a an Internet Drug Outlet Identification Program and ban such sales.

Fifth, let's increase criminal penalties for doctors like Lisa Tseung who make a living through the irresponsible distribution of drugs. Do you know what happened to her so far? She's having her license removed, and there's certainly the possibility of civil suits from the families. But I call it criminal negligence tantamount to manslaughter.

Finally, let's re-educate ourselves and our children about how to deal with pain. We simply have to toughen up, America, settle for aspirin and ibuprofen, and stop looking at pills with the attitude that if a drug company says its safe, we can just pop a pill at will.

REFERENCES

"Crossing borders: importing prescription drugs...." The Free Library, http://www.thefreelibrary.com/Crossing+borders%3A+importing+prescription+drugs,+illegally+or+legally,...-a0126156030.

"Families of those who overdosed have questions for doctor who prescribed," Los Angeles Times, August 29, 2010. http://articles.latimes. com/2010/aug/29/local/la-me-overdose-new-20100829.

"Internet Drug Outline Identification Program: Progress Report for State and Federal Regulators," National Association of Boards of Pharmacy, January 2011. www.nabp.net/news/assets/InternetReport1-11.pdf.

"Prescription Drug Abuse," Nemours Foundation website "Kid's Health," 2011. http://kidshealth.org/teen/drug_alcohol/drugs / prescription_drug_abuse.html.

"Officials move to strip doctor of license," Orange County Register, August 31, 2010. http://articles.ocregister.com/2010-08-31/news/24636652_1_medical-office-dea-california-medical-board.

"Prescription drug abuse surged 400% in past decade," Christian Science Monitor, July 15, 2010. http://www.csmonitor.com/USA/2010/0715/Prescription-drug-abuse-surged-400-percent-in-past-decade.

"Prescription drugs find place in teen culture," USA Today, June 13, 2006. http://www.usatoday.com/news/health/2006-06-12-teens-pharm-drugs_x.htm.

"Prescription Drug Trends," Kaiser Family Foundation website, September 2008. www.kff.org/rxdrugs/upload/3057_07.pdf.

"Students talk of gangs, drugs," Los Angeles Times, August 20, 2010.

SAMPLE VALUE DEBATE

This value debate was recorded in one my classes, and it was a fiercely fought one. The students were both Hispanic, both friends, and they worked very hard at playing devil's advocate with each other on the proposition: **Illegal immigration is wrong for America.**

Prime Minister Constructive:

My parents immigrated legally to the U.S., and I am proud that they worked hard, got education, spoke English in the home and gave me a chance to get a good start as a citizen. Yet there are others who don't believe in the rules, do not work at assimilating into the U.S., and are disrespectful of our laws. If you're one of those who resents having to push a phone button to ask for services in our national language, or if you are a starving student who would happily take a low paying job currently held by non-citizens, you may agree that illegal immigration is bad for the country.

I'm going to argue that it's bad in two ways, it increases crime and it exploits our services, endangering both our health and education.

My standard for victory is that what is best for this great country in the long run is what's right and good.

Claim 1: My first claim is that illegal immigrants increase crime.

Warrant 1A: Illegal immigrants harm us on our roads.

Grounds 1A-1: A 2006 report by AAA found that 20% of fatal accidents involve at least one illegal immigrant. Another report conducted by the state of California, cited in the *World Daily News* of November 12, 2006, says that illegal immigrants are five times more likely to cause a fatal accident than licensed drivers. In New York, the Rockland County DA, Michael Bongiorno, estimated that two thirds of felony drunk drivers charged in his district are illegal immigrants.

Ground 1A-2: According to *The News & Observer* published in North Carolina, April 7, 2007. "In 2005, there were 37 alcohol-related crashes caused by Hispanic drivers for every 10,000 Hispanics in the state, according to the UNC Highway Safety Research Center. That is more than three times the rate of alcohol-related crashes among non-Hispanics."

Grounds 1A-3: *The World Net Daily* website of November 12, 2006, cites the case of Jose Trejo Encino, a 27 year-old illegal immigrant, who admitted to drinking a 12 pack of beer before running his Pontiac Grand Prix into a car in Tennessee, killing one passenger and seriously injuring the other. A drunken Vitalina Buatista Vargas ran her car into the house of a 91-year old woman, killing her in the same state.

Warrant 1B....

Leader of the opposition: Will you yield to a point of information?

Prime Minister: Yes.

Leader of the opposition: Your examples are both from Tennessee. Do you have others?

Prime Minister: I'll give you one more now. From the *V-Dare* website of Brenda Walker of Sierra Club on December 3, 2010, "Tricia Taylor, 18, of Clarkston, Michigan, and companion Noah Menard, were walking to his car after attending a concert in Pontiac when both were struck and severely injured by Jose Carcamo, whose car was traveling between 50 and 75 miles per hour on a street posted for 25 mph." By the way, Carcamo had 17 violations and continued to drive.

Warrant 1B: Our prisons are filed with criminal illegals. Please, note that the very act of evading authorities and entering illegally is a crime.

Grounds 1B-1: In Edwin Rubenstein's 2005 web article *"Criminal Alien Nation,"* his research found that 27% of prisoners in the Federal system are illegal aliens. His figures are supported by GAO report 05-337R from May 9 of the same year. Their report notes a 15% increase in illegals in prison and rising costs of $5.8 billion in the early years of this century. The GAO further estimated that of 55,000 illegal aliens studied, they averaged about 13 offenses per person. More than half had been convicted of felonies and nearly 20% of violent crimes.

Grounds 1B-2: The *"Immigration's Human Cost"* website of August 9, 2010, mentioned the case of Tina Davila, a Houston mother of five who was stabbed to death when Timoteo Rios tried to hijack her SUV, but she refused to give up the keys because her 4-month-old baby was in the vehicle.

Grounds 1B–3: *CNN News* of Febuary 11, 2011, reported a triple shooting homocide by Jose Oswaldo Reyes Alfaro in Virginia. Two others were shot and another was stabbed. The Sunday after the first crime, another illegal immigrant, Salvador Portillo-Saravia was arrested for raping an 8-year old girl.

Claim 2: Illegal immigration exploits our social services to the detriment of our health and education.

Warrant 2A: Our health care system is exploited by illegal immigrants. First, they bring diseases across the border that we had controlled. Second, they then force our taxpayers to pay for their illnesses and childbirth.

Grounds 2A-1: A June, 2009 article in the *New England Journal of Medicine* noted that a majority (57.8%) of all new cases of tuberculosis in the United States in 2007 were diagnosed in foreign-born persons. The TB infection rate among foreign-born persons was 9.8 times as high as that among U.S.-born persons.

Grounds 2 A-2: According to an article "Illegal immigration and public health," published on the *FAIR* website in 2009, "The pork tapeworm, which thrives in Latin America and Mexico, is showing up along the U.S. border, threatening to ravage victims with symptoms ranging from seizures to death.... The same [Mexican] underclass has migrated north to find jobs on the border, bringing the parasite and the sickness."

Grounds 2 A-3: And from the same article, "Another problem is immigrants' use of hospital and emergency services rather than preventative medical care. For example, utilization rate of hospitals and clinics by illegal aliens (29 percent) is more than twice the rate of the overall U.S. population (11 percent).[8]

Warrant 2B: Our education systems are strained by illegal's when we're already in a budget crunch.

Grounds 2B-1: According to The Texas Education Agency (TEA) report, the annual per pupil expenditure is $11,567. That brings the cost to educate the 60,000 illegal immigrant children born annually to nearly $700,000,000 and that is only for one year of their education! That's from the *Texas Insider Report* of February 10, 2011.

Grounds 2B-2: And from the same article, there is a new "birth tourism" industry that lures expectant mothers from all over the world, including China and Turkey, to give birth in the U.S. for the purpose of obtaining citizenship. The Turkish owned upper eastside luxury hotel, the Marmara Manhattan, markets birth tourism packages to expectant mothers abroad for a tidy sum of $8,000."

Leader of the Opposition: Well, I'm glad to hear that evidence referring to Turks and Chinese. There was so much scapegoating of our social problems on Hispanics... and from a fellow Hispanic. It's true. I come from a family of illegal immigrants. I am a so-called "anchor baby" who is here because my parents believed what it says on the Statue of Liberty, "Bring us your tired, our poor, your huddled masses.," and I am grateful for the chance to better this country in return for the chance.

I am both going to directly refute her arguments and build a single counter-argument that will outweigh them.

Claim 1: Her first claim is that illegal immigrants commit crime.

Warrant 1 A: Her first warrant says there is a disproportionate amount of DUIs among illegal immigrants. She has framed the problem incorrectly. Young people regardless of ethnicity are by far the most dangerous drivers.

Grounds 1A-2: The Census Bureau of the United States says that kids between the ages of 16–25 are involved in 4,700,000 accidents, 13,800 of which were fatal. People over 65 were involved in 1,340,000 accidents, 8100 of which were fatal.

Grounds 1A-2: *The Satellite Spotlight* daily news of April 1, 2007, quotes Bobby Dunn, a counselor for Hispanic DWI convicts,:" Clients are often young men far from home with money in their pockets for the first time. Many were too poor to have cars in Mexico, so they have little experience behind the wheel. They also see drinking as a way of showing their manhood." More specifically he says that 12 beers is the standard for showing that manhood and that they don't understand. Other experts say that the drinking is a byproduct of working long days, being far from family, and simply being lonely.

Grounds 1A-3: Mothers Against Drunk Driving report, on the same Brenda Walker website my opponent cited, notes that Hispanics believe it takes 6–8 drinks to affect their driving, while Americans think it takes 2–4.

Transition: In other words, they lack education, the very education that my opponent resents later in her case. These aren't bad men, they're uneducated ones. What's the excuse for young people in this country who have the training and have accidents anyway?

Warrant 1B: Her second warrant is that illegal immigrants have violent crime and over occupy our jails.

Grounds 1B-1: The most violent crime does not come from illegal immigrants. It comes from blacks who are legal citizens. According to the Department of Justice, "African Americans are victims of nearly half of the murders in the U.S. though they comprise only 13% of the population, " and most were killed by other blacks. "Young black men aged between 17 and 29 bore a disproportionately high burden in the grim statistics, making up 51 percent of African-American murder victims." White male murder victims in the same age group were only 37 percent. They also reported that there was more black rape and sex crime than, I quote, "Any other ethnic group except American Indians. "

Prime Minister: Will you yield to a point of information?

Leader of the Opposition: Yes.

Prime Minister: What was the year of that study?

Leader of the Opposition: The article was from 2007, but the figures are based on 2005.

Prime Minister: So they do not take into account recent growth in illegal immigration?

Leader of the Opposition: No, but some of your examples are no newer, and 2010 is a year in which the rate of illegal immigration lowered for the first time.

Grounds 1B 2 & 3: She has a couple of examples of violent crimes, and those are always terrible to hear, but that is not unique to Hispanics or illegal immigrants from anywhere.

She also refers to prison costs, but I'll handle that below with a counterargument.

Claim 2: My adversary argues that our social services are being exploited, both in health and education.

Warrant 2A: Her first warrant regards health, and she blames illegal's for a rise in disease and overcrowded emergency rooms.

Grounds 2A-1: *The New England Journal of Medicine* is a fine source, but look at what it actually says regarding TB. It says "foreign borns" but does not specify illegal immigrants.

Grounds 2A-2: Regarding the pork tapeworm, there is no source qualification for this nor quantification. It sounds scary, but how serious a threat is this really? No other disease increases are mentioned.

Grounds 2A-3: A *USA Today* article of January 22, 2008, mentions two very important facts: A) Quote, "Data on health care costs for illegal immigrants are sketchy because hospitals and community health centers don't ask about patients' legal status." In other words, the costs of illegals for health are all based on estimates. B) "Because most illegal immigrants are relatively young and healthy, they generally don't need as much health care treatment as U.S. citizens, studies show."

Warrant 2B: The affirmative argues that illegal's strain the education system.

First, let me say again that her first claim about crime, especially DUIs, can be related to lack of education. We complain about them not assimilating, but we turn around and deny them the education that helps them adapt.

Second, again, we're scapegoating a particular population sector for a budget problem that has many causes, including generally lousy economy.

Third, her claim is all based on estimates of an illegal population.

Finally, I want to agree with the affirmative that we should not accept a tourism industry that encourages people to come here to use their babies as a means of becoming citizens. I grant that point, but I also remind you that rich tourists are not the same as a hard working poor people contributing to our economy and having a normal family life.

And that leads to my counter-argument.

Claim 3: Illegal immigrants are an economic benefit to this country.

I will be referring to government figures and testimony from an article from *Yahoo News* called, "Benefits of Illegal Immigration Offset Costs on the U.S. Economy," from December 5, 2007.

Warrant 3A: They provide cheap labor that keeps the costs of goods down. The stereotype is that they take American jobs. The facts say otherwise.

Grounds 3A-1: Thomas Donohue, president and chief executive of the U.S. Chamber of Commerce, reports that "less-skilled workers experience very little downward pressure on their wages from competition with illegal immigrants.... American workers are moving into higher paying jobs, and immigrants have filled the gap by taking manual labor jobs that American workers are unwilling to take."

Grounds 3A-2: A study cited in *Forbes*, July 2007, revealed the impact of immigration on prices in twenty-five large U.S. cities. It found that a 10% increase in immigration lowered the price of low-skilled intensive goods and services by 1%." Another study by the National Research Council reported that "Americans gained between $1 and $10 billion per year from immigration's labor market impacts alone."

Warrant 3B: Illegal immigrants pay taxes.

Grounds 3B: According to the National Council of La Raza, a Washington-based Latino Civil Rights and Advocacy Organization, "the majority of undocumented immigrants pay income taxes using individual taxpayer identification numbers or false social security numbers." In comparison, a corporate law firm called the Washington-based American Immigration

Lawyers Association, states that "immigrant households paid an estimated $133 billion in taxes to federal, state, and local governments in 1997."

These taxes offset the costs to services provided. They will receive no benefit from the Social Security that they help buoy, but they pay to give back for the opportunities we humanely provide.

(**NOTE:** Again, while it is traditional in tournament debate to reverse rebuttal order between the affirmative and negative, I do not follow that convention in my classes).

Prime Minister Rebuttal

Claim 1: Illegals increase crime.

Warrant 1A: With regard to disproportionate DUIs, my opponent reframes the statistics in terms of young people, but a disproportionate number of people in all accidents are illegals, and it's worse because they are not insured, so the damages are multiplied.

Grounds 1A-1: In North Carolina, for instance, according to *NPR News* of July 21, 2007, "Hispanics account for disproportionate number of drunk driving deaths. In North Carolina where the Latino population has grown by more than a third in this decade largely due to illegal immigration, alcohol-related crashes have become a leading killer of Latinos."

Also, some of those young American deaths come from illegals.

Grounds 1A-2: In Virigina, according to the *World Net Daily* article previously cited, two college students and a high school boy were killed by a drunken illegal in October of 2005, along with a young woman in a head-on crash in January of 2006, with the killer fleeing the scene of the crime and leaving his own young injured companion in the car, and that was followed by a pregnant woman and her unborn child killed by an in February.

And, I'm sorry, but trying to explain away such deaths based on cultural norms in Mexico is no excuse. We don't need macho drinking habits of 12-pack driving here, especially when they aren't insured and the medical costs are dumped on innocent victims and taxpayers.

Warrant 1B: Concerning prison overcrowding of, my opponent says that I haven't really quantified the costs.

Grounds 1B: In the web article, "The Dark Side of Illegal Immigration," the federal government spends about $1.4 billion a year to house illegal prisoners. That does not count the costs to border state law enforcement who are only partially reimbursed for their expenses. At any given time, there are an average of 400,000 illegal criminals on the loose costing law enforcement before we even put them in jail. And illegal's are responsible for 1,288,619 crimes including 2,158 murders a year. Those last figures were based on a February 12, 2011, *World Daily News* article.

How can we possibly estimate the cost in dollars as related to the lives of those victims. Yes, blacks kill blacks. It's a national tragedy. But illegal aliens kill us. And that's not even counting the drug deaths caused by the importation of cocaine by illegal's, approximately 72,000 pounds a year.

Claim 2: Illegals exploit our social services.

Warrant 2A; Regarding health care, my opponent argues that the statistics cited refer to Hispanics but not illegals. Not true.

Grounds 2A: According to a Kaiser Foundation study in 2008, the annual costs of uncompensated care are $56 billion annually. They calculate that a minimum of 15% of that cost is from illegals, or $8.4 billion. According to a May 2009 study by Families U.S.A., a nonprofit organization, the annual cost from uncompensated care if $73 billion. So, at a minimum of 15% illegal's, that's roughly %11 billion dollars, possibly more.

Who pays? We do, in increased medical costs and insurance costs. Acccording to the same Slate magazine article of November 20, 2009, These costs raise the average family insurance premium by over $1000 annually.

Warrant 2B: Regarding education, my opponent says that this is all based on estimates. That's true. We can't account for the exact number of illegals, although the estimates by all sources say that we have about 11 million in the country. But let's keep in mind that his rationale for his counterargument on economic benefit also depends on estimates.

Which leads me to my opponent's counter-claim.

Claim 3: Illegal immigrants do not benefit the economy.

Warrant 3: When you ad up the criminal costs of incarceration, note to mention the human pain and suffering that come from those crimes, and the costs to health care of $11 billion a year cited in my first speech, which by itself outweighs the $10 billion dollar economic advantage cited by the opposition, and add the education costs just cited for one state alone,— that was $700,000,000 in Texas alone—and I think you'll have to agree that illegal immigration just doesn't add up in our favor.

Leader of the opposition rebuttal

I'm going to start with my counter claim 3 then use that to refute the rebuilding of the affirmative case. As you notice, the affirmative offered no direct attacks to my argument other than that the other costs outweigh them.

Claim 3: Illegals DO help the economy.

Warrant 3A: Certain new factors reduce the affirmative concern with crime specifically. First, you heard me mention earlier that there are fewer immigrants for the first time in many years. Second, those that are staying are the most productive.

Grounds 3A: According to *CBS News*, February 11, 2011, "The Department of Homeland Security reported that illegal immigrant population dropped to 10.8 million in 2009 compared to 11.6 million in 2008. It was the second consecutive annual decline and the largest in at least three decades." According to Reverand Lewis Estrada of Los Angeles, "Millions of people here are good citizens and workers who pay taxes and own homes.... The reality is that they are not going back." The DHS report further notes that the vast majority, 63% are immigrants who came before this century.

Transition: In other words, these are the people who have invested themselves in this culture, found productive jobs, and are not a part of the kind of problems the affirmative is concerned with. And do not forget the $10 billion per annum contribution to the economy. That's not coming from the criminals. It's coming from productive taxpayers who stay. Let's return to the affirmative case.

Claim 1: Illegal crime is not as bad as the affirmative says.

Warrant 1A: The affirmative says that I've misframed the statistics be pointing out that young and old account for more fatal accidents. Did you hear an actual quantification of how many of those illegal youths were illegal immigrants? No you did not. You heard a variety of ugly cases of individuals, which we can find about any sector of the population. I also want you to recall how much of her evidence mentions Hispanics but does not actually distinguish illegal's among them. The Carcomo case, for instance, says that he was Hispanic and had 17 previous violations before a fatal one, but it does not specify that he was an illegal immigrant.

Warrant 1B: I want you to notice that the affirmative had virtually no direct response to my evidence that black on black crime is by far the most violent in this country. Half the murders in the country. Not a word. Further, I want to ask, why are we keeping criminals here and assuming the cost? Why are we not just deporting them to Mexico? Do you think that productive illegal's, the children of productive illegals like me, trying hard to get educated and be a contributing citizen want these guys around? The don't represent the vast majority of illegals who come to this country to get a decent life and to give back.

Claim 2: Illegals do not exploit our social services.

Warrant 2A: Do they use some health services, yes. But the affirmative ignores that the illegal population is generally young and healthy and uses less medical service. Also, they use health services sparingly because they're afraid of getting caught.

I agree about there being some increase in TB. Notice she dropped my pork tapeworm challenge. But isn't the affirmative in a dilemma? On one hand, the argument is that illegals bring disease, but then we should deny them health care? They're uninsured? That's not unique in America.

Grounds 2A: According to a *U.S.A Today* article of September 17, 2011, the Census Bureau says that 50.7 million Americans have no insurance, and it's getting worse. The health care system is broken folks, let's not scapegoat one portion of the population for it.

In fact, use the affirmative's own figure that about 70% of illegal's have no health insurance. There are 10.8 estimated illegals. That's about 7,500,000 uninsured illegals of 51 million uninsured Americans, if they're even counted . We're paying for everyone, folks, roughly a sixth of all Americans. Stop scapegoating illegals.

Warrant 2B: Regarding education, education is good. Again, the affirmative is in a dilemma. We don't like illegals because they're different, they don't assimilate, then we cannot deny them the education that would keep them from DUIs, keep them from crime, teach them preventative health, trades, and make them productive citizens. And, again, we have a nation-wide problem. The economy as a whole has hurt education. I say again, stop scapegoating illegals with racist charges.

REFERENCES

"Cop murder spotlights crisis of killer aliens," World Net Daily, September 28, 2006. http://www.wnd.com/news/article.asp?ARTICLE_ID=52198.

"Federal Immigration Law Enforcement: Procedures and Complaints," Center for Immigration Studies. http://www.cis.org/articles/2001/crime/law.html.

"Hispanic DWIs rooted in immigrants' culture," The Raleigh News & Observer, April 1, 2007. http://www.tmcnet.com/usubmit/2007/04/01/2456644.htm.

"Hispanics lead drunk driving arrests, accidents," World Net DailyNovember 12, 2000. http://www.wnd.com/?pageId=4336.

"Illegal Immigration and Public Health,: FAIR website. http://www.fairus. org/site/News2?page=NewsArticle&id=16742&security=1601&news_iv_ctrl=1007.

"The Nativism Tax: What it will cost you to deny illegal immigrants health insurance," Slate, November 20, 2009. http://www.slate.com/id/2236288/.

"Nearly half of US Murder victims are black," Breitbart News Alert, August 9, 2008, http://www.breitbart.com/article.php?id=070809202217. 9us2orhu.

"Number of Illegal Immigrants Plunges by 1M," CBS News, February 11, 2010. http://www.cbsnews.com/stories/2010/02/11/national/ main6197466.shtml.

"Number of uninsured Americans rises to 50.7 million," USA Today, September 9, 2010. http://www.usatoday.com/news/nation/2010-09-17-uninsured17_ST_N.htm.

"12 pack illegal in fatal car crash," World Net Daily, November 12, 2006. http://www.wnd.com/?pageId=38841.

Rubenstein, E.S. "Criminal alien nation," The V-Dare Web site, July 30, 2010. http://www.vdare.com/rubenstein/050630_nd.htm.

Wagner, P.F. "The Dark Side of Illegal Immigration," Website, 2011. http://www.usillegalaliens.com/forward.html.

Walker, Brenda. "Diversity is strength! It's also drunk driving." The V-Dare Website, May 4, 2004. http://www.vdare.com/why_vdare.htm.

This is one of those dot.com websites we have to be careful about. It was founded for Virginia Dare, the first child to be born in the colonies. It has the explicit purpose of challenging illegal immigration and, thus, could be charged with bias. The excerpts here are only from government sources on this website that can be otherwise substantiated.

don't assimilate, then we cannot deny them the education that would keep them from DUIs, keep them from crime, teach them preventative health tidbits, and make them productive citizens. And again, we have a nationwide problem. The economy as a whole has hurt education. I say again, stop scapegoating illegals with racist charges.

REFERENCES

[illegible] September 28, 2006 http://www.[illegible]

[illegible] Immigration Law Enforcement Procedures and Complaints," Center for Immigration Studies, http://www.cis.org/Articles/2004/[illegible].html

[illegible] "[illegible] immigrants' culture," The Raleigh News & Observer, April [illegible], 2007 http://www.[illegible]/2007/04/[illegible].html

[illegible] drunk driving arrests [illegible]," World Net Daily, November 12, 2009 http://www.wnd.com/?pageId=[illegible]

"[illegible] Immigration and Public Health," [illegible] website http://www.[illegible].org/site/News?page=NewsArticle&id=[illegible]

"The [illegible] will cost you to [illegible] illegal immigrants health insurance," Slate, November 10, 2009 http://www.slate.com/id/[illegible]

"[illegible] of US Mexican [illegible]," [illegible], August [illegible], 2008, http://www.[illegible].com/article.php?id=[illegible]

"[illegible] of Illegal Immigrants [illegible] by [illegible]," CBS News, February 11, 2010, http://www.cbsnews.com/stories/2010/02/11/[illegible].shtml

"[illegible] of unmarried [illegible] 2007 [illegible]," USA Today, [illegible] http://www.usatoday.com/news/nation/2007-[illegible]

"[illegible]," [illegible] 2006 http://www.[illegible]/?pageId=[illegible]

[illegible] The [illegible] Website, July [illegible], 2010 http://www.[illegible]

[illegible] "[illegible] Illegal Immigration," [illegible], 2011 http://www.[illegible].html

[illegible] The Virginia Dare Website, March [illegible], 2004 http://www.vdare.com/[illegible].htm

This is one of those dubious websites we need to be careful about. It was founded for Virginia Dare, the first child to be born in the colonies. It has the explicit purpose of challenging illegal immigration and, thus, could be charged with bias. The documents here are only from government sources on this website that can be otherwise substantiated.

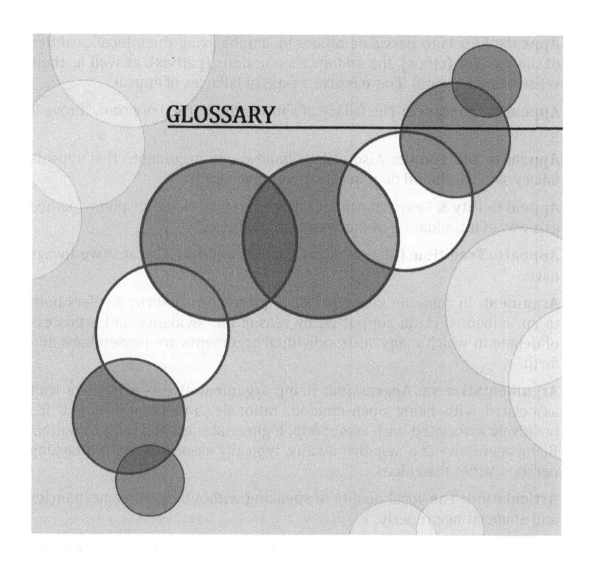

GLOSSARY

Ad Hominem: Literally argument "to the man." The appeals fallacy of attacking the person rather than his arguments. See typical presidential election.

Advocate: The speaker who takes the affirmative side in a debate, advocating a change from the present view of things.

Affirmative: The side in a debate that supports a proposition for change.

Analogy: Reasoning that since two things are similar, we can't expect similar things of them.

Appeals: Efforts to persuade others by emphasizing the ethical qualities of the speaker (ethos), the audience's emotions (pathos), as well as their sense of logic (logos). There is also a class of fallacies of appeal.

Appeal to Ignorance: The fallacy of shifting the burden of proof. "Prove it isn't so."

Appeal to the People: Also called "bandwagon argument," this appeals fallacy says we should do it because everyone else is.

Appeal to Pity & Fear: The appeals fallacy of fear tactics or phony pathos as a way of intimidating or motivating an audience.

Appeal to Tradition: Fallacy that argues we should do it because we always have.

Argument: In common language, it's a quarrel. In rhetoric, it refers both to an individual claim supported by reason and evidence and a process of debate in which many such individual arguments are passed back and forth.

Argumentative vs. Aggressive: Being argumentative is a positive trait associated with being open-minded, rationale, and issue-oriented. It's positively associated with leadership, higher salaries, and job promotion. Being aggressive is a negative quality, typically associated with attacking persons rather than ideas.

Articulation: The vocal quality of speaking without excessive hesitancies and enunciating properly.

Artifacts: Objects of proof, like fingerprints, fossils, or "the smoking gun."

Assertion: Making a claim without any reason or evidence to support it.

Attractiveness: A positive indicator of credibility.

Burden of Proof: The obligation of the advocate to clearly demonstrate the need for a change with *a preponderance of evidence* over his opponent on the negative.

Cause to Effect: One of the basic patterns of reason. A leads to B.

Circular Reasoning: Also called "begging the question." A warrant simply repeats the claim. Chasing one's own tail in reasoning.

Citation: Naming the source for your evidence out loud in a speech, as well as including a bibliography. You should include who said it, their qualifications, the publication, and the date.

Claim: The statement to be proven in Stephen Toulmin style argument.

Classification: The process of putting different persons, concepts, and things into groups of like qualities. Generalization.

Common Ground: Establishing a sense of community with your audience, the feeling that you have more in common than not.

Competence: A positive indicator of credibility. The ability to speak expertly about a given area of study.

Complex Question: The fallacy of asking "yes or no" questions when its reasonable to offer a more nuanced answer.

Conclusionary Evidence: Quotations from experts that simply say something is so without explaining why.

Consistency: A test of evidence and of speaker credibility. You should avoid self-contradiction.

Constructives: The speeches in a debate when positions are built and maintained.

Costs vs. Gains Analysis: Comparing the benefits and detriments of a position to determine the worth of that position.

Counter-Argument: Building arguments of your own against an advocate's case.

Credibility: Personal qualities and rhetorical actions that make some speakers more believable and persuasive than others. Aristotle called it "ethos."

Criteria/Criterion: Plural and singular, respectively. A specific principle for deciding what's most important or what constitutes a threshold for winning an argument.

Critical Thinking: An attempt to achieve more than a merely conditioned response to controversial opinions. It requires open-minded objectivity and an empathic response to opinions other than our own.

Cultural Conditioning: The process by which a culture influences and continually reinforces the beliefs of its citizens.

Definitions: Clarifying potentially vague terms in a proposition by these means: dictionaries, including field specific dictionaries; inclusive/ exclusive definitions that tell what is included and excluded; operational definitions describing the particular functions of proposed change.

Delivery: The act of speaking the speech out loud and supporting it with appropriate nonverbal behavior.

Demonize: A form of propaganda that reduces opponents to negative stereotypes.

Direction of Change: An aspect of the proposition that calls for a particular kind of change—more or less of something, a ban, a curtailment, an improvement in funding—something more specific than "we should change."

Disinformation: Intentionally leaking false information to media to manipulate public reactions and embarrass political enemies.

Documentation: The process of keeping track of your sources of evidence, so that you can say where you got their proofs.

Double Standard: When an adversary uses one set of standards for himself and another for his adversary.

Dynamism: The quality of projecting energy and excitement as a speaker, a positive indicator of credibility.

Emotive Language: Fallacy of language that use extremely emotional language to incite.

Empathy: Taking the perspective of another. Feeling with someone, identifying with their point of view. Differs from sympathy, which is feeling sorry for someone without necessarily relating to their condition or point of view.

Equivocation: Fallacy of language that uses words that can mean more than one thing.

Euphemism: Literally "words of good omen." Considered a courtesy in everyday conversation, it can also be used to conceal odious political maneuver as a lesser offense. For instance, calling civilian deaths "collateral damage."

Evidence: Documented proofs offered as grounds to support a claim. It includes evidence *of fact* (artifacts, specific examples, figures, statistics) and evidence *of opinion* (personal testimony or testimony by qualified experts).

Examples: Specific narratives demonstrating individual cases of an event, often to create identification and sympathy for parties affected by social problems.

Extemporaneous: A style of speaking in which you may have a few brief notes or an outline, but you makes word choice spontaneously.

Extension: Not merely repeating arguments during supporting speeches in a debate, but adding new evidence and analysis, as well as countering refutation.

Fallacies: Errors in reason, appeal, or language that mar the quality of an inference or argument. See Chapter IV and Chapter VII for complete lists.

False Analogy: The fallacy of comparing unlike things.

False Cause: The fallacy of arguing that because A follows B, B must have caused A.

False Sign: The fallacy of making superstitious connections among things that don't really correlate.

Flow Sheet: A paper folded twice to make columns then used to take notes during a debate.

Forcing an Argument: Pressing an advocate's burden of proof.

Forcing the Dichotomy: The fallacy of forcing a dilemma upon an adversary when there are three or more choices, not just two.

Furthest Logical Extent: A refutation tactic in which you push an adversary's reason to comparable yet absurd points, revealing the weakness of the reason.

Generalization: Reasoning by classification. You observe and characterize sufficient similarities among things, people, and events to group them into a class.

Glittering Generalities: Words so imbued with positive feelings that it's hard to argue against them, although they may conceal less idealistic intentions. For instance, calling something "patriotic" more as a matter of persuasion than real patriotism.

Good Will: Showing that you really care about the audience to which you speak, a positive indicator of credibility.

Government: The affirmative side in a parliamentary debate consisting of a Prime Minister who speaks first and last and a Member of the Government.

Grounds: The part of a Toulmin argument in which evidence is presented.

Hasty Generalization: Making generalizations based on too few examples.

Hidden Presumption: Ideas that we assume to be true without really knowing how we came to them or why we believe them. Assuming facts not in evidence.

Hierarchy: Standards or principles listed in order of importance.

Honesty: A positive indicator of credibility.

Identification: When an audience has a sense of empathy and personal involvement with a topic or a speaker.

Imaginary Opponent: The person you imagine will argue against your position. by anticipating what the opponent might argue, you can take a dialectical view of your own arguments and improve them.

Inclusive/Exclusive Definition: Saying specifically what your proposition does and does not include.

Inference: The use of reason to arrive at conclusions not necessarily self-evident in the grounds for an argument.

Inherency: A stock issue used in both proposition of fact and policy speeches. What is the cause or causes of a significant event? Inherency may be structural, a matter of established law and organization, or it may be attitudinal, a matter of public resistance to an unpopular idea.

Instrumental Communication: Communication as a tool for achieving specific ends, rather than for mere expression or conversational purposes.

Intrapersonal Communication: The interior conversations we have with ourselves.

Invention: The act of creating arguments, often by use of stock issues, which are sometimes called "the inventional system."

Issue: A question to be answered about a controversial subject. "Stock Issues" are particular sets of questions that go with particular kinds of propositions.

Jargonese: Using specialized vocabulary to confuse an adversary or to boost your credibility by looking smarter, even when you're not being clear.

Jingoism: Reducing complex social problems in to bumper sticker phrases. For instance, "Guns don't kill people; people kill people." People with guns do kill people, and it's much easier than doing it by other means. One could just as easily say "People who make guns kill people," another oversimplification.

Knowledge: The impression that a speaker is well informed about a topic, a positive indicator of credibility.

Lincoln-Douglas Debate: A one-on-one style of debate, as opposed to the usual two-on-two team debate formats, named for Abraham Lincoln's famous debates with Douglas during a Senate campaign.

Moral Character: Audience perception that a source or speaker is a good person, a positive indicator of credibility.

Multiple Causation: The usual circumstance among social problems is that they have complex cause of several factors, not merely one thing.

Mutually Exclusive: A necessary condition for arguing dilemma. You cannot have both of the two choices. One thing necessarily precludes the other.

Negative: The side in the debate that opposes a proposition for change and supports the present view of things.

Non Sequitur: Literally "does not follow." The fallacy that occurs when wild inferences without warrants are made. Great leaps of logic.

Nonverbal Communication: All aspects of speech delivery except for the words themselves, stance, gesture, eye contact, etc.

Non-unique: A refutation tactic by which you point out that a criticism of a particular thing is not unique to that thing, since it also occurs with your adversary's position. Also, an advantage claimed by an adversary may really already exist in the present view of things.

Opponent: The person who defends the present view of things, to one degree or another, and opposes the advocate.

Opposition: The negative side in a parliamentary debate consisting of a Leader of the Opposition who speaks first and last and a Member of the Opposition.

Oregon Debate: A form of debate with designated cross-examination periods after each constructive speech.

Oversimplification: The fallacy of ignoring multiple causes to a problem.

Oxford Debate: A research-oriented form of debate without cross-examination.

Parliamentary Debate: A form of debate modeled after British Parliament, emphasizing reason over research.

Peroration: A persuasive and inspiring conclusion to a speech in Greek rhetoric.

Persuasion: The process of using appeals and imagery to motivate an audience.

Plagiarism: Borrowing ideas and language from other authors without acknowledging them. That includes not using quotation marks for the borrowed material.

Presumption: The advantage enjoyed by the negative in a debate. The present view of things is presumed innocent, until the advocate satisfies his burden of proof to a degree that we suspend presumption and consider change.

Prima Facie Case: A set of arguments by an advocate sufficiently persuasive to counter the presumption of the present view. It can be measured by whether the advocate has satisfied his burden of proof in each of the relevant stock issues.

Primary Certitude: An immediate and strong reaction that one knows the real truth about an issue, even when little is actually known about it. One result of cultural conditioning.

Projection: Breathing out with your vocal delivery to support appropriate volume. The quality of speaking loudly enough for an audience to be compelled to listen.

Propaganda: The use of untruthful language and images to attack others and to unfairly manipulate public opinion. To "short circuit" critical thinking by taking advantage of the public's cultural conditioning.

Proposition: A complete sentence that declares your opinion on an issue, the basic particle of an argument. Propositions of fact deal with what has or has not occurred, what does or does not exist, and what will or will not occur. Propositions of value deal with what is good or evil, ethical or unethical, morally acceptable or a higher priority. Propositions of policy deal with what actions we must take to solve a social problems.

Qualifications: The training, relevant academic degrees, or official recognitions of achievement that make a source seem worthy of attention.

Qualifiers: Words and phrases used to limit the extent of a claim. They suggest the degree of probability to which something may be true. A part of Toulmin's secondary triad.

Quantify: To demonstrate how big, how long, how much in actual figures and statistics.

Rate: How fast or slow one speaks, as well as the punctuation provided by appropriate pauses.

Reaction Formation: Immediately strong, negative reaction against something, often a defensive response to having one's ideas successfully challenged. A person experiencing reaction formation may not even consider it possible that they could have anything in common with someone who thinks differently.

Reason: The ability of people to make logical inferences in one of seven ways: analogy, sign, cause to effect, generalization, definition, dilemma, and authority.

Reasoning from Authority: Reasoning that something is true based upon one's own expertise or that of a recognized authority.

Reasoning from Definition: Applying known standards for belonging to a generalized class to particular people, events, and things, in order to identify them.

Reasoning from Dilemma: Having to decide between two mutually exclusive choices based on costs vs. gains analysis.

Rebuttals: The closing speeches of a debate in which positions are summarized and final refutations are made, but no new arguments may be issued.

Red Herring: The fallacy of throwing irrelevant though perhaps well-worded arguments in a debate to distract one's adversary.

Refutation: Attacking an adversary's arguments. Straight refutation means you only attack, building no arguments of your own.

Relevance: A test of evidence and arguments and whether they are topical, or germane to the subject matter.

Representative: A test of evidence, especially statistics. Is the sample population a true picture of the people, or is it a unique or atypical sector of the population.

Rhetoric: According to Aristotle, using "the best available means of persuasion." Adapting messages on social issues to particular people, at particular times and places. It combines the use of both argument and persuasion.

Rhetorical Demand: An impending necessity in the human community that calls for advocates to speak to a particular issue.

Shifting Ground: The fallacy of abandoning your original position once it's been attacked to adopt a more convenient one.

Side Effects: A stock issue in policy speeches calling for one to claim advantages for a solution beyond solving the harm, or to defend against anticipated disadvantages of the solution.

Sign: Observing and reasoning from correlations among beings, things, and events.

Significance: A stock issue for both proposition of fact and value speeches. Something significant, usually a social harm, is occurring.

Slippery Slope: The fallacy that one event will start an avalanche of events without providing proof for each link in the chain.

Source-based Evidence: Evidence of opinion from quoted experts.

Speaker Apprehension: Nervousness and fear that interfere with speaker confidence.

Spin: The process of altering story details to influence reaction to the news.

Stereotype: Oversimplifying the unique characteristics of an individual to brand him with exaggerated qualities of a particular group. Sweeping generalization.

Stock Issues: A particular set of questions, questions that vary among fact, value, and policy speeches, that an advocate must answer to satisfy the burden of proof.

Sufficiency: A test of evidence. Is the grounds really enough to justify the full extent of the claim.

Sweeping Generalization: Over-applying a general principle that is true to one degree or another as if it were always true of each individual case.

Thesis/Antithesis/Synthesis: A model of dialectical thinking. You propose an idea, opposes it then synthesizes the strongest position between the two poles.

Threshold: A level at which an audience would agree that the advocate's burden of proof has been met. The advocate can and should define what he has to prove in order to meet that burden.

Tolerance of Ambiguity: The ability to resist jumping to conclusions, especially in the face of limited information, or an abundance of information so great that it requires consideration.

Topical: A stock issue. Does the argument or evidence fit in with the proposition discussed.

Trend: The minimum level of inherency by which you demonstrate the worsening of a problem, calling for some solution, without knowing the cause.

Turns: Using an opponent's own grounds against him or her, usually by providing an alternative warrant.

Urban Folklore: Word of mouth myths and stories, usually with some moral caution or attempt to frighten, that gets passed along as truth. Often accompanied by the Opening phrase, "I knew a guy who . . ."

Value Standard: A set of principles used to measure the worth of particular values.

Verifiability: A test of evidence. Is the proof a rumor, the result of only one account, or can it be proven true by multiple sources?

Workable Solution: A practical solution for social harms in a policy speech.

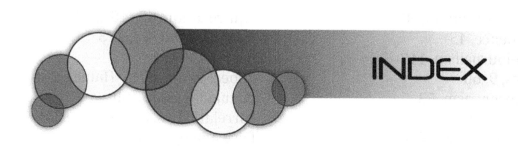

INDEX

Adversary, 252
Advocate/affirmative, 20–21
Alternative causation, 276–278
Appeals: ethos, pathos and logos, 9
Appeals and evidence selection,
        82–84
Argument, definition of, 2
Argumentative ground, 14–16
Argumentative vs. aggressive,
        37–38
Argumentum ad nauseum, 52
Articulation, 238–241
Artifacts, 68–69
Assertion, 6
Attitude, bad, 34–37
Attitudinal inherency, 210–211
Audience adaption, 29–30

Bias, in news, 104–105
Bias, in news sources, 109
The Big Lie, 58–60
Burden of proof, 21

Cable news, 110–123
Causal link, 176
Centrist magazines, 138–141
Cherry picking, 102

Citation, 79, 88, 90–91
Claims, 3–7
Clash, 252
Classification, 163
Common ground, 9
Conservative magazines, 128–132
Constructive speech, 257–258
Contradiction and dilemma,
        278–280
Costs vs. gains analysis, 183, 217
Counter-evidence, 275–276
Counter-productivity, 283–284
Credibility, 79–82
Critical thinking, 11–12
Cross-examination, 273
Cultural conditioning, 52–55

Debate, 10, 20–21, 255–256
Definitions, 16–18
Delivery, physical techniques,
        241–245
Demonization, 57–58, 59
Dialectical thinking, 38
Direction of change, 14
Disinformation, 56–57, 59
Documentation, 90–91
Double standards, 280–281

Either or thinking, 35
Eloquence, 45
Emo-journalism, 112
Ethics, 9, 60
Ethnocentrism, 53–54
Euphemism, 51–52
Evidence, types of, 68–78
Evidence and counter-argument,
    266
Evidence and persuasion, 78–79
Evidence attacks, 273–275
Evidence of fact, 68–76
Evidence of opinion, 76–78
Evidence tests, 84–87
Exaggeration, 54
Examples, 69–71
Extemporaneous thinking, 287
Eye contact, 237, 238, 242–243

Fairness doctrine, 105–106
Fallacies of appeal
    ad hominem, 38–39
    appeal to ignorance, 42–43
    appeal to pity and fear, 40–41
    appeal to snobbery, 40
    appeal to tradition, 42
    bandwagon argument, 39
    reductio ad absurdum (appeal to
        humor), 43–44
Fallacies of evasion (relevance),
    94–95
    avoiding the issue, 94
    red herring, 94–95, 272
    seizing on a trivial point, 94
    shifting ground, 95
Fallacies of language
    emotive language, 48–50

equivocation, 45–48, 273
jargonese, 50–52, 273
Fallacies of logic
    appeal to authority (fame), 186
    circular reason, 268
    correlation vs. causation, 180
    false analogy, 162
    false cause, 178–179
    false sign, 174–175
    forcing the dichotomy,
        183–185, 280
    hasty generalization, 166–168
    non sequitur, 269
    oversimplification, 179–180, 276
    slippery slope, 180–181
    sweeping generalization,
        171–172
    transfer fallacy, 269
    composition, 270–271
    division, 271
Figures, 71, 75–76
Flow sheets, 290–291

Glittering generalities, 46–47
Grounds, 3–7

Hidden presumptions, 53,
    74–75, 195

Imaginary opponent, 14, 38
Imperialism, 55
Inclusive/exclusive definitions, 17
Induction vs. deduction, 157–158
Inference, 6–7
Infotainment, 106–108
Interpersonal communication, 1–3
Intrapersonal communication, 232

Invention, 25
Issue, 14, 22–23, 25

Jingosim, 47–48
Just plain folks, 40

Liberal magazines, 133–138
Listening, 253–254
Longitudinal studies, 74

Media bias, 102–104
Modal qualifiers, 18–19

Newspapers, 141–142
Nonverbal communication, 241–244

Online sources, 143
Open-mindedness, 34–35
Operational definitions, 17–18
Opponent/negative, 21

Parliamentary debate, 257–260
    leader of the opposition speaker,
        257, 258
    member of the government
        speaker, 257
    member of the opposition
        speaker, 258
    Prime Minister speaker duties,
        257, 258
Pauses and rates, 240, 242
Performance, 246–247
Personality news, 106–7
Personal testimony, 77
Persuasion, 8
Persuasion and evidence, 78–79
Plagiarism, 90

Pre-critical thinking, 34–37
Presumption, 20–21
Prima facie case, 21–22
Primary certitude, 34–35
Print news, 128–142
Probability, not certainty, 18
Propaganda, 56–60
Proposition of policy, 202–203
Propositions, 12–14
Propositions, grammar of, 25–27
Propositions, types of, 22–25
Propositions of fact, 192–193
Propositions of value, 218–220

Qualifiers, 8, 18–20
Quarrel, 2
Questions, 262–264

Radio news, 126–128
Reaction formation, 36
Reasoning, patterns of
    authority, 155, 185
    cause, 175–178
    definition, 168–171
    dilemma, 182–183
    generalization, 163–166
    parallel reason, 159–162
    sign, 156, 172–174
Rebuttal, 258, 264–265
Refutation, 254–255, 265–287
Rehearsal, 245–246
Research, 87–90
Research reviews, 74
Resistance to change, 34
Rhetoric, 8–11
Rhetorical demand, 27, 192
Rules and roles, 20–22

Socio-centrism, 53–54
Source splitting, 88
Spin, 102
Statistics, 71–74
Stereotype, 54
Stock issues, 23, 24
   of fact, 193–195
   of policy, 204
      inherency, 208–212
      side effects, 217–218
      significant harm, 205–208
      topicality, 261–262
      workable solution, 212–217
   of value, 220
Structural inherency, 209–210
Subject matter for argument, 27–29
Surveys, 73–74

Thesis, 13

Thesis-antithesis-synthesis format,
   14, 38
Threshold, 19
Tolerance of ambiguity, 35–36
Topicality, 261–262
Toulmin, Stephan, 3, 18
Toulmin argument, 3–8, 91–93

Values, core American, 227–228
Values, definition of, 225
   instrumental values, 226
   terminal values, 226
Value standards, 221–224
Value systems (Rokeach), 226–227
Voice, 238–241

Warrants, 3–7

Yellow journalism, 104